PHILOSOPHICAL WRITINGS

The text of this work is reprinted from
The Nelson Philosophical Texts

General Editor
RAYMOND KLIBANSKY

Emeritus Professor of Philosophy
McGill University and *University of Heidelberg*
Fellow, Wolfson College, Oxford University

PHILOSOPHICAL
WRITINGS

A Selection

WILLIAM OF OCKHAM

Translated, with Introduction and Notes, by

PHILOTHEUS BOEHNER, O.F.M.

late Professor of Philosophy at the Franciscan Institute
St. Bonaventure, New York

Latin texts and English translation revised by

STEPHEN F. BROWN, 1989

New Foreword and Bibliography by

STEPHEN F. BROWN

Professor of Theology at Boston College

HACKETT PUBLISHING COMPANY
Indianapolis / Cambridge

WILLIAM OF OCKHAM: ca. 1285–1349

New materials copyright © 1990 by Hackett Publishing Company
All rights reserved
Printed in the United States of America

Cover design by Listenberger Design & Associates

06 05 04 03 02 01 00 99 98   2 3 4 5 6

For further information, please address
Hackett Publishing Company
P.O. Box 44937
Indianapolis, Indiana 46204

TO
PACIFICUS BORGMANN
O.F.M.

Library of Congress Cataloging-in-Publication Data

Ockham, William of, ca. 1285–ca. 1349.
   [Selections. English. 1990]
   Philosophical writings: a selection/William of Ockham.;
translated, with introduction and notes by Philotheus Boehner:
Latin texts and English translation revised by Stephen F. Brown,
1989; new foreword & bibliography by Stephen F. Brown.
      p.   cm.
   Includes bibliographical references.
   ISBN 0-87220-079-5 (alk. paper)—ISBN 0-87220-078-7 (pbk.: alk.
paper)
   1. Philosophy.   I. Boehner, Philotheus.   II. Brown, Stephen
F.   III. Title.
   B765.O32E5   1990   89-48587
   189′.4—dc20   CIP

The paper used in this publication meets the minimum
requirements of American National Standard for
Information Sciences—Permanence of Paper for Printed
Library Materials, ANSI Z39.48-1984.
                        ∞

PREFACE

Any selection from the works of a philosopher, even if it purports to give a general picture of his thought, will at best be an introduction. It can present only parts or pieces of his system, usually taken out of their context and organised according to the view of the compiler. None the less, such a procedure has this advantage : the reader is informed by the philosopher himself about his own thought.

The present selection suffers not only from the short-comings necessarily connected with such a work, but also from difficulties of its own. First, and this is a major handicap, there are hardly any critical editions of the works of Ockham. Birch's edition of *De sacramento altaris* cannot satisfy a critical reader, and the few texts edited by the present writer are of minor importance for our present purpose.

The main task, therefore, was to prepare texts which could be considered reliable. For that reason I have compared all the Latin texts with a number of good manuscripts. Though they make no claim to be critical in the technical sense of the word, nevertheless they can be rated as *safe* texts. I hope to be excused from indicating and describing these manuscripts, since most of them have already been given place in our various publications.

A second handicap derives from the highly technical Latin used by Ockham. His language makes it impossible simply to *read* him ; he needs to be studied, or rather, as St Bonaventure demanded for one of his writings, the *Venerabilis Inceptor* must be *ruminated*.

The purpose of the present translation is to make this ruminating process less laborious for the ordinary reader, although my chief concern was to render faithfully Ockham's thought. And to attain this latter objective,

I have frequently sacrificed fluency of style. As a further help in understanding the texts, I have added an Introduction to Ockham's philosophy. In its general outline, this Introduction follows the order of the selection.

I am deeply indebted to my colleague and confrère, the Rev. Allan Wolter, o.f.m., for the tedious work of checking the translation. With gratitude I dedicate this work to my teacher and friend, the Rev. Pacificus Borgmann, o.f.m., who not only first led me to an understanding of Ockham's thought, but also, by many personal sacrifices, has made possible my studies in the field of medieval philosophy.

PHILOTHEUS BOEHNER

The Franciscan Institute,
St Bonaventure, N.Y.
1955

CONTENTS

PHILOSOPHICAL WRITINGS

EDITORIAL NOTE

FATHER PHILOTHEUS BOEHNER died suddenly, on 22 May
1955. At that time the present volume was in the proof-
stage. In seeing the book through the press, it was considered proper to alter his text and translation as little as
possible. Changes were necessary to correct obvious slips,
to emend those sentences which Father Boehner himself
had queried, and to clarify a number of passages of
particular difficulty. In accordance with his wishes, the
Bibliographical Note was revised and enlarged.

Special thanks are due to Mr Peter Geach, Lecturer
in Philosophy at the University of Birmingham, for many
valuable suggestions and helpful comments. Mr Storrs
McCall, of McGill University, kindly assisted in correcting the proofs. I also wish to express my gratitude to
Father Eligius Buytaert, O.F.M., Father Boehner's suc-
cessor as Director of the Franciscan Institute, both for
his help in compiling the bibliography and for his
readiness to answer queries which arose in the last stages.

To arrive at a just estimate of Ockham's thought and
to remove the many misconceptions which for centuries
have stood in the way of a true understanding of the
Franciscan master, was the aim to which Father Boehner
devoted much of his scholarly work. With this end in
mind, he accepted our invitation to prepare a repre-
sentative selection of texts for the present series. At the
same time, he was engaged in laying the foundation for
the first comprehensive critical edition of Ockham's
philosophical and theological works. His untimely death
cut short his own participation in this design ; but thanks
to the provisions he made, this important undertaking
will be carried on by the Franciscan Institute.

RAYMOND KLIBANSKY

McGill University
  Montreal
    1955

viii

INTRODUCTION

SCHOLASTIC philosophy found its mature expression
during the thirteenth and fourteenth centuries. The
scholasticism of the thirteenth century was predominantly
receptive and constructive in its tendencies. Its chief
exponents were mainly interested in absorbing the wealth
of philosophical learning that came to them from Greek
and Arabic sources, and in constructing articulate
systems comprising the thought of their time. Their
work can perhaps best be called 'synthetic'. By contrast,
fourteenth-century scholasticism was occupied in sifting,
revising and adapting its rich legacy of ideas. Its chief
exponents focused their attention on the structure of the
traditional philosophy itself ; they tested its basis and
examined the solidity of its parts. Their philosophy may
therefore be characterised by the term 'critical'. These
labels must not, however, be taken as mutually exclusive.
Neither the thirteenth nor the fourteenth century was
without originality ; and while in the thirteenth century
a sound sense of criticism was visibly active and alive,
the fourteenth proved itself by no means incapable of
building systems.

In one aspect the two centuries are two parts of a single
whole—the period of classical scholasticism. There is
a tendency on the part of historians who have mainly
studied the thirteenth century to look upon them as two
distinct or even opposing periods. In their view the
thirteenth century is unmistakably the golden age, the
fourteenth a period of decline and decadence. Yet it
remains an historical fact that there was a unity of
civilisation and religion ensured by an agreement in
holding the dogmas of the Catholic faith, dogmas which
it was their main endeavour to elucidate. There was
the unity of an unbroken academic tradition guaranteed

by the use of common textbooks, viz. the writings of
Aristotle, the *Sentences* of Peter Lombard and others,
which had to be read and publicly interpreted by anyone aspiring to academic degrees. Within this unity
there was a lively discussion of the various conflicting
solutions of the common problems, but, in contrast to
the terminological confusion of modern philosophy, this
discussion was grounded on the use of a generally
accepted common technical language.

The great Scottish philosopher John Duns Scotus
(*d.* 1308) is in many respects the connecting link between
the thirteenth and the fourteenth centuries. His outlook
is deeply rooted in the philosophical movement of the
thirteenth century ; he is the builder of one of the most
impressive systems of the Middle Ages ; but at the same
time his work reveals many characteristics of the period
which follows him. Because of his keen logical analysis
and his penetrating criticism, his contemporaries called
him the *Doctor Subtilis*. Not only did his life and teaching
bridge the two classical centuries ; not only did he unite
in an unprecedented manner the theological and philosophical tradition of Oxford and of Paris ; he also had
the rare gift of awakening a great number of disciples,
who at the same time were in varying degrees independent
thinkers. No schoolman of the day could afford to
ignore his teaching ; everyone was forced to define his
position.

A prodigiously varied school, composed mostly, though
not exclusively, of members of the Franciscan Order,
achieved the firm entrenchment of Scotus's doctrine in
scholasticism for centuries to come. It was natural that
the followers of the older scholastics, in particular of
St Thomas, should strongly oppose the innovations of
Duns Scotus and his criticism of their own position. But
these were not his only critics ; some of those who readily
acknowledged their great indebtedness to him nevertheless felt free to go their own way. Two of these inde-

pendent-minded followers are known as the originators
of conceptualism, viz. the saintly French Franciscan,
Archbishop Peter Aureoli (*d.* 1321 or 1322), and the
English Franciscan, William Ockham.

Aureoli and Ockham have many doctrines in common ;
both were in immediate contact with Scotus's work, and
perhaps both heard the lectures of the Subtle Doctor,
whom, in any case, both deeply admired. But their
admiration is that of independent thinkers who are
constantly criticising and sifting the teachings of Scotus.
Both reject the realistic interpretation of universal concepts and the connected doctrine of 'formal' distinctions
so characteristic of Scotus's teachings, and both went
far beyond the work of the great Master.

Though we must not underrate the importance of
Aureoli for medieval thought or deny the possibility of
his having influenced Ockham, it nevertheless seems
justifiable to consider Ockham as the central figure of
a new movement, known as the school of the nominalists,
the *schola* or *via nominalium*. This school grew to such
importance that every historian of fourteenth-century
scholasticism is forced either to go back to, or to start
with, the *Doctor plusquam subtilis*, the *Venerabilis Inceptor*,
William Ockham.

II. OCKHAM'S LIFE

Documentary evidence about the life of Ockham is
scanty. For most of the events of his life we have only
more or less probable conjectures. It is not our task
to substantiate these conjectures here, since we have
done so elsewhere.[1]

William Ockham was probably born at Ockham, in
the county of Surrey near London, perhaps closer to

[1] *Cf. The Tractatus De Successivis attributed to William Ockham*,
Franciscan Institute Publications No. 1 (N.Y. 1944), pp. 1–15.

1280 than 1290. A document discovered lately by Fr Conrad Walmesly, O.F.M., informs us that he was ordained subdeacon on 26 February 1306.[1] We know nothing definite about his earlier studies or of any of his early life. It is most probable that he pursued his higher studies in theology at Oxford from about 1309 to 1315, lectured on the Bible from about 1315 to 1317, lectured on the *Sentences* from about 1317 to 1319, and was a *Baccalaureus Formatus* from about 1319 to 1323. It seems that Ockham was a *Magister Theologiae*—that is to say, he had fulfilled all the requirements necessary for that degree—but he never became a *Magister actu regens*, a Master occupying an official chair of theology ; that is the reason why he was called *Inceptor*, and that is the meaning of this title so often misinterpreted in the sense of 'originator of the nominalistic school'.

Why did Ockham remain an *Inceptor* ? The most likely reason is that he was prevented from holding a chair by Lutterell, former Chancellor of Oxford University. Lutterell, an overzealous Thomist, was apparently in opposition to the majority of the University. At the request of the University itself he was deposed by the Bishop of Lincoln, Henry Butwolsh.[2]

Whether or not Ockham's teaching was already the subject of this dispute, we do not know. However, it is certain that after his deposition Lutterell made Ockham his victim. Lutterell was no longer Chancellor by the middle of the year 1322. For we know that in a letter dated 12 August 1322, Edward II forbade Lutterell to leave England for the Continent and warned him not to jeopardise the reputation of the University by taking a domestic affair to other places. However, in another

---

[1] *Cf. Guillelmi de Ockham Opera politica*, accuravit J. G. Sikes (Manchester 1940), p. 288.

[2] *Cf.* Fritz Hoffmann, *Die erste Kritik des Ockhamismus durch den Oxforder Kanzler Johannes Lutterell (nach der Hs.* ccv *der Bibliothek des Prager Metropolitankapitels)*, in Breslauer Studien zur historischen Theologie, Neue Folge Band IX (Breslau 1941), pp. 1 sqq.

letter, dated 20 August 1323, the King gave permission for Lutterell to go to Avignon, the residence of Pope John XXII. His permission (we would say 'passport') was given for two years. From a letter written to the King in 1325 by the Pope, requesting an extension of this permission, we know that one reason, even if not the only one, why Lutterell had gone to Avignon was to accuse Ockham of expounding heretical doctrines.

We have, too, several of Lutterell's own documents presented to Pope John XXII in order to justify the accusation that Ockham taught dangerous doctrines.[1] These documents certainly do not constitute a faithful account of Ockham's teachings. However, they caused Ockham to be summoned to Avignon by the Pope. Thus Ockham went to Avignon, probably early in 1324. Most likely in the same year, the Pope appointed a commission to examine Ockham's teachings in his *Commentary on the Sentences* (BKS I–IV). The trial dragged on for three years. Two acts had been drawn up by 1326, both based upon fifty-six articles of accusation composed by Lutterell. However, the inquiry was never finished, and none of the doctrines censured by the commission were ever formally condemned.

During the years 1324 to 1328 Ockham may have stayed at the Franciscan Convent in Avignon. We have no record, nor are there any contemporary insinuations that the English friar suffered imprisonment. On the contrary, it is extremely probable that he was free to go anywhere, except to leave the town. It was in the third year of his stay at Avignon that he became involved in the debate over Franciscan poverty. Up to that time he had taken no active part in this hotly disputed question which, in its purely theoretical aspect, concerned the statement that Christ and his Apostles did not possess property whether privately or in common, in its practical aspect, the ideal of poverty cherished by some

---

[1] *Cf.*, for further literature and documentation, *op. cit.*, pp. 6 sqq.

of the friars and loathed by others. The Order was divided into two parties. Together with the General of the Order, Michael of Cesena, a large majority took up a radical stand against the decision of the Pope. Called to Avignon, Michael openly resisted the Pope in an audience. He was detained in Avignon. During his stay in Avignon, and probably soon after his arrival, Michael ordered Ockham to study the question.

As Ockham tells us,[1] it was only then that he became interested in the whole problem, and that he discovered that the Constitutions of Pope John XXII were in contradiction with statements of earlier Popes. Passionately he took sides with his superior against the Pope. This decision, however, was much more far-reaching than Ockham may have realised at this time ; for the German Emperor, Louis the Bavarian, seized the opportunity of the debate over poverty to further his own political purposes. This unfortunate mixture of political and theological struggles plunged the Order into the greatest crisis of its existence, and drove Ockham finally into the camp of the Pope's enemies.

The year 1328 can be considered as the crucial turning-point in Ockham's life. Convoking a General Chapter of the Order, the Pope commanded it to elect another General. Probably it was to counter this move that Michael decided to leave Avignon secretly. United with him in this enterprise were three loyal friars, one of whom was William Ockham. They left Avignon on 26 May 1328 and fled to the German Emperor, Louis of Bavaria. Ockham and his companions met the Emperor in Pisa on his return from Rome, where he had just installed an Anti-pope and received from him the crown of the Roman Empire. The rebellious friars followed the Emperor to Munich, which then became the centre of the intellectual struggle against Pope

[1] *Cf.* L. Baudry, 'La Lettre de Guillaume d'Occam au chapitre d'Assise,' in *Revue d'histoire franciscaine* III (1926), p. 202.

John XXII. Though there is no historical evidence
that Ockham at his first meeting with the Emperor
said 'O Emperor, defend me with your sword, and I
will defend you with my pen', this famous dictum nevertheless expresses a fact. For Ockham became one of the
intellectual leaders in the struggle of the Emperor
against the Popes.

The fugitive Franciscans at Munich were excom-
municated by the Pope and by their own Order ; but
the seal of the Order was still in their keeping, and
when, in 1342, Michael died, Ockham took possession
of it. It appears that Ockham never left Munich, where
he was occupied in writing his works concerning the
question of poverty, and (in his later period) concerning
the relation between state and church.

After the death of Louis of Bavaria in 1347, Ockham's
situation became hopeless. There is good evidence that
he sought a reconciliation with the Pope and his Order.
We know that he sent back the seal of the Order, and
we also know the wording of his submission : 'I confess
that I hold and held what the holy mother, the Roman
Church, believes, holds and teaches ; and that I believed
and even now believe that the Emperor has no authority
to depose the Pope, the highest Pontiff, and to elect and
create another. On the contrary, I consider it heretical,
and condemned, as such, by the same Church. Furthermore I swear that I will await and obey the orders of the
Church and of our lord the Pope. . . . (I swear too)
that in future I will be . . . faithful to the Pope and
that I will not adhere to the heresies, the errors, the
opinions and the rebellions of Louis of Bavaria and
Michael of Cesena against the Church. . . .' [1]

It is worth while to note that this formula of submission
speaks principally about certain political errors concerning the relation between the Pope and the Emperor,
and of Ockham's disobedience, and further that it does

[1] *Bullarium Franciscanum*, TOM. IV, n. 508a.

not mention any errors of Ockham in his teachings on
theology and philosophy during his first period in
Oxford. Thus ended the career of one who was a
brilliant philosopher, a great theologian, and too modern
a politician. Ockham died soon after the formula of
submission was drawn up. Whether he signed it or not,
we do not know. It seems that he died *c.* 1349 (or
1347 ?), probably a victim of the Black Death.[1] Ockham
was buried in the old Franciscan Church in Munich.
His tomb, in the choir before the altar, was removed
in 1802 and his remains brought to a place still unknown.

III. OCKHAM'S PHILOSOPHY [2]

Before drawing the broad outlines of Ockham's philosophy, we must remind the reader that Ockham never
expounded it systematically and in its entirety. The
Cursus philosophicus in several ponderous tomes is a
characteristic product of sixteenth- and seventeenth-
century scholasticism, but no scholastic philosopher of
the thirteenth or the fourteenth century has handed
down to us anything like that. The scholastics of the
thirteenth and fourteenth centuries were theologians
essentially, philosophers only incidentally. Their reasoning was a concentrated effort to penetrate the mysteries
of the Christian faith ; their philosophy was the hand-
maid of theology. None the less, it is a striking historical
fact that these great theologians were equally great as
philosophers. Being theologians, they did not care to
start by developing a complete philosophy. Rather they
developed their theology and philosophy in organic
integration, so that theology was constantly fertilised by
philosophic speculation and philosophy remained under

---

[1] *Cf.* Rudolf Höhn, o.f.m., 'Wilhelm Ockham in München', in
Franziskanische Studien, XXXII (1950), 142 sqq.
[2] A complete list of Ockham's writings is given in the Bibliographical Note below, pp. li–lix.

the guidance of Christian dogma. It was due to this organic unity of medieval speculation that little need was felt for composing a complete philosophical *Summa*. It is in the theological writings that the best scholastic philosophy is hidden, and it is the task of the historian to extract it from its theological context.

This will be our task, also, when giving an outline of Ockham's philosophy. Some of our texts, in fact a considerable number, have been taken from writings devoted to purely philosophical subjects, many from the *Summa logicae*, some from his writings on the *Physics* of Aristotle. But this has been done for practical purposes, because in these later writings Ockham usually presents his thoughts in a more systematic and precise manner. Nevertheless, his epistemology, psychology, ethics and a large part of his metaphysics have to be reconstructed from fragments scattered throughout his theological works. To present these separate pieces as a part of an ordered system inevitably produces a somewhat artificial synthesis ; but we hope that our reconstruction will not be too far removed from what may properly be called the philosophy of William Ockham.

1. *The leading ideas of Ockham's philosophy*

In order to achieve a general understanding of Ockham's work we have to view him as a theologian, who at the same time was a great logician, a keen observer of facts and a man endowed with a sharp critical sense.

Ockham is first and foremost a theologian who by entering the Order of Friars Minor devoted his whole life, and especially his intellectual activity, to the service of God. Hence he is a religious thinker ; for him, there can be only one absolute in this world, one thing which alone is necessary, only one reality which is completely self-sufficient, namely God, the supreme author alike of creation and of revelation. In this world, it is God

who ultimately matters. God—the living, the wise, the loving, the just, the all-powerful—God alone is absolutely independent ; and by *God* Ockham means a God of absolute unity and simplicity, and at the same time a God threefold in His personality. With due humility the theologian as such submits and bows to this God of his in an act of uncompromising faith. God's revelation, whether as deposited in holy scripture or as embodied in the living tradition of the Church, is accepted by Ockham as the rule of faith. This rule is throughout the guiding principle of his investigations. Once at least he has expressed it in the following words : 'This is my faith, since it is the Catholic faith. For whatever the Roman Church explicitly believes, this alone, and nothing else, I explicitly or implicitly believe'.[1]

However, Ockham is also a logician, perhaps the greatest logician of the Middle Ages. Reason is something sacred, a gift from God ; hence the laws of reason are to be respected. Passionately, Ockham denounces any encroachment on the duty to follow one's own reasoning, except, of course, the intervention of that higher authority which is the source from which reason itself flows : 'I consider it to be dangerous and temerarious to force anyone to fetter his mind and to believe something which his reason dictates to him to be false, unless it can be drawn from holy scripture or from a determination of the Roman Church or from the words of approved doctors'.[2]

While Ockham apparently enjoys the display of logic, we look in vain for lofty speculations. Wherever possible, he tries to get a solid footing on experience and observation. We have to find out how things are, we have no right to dictate how things must be. Ockham's philosophy is empirical, but he is no empiricist. He is an

---

[1] *De sacramento altaris*, cap. 1 ; ed. Birch, p. 164, 3–5.
[2] *De corpore Christi* (*De sacramento altaris* in the ed. of Birch), ed. Birch, p. 126, 18–23.

empirical thinker, because he is a Christian firmly believing in the contingency of this created world of ours.

Since God is the only absolute and necessary being, knowledge about created beings requires that we should examine them and investigate what they actually are ; for, so far as God is concerned, they might be different. Ockham never loses sight of this basic Christian idea— so radically opposed to the necessitarian view—that there is no *inherent* necessity for anything in this world to be what it is. Even in his investigation of the problems of physics or psychology Ockham never forgets that this world is absolutely dependent on the will of God ; always he takes the stand of a Christian, who firmly believes in the omnipotence of God and the contingency of creatures.

Thus the following maxims are the guiding principles of all Ockham's work :

1. *All things are possible for God, save such as involve a contradiction.*

In other words, God can do (or make or create) everything which does not involve a contradiction ; that which includes a contradiction is absolute non-entity. Ockham expressly bases this principle on an article of faith : 'I believe in God the Father Almighty'.[1] From this Ockham immediately infers a second principle which is encountered everywhere in his writings :

2. *Whatever God produces by means of secondary (i.e. created) causes, God can produce and conserve immediately and without their aid.*[2]

Hence any positive reality which is naturally produced by another created being (not of course without the aid of God who is the first cause) can be produced by God alone without the causality of the secondary cause. In

---

[1] *Cf. Quodlibeta* VI, qu. 6, of the Strasbourg edition.
[2] *Ibid.*

other words, God is not dependent on the causality of created causes, but they are absolutely dependent on His causality.

This is stated in a more general manner :

3. *God can cause, produce and conserve every reality, be it a substance or an accident, apart from any other reality.*[1]

Hence God can create or produce or conserve an accident without its substance, matter without form, and *vice versa*. In order to bring anything under the operation of this principle, it is sufficient to prove that it is reality or entity.

These rules or guiding principles are theological in nature, as Ockham does not fail to emphasise. The following is, however, a scientific principle of general application :

4. *We are not allowed to affirm a statement to be true or to maintain that a certain thing exists, unless we are forced to do so either by its self-evidence or by revelation or by experience or by a logical deduction from either a revealed truth or a proposition verified by observation.*

That this is the real meaning of ' Ockham's razor' can be gathered from various texts in Ockham's writings.[2]

---

[1] *Cf. Reportatio* II, qu. 19F.

[2] *Cf. De sacramento altaris*, cap. 28 ; ed. Birch, p. 318. In *Ordinatio* d. 30, qu. IE, we read : 'Nothing must be affirmed without a reason being assigned for it, except it be something known by itself, known by experience, or it be something proved by the authority of holy scripture'. *Reportatio* II, qu. 150 has the following wording : 'We must not affirm that something is necessarily required for the explanation of an effect, if we are not led to this by a reason proceeding either from a truth known by itself or from an experience that is certain'. It should be noted that various formulations of ' Ockham's razor' are already found before Ockham, for instance in Duns Scotus. The oldest scholastic thinker, so far as we know, who formulated it, gives this version : '*Frustra fit per plura quod potest fieri per unum*' ; Odo Rigaldus, *Commentarium super Sententias*, MS. Bruges 208, fol. 150*a*.

It is quite often stated by Ockham in the form : 'Plurality is not to be posited without necessity' (*Pluralitas non est ponenda sine necessitate*), and also, though seldom : 'What can be explained by the assumption of fewer things is vainly explained by the assumption of more things' (*Frustra fit per plura quod potest fieri per pauciora*). The form usually given, 'Entities must not be multiplied without necessity' (*Entia non sunt multiplicanda sine necessitate*), does not seem to have been used by Ockham. What Ockham demands in his maxim is that everyone who makes a statement must have a sufficient reason for its truth, 'sufficient reason' being defined as either the observation of a fact, or an immediate logical insight, or divine revelation, or a deduction from these. This principle of 'sufficient reason' is epistemological or methodological, certainly not an ontological axiom.

The scholastics distinguished clearly between a *sufficient* reason or cause (usually expressed by the verb *sufficit*) and a *necessary* reason or cause (usually expressed by *requiritur*). As a Christian theologian Ockham could not forget that contingent facts do not ultimately have a sufficient reason or cause of their being, inasmuch as God does not act of necessity but freely ; but our theological and philosophical, and in general all our scientific, assertions ought to have a sufficient reason, that is a reason from the affirmation of which the given assertion follows. All created things can be explained ultimately only by a necessary reason, i.e. a cause which is required to account for their existence. For every creature is contingent. The guiding idea of Duns Scotus, to safeguard contingency (*servare contingentiam*), is present everywhere in the work of Ockham. We can formulate it as follows :

5. *Everything that is real, and different from God, is contingent to the core of its being.*

If we bear in mind these guiding principles of Ockham, then his philosophical work becomes intelligible as the effort of a theologian who is looking for absolute truth in this contingent world, viz. for truth independent of any of those thoroughly contingent worlds which are equally possible. He is a theologian who views the world from the standpoint of the absolute. Consequently he sees many truths which were called 'eternal' dwindling away in the light of eternity, which is God Himself. The actual order of creatures remains contingent ; the possible order of creatures is above contingency. Hence the tendency of Ockham to go beyond the investigation of the actual order, by asking what is possible regardless of the state of the present universe. What is absolutely possible can never be impossible ; and in that sense statements about absolute possibility are always true and free from contradiction, and for that reason are necessary. Thus the work of Ockham also becomes intelligible—and this is only the converse of the former viewpoint—as the effort of a philosopher who is constantly reminded by the theologian in himself that he must not call any truth necessary unless it can be shown that its denial implies a contradiction.

Such a theologian, and such a philosopher, stands in need of a refined and powerful logic, since he is always looking beyond facts and the actualities towards absolute being and absolute possibility. Ockham was, therefore, bound to be more interested in logic than any of his predecessors. This being so, we must acquaint ourselves as closely as possible with Ockham's highly developed logic, and it is for this reason that so much of our text consists of passages from his writings on logic.

It will now be our task to present a rounded picture of Ockham's philosophy as reflected by the texts in this volume. We shall do it according to a certain system, but we wish to repeat that Ockham himself never presented a system of philosophy.

2. *Epistemology*

Right at the beginning of our exposition we are faced with difficulties of terminology. The highly technical language of Ockham does not always allow of a simple rendering into English. Such is the case with the term '*scientia*', which may assume various shades of meaning, ranging from the unqualified knowledge of a truth to scientific knowledge in the strict sense ; and again, it might mean groups of such pieces of knowledge (for instance a demonstration), or a system of such pieces of knowledge, e.g. the science of logic or of physics. Here we shall merely describe one very important meaning.

Scientific knowledge in the strict sense. Ockham's ideal of scientific knowledge is extremely high. He knows that any cognition of a truth may be found in the various sciences ; however, his ideal of a strictly scientific knowledge is the same as that developed by Aristotle in the *Posterior Analytics*. According to Aristotle those propositions only are scientifically known which are obtained by a syllogistic process from evident propositions which are necessary, i.e. always true and never false. Hence Ockham will admit that there is scientific knowledge in this strict sense only when we know a proposition which remains true regardless of our existing world. All the truths of logic and of mathematics, and some statements about God, and many metaphysical propositions, conform to the definition of scientific knowledge given above, for they are necessary conclusions obtained from necessary

and evident premises. But no statement of actual fact about this world is in this sense truly a scientific statement. However, modal or conditional propositions about our world may have the necessity required by the definition of scientific knowledge. It is understood that a revealed truth which cannot be known by natural reason fails to satisfy the definition, since it lacks the required self-evidence. When reading Ockham, we must always keep it in mind that scientific knowledge in the strict sense is the result of a demonstration ; Ockham admits that we can have evidence for, and convincingly prove, many statements, but they are scientifically or demonstratively known only if they fulfil the requirements of the above definition.

Intuitive and abstractive cognition. The field of scientific knowledge is limited. But many statements outside this field are true and evident and even necessary, and therefore known with certainty. How do we arrive at them? The answer to this question is of ultimate importance. Our cognition starts with the apprehension not of necessary but of contingent facts. No knowledge of any kind is possible without a direct or indirect contact with some object that is experienced. Since it is generally admitted that in the real order only individuals exist, the realities primarily known to us must be individuals or singular facts, whether these be objects of sense or of intellect, whether outside or within the mind. This first, immediate cognition is called by Ockham, following Duns Scotus, *intuitive cognition.* It is the basis for a self-evident existential statement, viz. that the thing which is experienced exists, is present, has such and such a condition, etc. It is to be noted that the existential judgment is an operation of the intellect alone, and that the intuitive cognition which is at the basis of it, even if it concerns an object of sense, is an *intellectual* intuitive cognition or a primary *intellectual* awareness of an object. The intellect could not have an intuitive cognition of a

sensible object without the help of sensory cognition, at least in the natural order ; but the intellectual awareness relates to the sense-object as immediately as the sensory cognition does.

Now there is another sort of cognition of an object in which we are not aware of its actuality ; it is knowledge simply and solely of the object and therefore abstracts from its existence or non-existence. For instance, a few minutes ago I saw a cloud ; I had an intuitive cognition of this cloud, and on the basis of this cognition I gave my assent to the evident judgment 'There is a cloud'. I do not now see this cloud any more, but I think of it, I have it in my mind ; this latter knowledge or cognition cannot be the ground for assent to the evident existential judgment 'This cloud exists', for it does not imply the actual existence of this cloud at this time. It abstracts, therefore, from the existence or non-existence of the object and for that reason is called an *abstractive cognition* ; it need not be abstract in the sense of 'universal'. Both cognitions are caused by the object and the intellect. They are the result of a causality in which the object and the intellect co-operate to produce an act of intellection or cognition. Hence both intuitive and abstractive cognition represent real objects outside or inside the mind. Ockham, therefore, is a realist in his epistemology.

Intuitive cognition of non-existents. Ockham thus holds that intuitive cognition must be caused by two part-causes. There is no doubt that there cannot be an intuitive cognition without the knowing subject ; is it possible that there can be an intuitive cognition if the object itself or its causality is lacking ? It would seem that if the only part-cause present is the intellect, this is impossible ; and Ockham does not deny this. However, Ockham as a Christian theologian believes in the omnipotence of God ; one of the guiding principles of his work is that everything that can be produced by a

secondary cause can also be produced by the first cause,
God. No object, therefore, is necessary, because God
can supply the causality of the one secondary partial
cause, viz. the object, and co-operate with the other
part-cause, the intellect, to produce an intuitive cognition.
This He can do, even if the object so known is far away
or is for other reasons inaccessible to a direct contact
with the intellect. Thus far we are dealing with an
object that really exists but is intuitively known and
judged to exist only by supernatural aid. But is intuitive
cognition also possible, if there is no object ?

Ockham's complete definition of intuitive cognition is
that it makes possible an evident judgment that a thing
exists (or is present etc.) if it exists, or that a thing does
not exist if it does not exist. By definition, therefore,
intuitive cognition has reference to the existent order.
Hence when it is said that one can intuitively know an
object which does not exist, it must immediately be
stipulated that the object—though not existing in fact
—must be an object that might exist. Pure nothingness
(i.e. what involves a contradiction, or an impossibility)
cannot be known intuitively.

At first sight this may seem surprising. Is it not indeed
a contradiction to say that we can have an intuitive
cognition of something which does not exist ? Ockham
does not think so, because as a Christian theologian he
knows that God Himself has immediate and non-
inferential cognition of everything, whether it exists or
not. God knows immediately—and that is to say intuitively—not only all that exists, but also all that could
exist, but does not. If such a cognition is possible to
God, we must allow that it is possible absolutely speaking ; therefore it cannot involve a contradiction. And,
according to Ockham's other guiding principle, that
which does not involve a contradiction can be realised
by God. As a Christian theologian, Ockham maintains
that an intuitive cognition of non-existent things is

possible with the supernatural help of God ; as a philosopher, he maintains also that even in this case the statement 'This thing does not exist' is evident— because intuitive cognition is the basis of an evident and hence absolutely true statement that a thing exists or does not exist, as the case may be. Ockham never doubted the infallibility of evident knowledge.

Abstract universal cognition. Though an intuitive cognition could itself be called a concept, usually the term 'concept' is reserved for that abstractive cognition which results from comparing together several abstractive cognitions of singulars. By this process of comparison a more general abstractive cognition is formed : a *universal* concept, predicable of many singulars. What does the universal concept represent ?

Ockham refuses to admit that in the real world there is anything that corresponds to the universality of a concept ; in other words, he does not admit any universal *in re*, common nature, etc.—anything which is not completely individual. It is by no means self-evident, says Ockham, that in its own right the nature or essence of a thing is not individual. Almost all his predecessors had maintained that natures and essences considered in themselves had some kind of generality or commonness ; in order to become numerical units or individuals or singulars, natures had to be individualised by a principle of individuation. Ockham's predecessors had thus approached this problem from the side of the universal ; Ockham attacked it from the side of the individual; a change of outlook almost as epoch-making as the Copernican revolution in astronomy.

Here it is instructive to take a quick glance in passing at the teaching of Duns Scotus. He still held that concerning universals two questions may properly be asked : (1) How can a nature or essence which by itself is not singular become singular ? (2) How is it that the same nature or essence becomes a universal concept in the

mind ? The first question Scotus answers by his theory
of individuation. Ockham, however, considers this
question a pseudo-problem. To him it is self-evident
that everything that exists is individual and singular, so
that it does not need to be individualised or singularised.
We do not need an explanation for the fact that something is an individual—though of course we need an
explanation for the facts that it exists and that it has
such or such a nature. Thus Ockham reduces the questions that can properly be asked concerning commonness
and individuality to one question, viz. 'What is it that
makes a concept a *universal* concept ?' or 'How, by means
of universal concepts, can I know individual natures ?'

As already stated, Ockham's answer is that a concept,
for instance the concept 'man', arises out of the combina-
tion of an intuitive with an abstractive cognition. The
abstractive cognition alone survives and is stored in the
memory as habitual knowledge ; it is generalised by
way of comparison with other similar abstractive cognitions to represent, not just one, but many similar individuals. Because of its origin, and because of the similarity between the individuals, it is common to all
individuals of the same kind, in the sense that it is
predicable of them. Universality, therefore, is simply
a manner in which a sufficiently generalised abstractive
cognition is predicable, and thus it exists wholly within
the mind. On the side of the individuals that are
known, there exists only individuality and the similarity
of individual natures.

The nature of the universal concept. In answer to the
question stated above, Ockham did not hesitate between
various possibilities. But there is a further question.
What is the nature of a universal concept considered in
itself ; what kind of being does a universal concept have
in the mind ? At different periods Ockham gave different answers to this question. Originally he had believed
that the universal concept (for instance 'man' or 'animal'

in the mental proposition 'Man is an animal') is something different from the act of thinking it, (that is, the
intellection), and that the concept has no reality but
only a logical being, as an object of the act of thinking
(or, in medieval language, that it has no *esse subiectivum*
but does have *esse obiectivum*). As a mere thought-object
it has neither a spiritual, or psychic, nor a material
reality ; it is something mentally imaged, and for that
reason Ockham calls it a *fictum*. A *fictum*, however, is
not a *figmentum*, or a fiction in the modern sense ; the
latter being defined as something that is quite impossible,
or purely fictitious. This logical picture or *fictum* is
considered to be a true representation of the object in
connexion with which it was first constituted in its
proper being by the process of intuitive and abstractive
cognition.

This theory was held not only by Ockham in his earlier
period, but also by his contemporary Aureoli. Ockham
and Aureoli seemed to have arrived at it independently
of one another ; but it appears that when Ockham
became acquainted with Aureoli's *Commentary on the
Sentences* he gradually gave up his *fictum* theory in favour
of another. This other theory we shall call the 'intellection theory'. According to this, the concept or universal
involved in a cognition is identical with the very act
of abstractive cognition, hence it is a psychical entity ;
this act of cognition, immediately caused by the object
known and the intellect working together as two part-
causes, represents the object, and as such can function
as predicate in a mental proposition.

All the evidence suggests that Ockham finally held
only the intellection theory and, in his later years,
completely abandoned the *fictum* theory.

3. *Logic*

Once it becomes capable of conceptual and universal knowledge, the mind can proceed to develop the various sciences. Physics, mathematics, metaphysics and all the other sciences need universal notions as material. Logic, however, teaches us how to arrange these notions to form propositions and arguments in order to obtain truth and an organised body of truths, i.e. a science. Since a practical science teaches us how to do certain things in the right manner, logic is a practical science ; it is a tool of scientific work. It was especially in this field that Ockham made himself a great master.

Ockham divided the subject into three parts : the logic of terms, of propositions and of reasoning. This division has become classical and has its root, not so much in the nature of logic as such, as in those writings of Aristotle called the *Organon*. It is important to note that Ockham's logic (like all medieval logic) deals mainly with spoken sentences, a fact that is often overlooked. But this did not prevent Ockham from clearly distinguishing between mental, spoken and written sentences, and their elements.

Some divisions of terms. The elements of propositions are called *terms*. Terms function as signs, since they call or represent objects to our mind ; in a word, they *signify*. Nouns, for instance, are terms ; they are instituted by man in order to be names of objects and (in their significative capacity) to act in discourse as substitute for the things themselves. Language is thus, in Ockham's view, a system of artificial signs. Prior to these artificial signs are the natural signs, our concepts, which are not dependent on, or caused by, man's activity in instituting languages ; they are products of nature, caused simply by the interaction of object and intellect as two part-causes. Now, according to Ockham, the artificial signs, our spoken words, are dependent on the

natural signs of our mental language. An artificial sign is associated with a concept ; the word, however, the artificial sign, does not signify the corresponding concept ; properly speaking, the word and the concept both directly signify the same object ; the only difference is that the word does so only in subordination to the concept.

Categorematic and syncategorematic terms. In any proposition we can distinguish formal and material elements. For instance, in the proposition 'Every man is not white', the material elements are 'man' and 'white' ; the formal elements 'every' and 'is not'. The latter constitute the *form* of a proposition, and are *syncategorematic* terms; the former are called *categorematic* terms. Examples of syncategorematic terms are 'every', 'is', 'not', 'or', 'and', 'if—then', etc. ; modern logicians would call them constants. Ockham would say that categorematic terms signify definite objects, whether naturally or by convention, so that we can point at a definite object and predicate the term of it. 'Man' is thus a categorematic term, for we can point at a definite object and say 'This is a man'. Syncategorematic terms, on the other hand, do not signify a definite object or objects. They do have meaning, of course, but they have no signification when taken by themselves. Thus, if we take 'every' in its proper meaning, it is simply nonsense to say 'This is every'. Syncategorematic terms thus have a *contextual* meaning ; they signify only in conjunction with categorematic terms. It is these formal elements or syncategorematic terms which enable us to make inferences, and for that reason they are the main subject of logic.

Absolute and connotative terms. As regards categorematic terms, Ockham explains several distinctions ; the most fundamental appears to be the division into absolute and connotative terms. An *absolute* term signifies its object directly and without at the same time signifying something else indirectly or secondarily ; in other words, an absolute term is one that calls an object to mind, and

only that object. Correspondingly, a *connotative* term is
one which calls to mind not only the object it signifies
directly, but also something else which it signifies indirectly. For instance, the term 'white' is a connotative
term. Directly, it signifies the *thing* that is white, or,
to use the medieval terms, the *subject* that has whiteness ;
but along with this object it also brings to mind, and
signifies indirectly or connotes, another object, *whiteness*.
The term 'white' does not directly and primarily signify
the whiteness of a thing. For if that were true, then the
proposition 'This [pointing at the quality whiteness] is
white' could be true. But whiteness is not white ; rather
it is a white thing that is white, or *has* whiteness. 'Whiteness' on the other hand is an absolute term. We can
point at a certain colour and say 'This is whiteness'. In
this case, the real quality of whiteness is signified, and
there is nothing else 'connoted'. Similar absolute terms
are 'man', 'horse', 'stone', 'intellection', etc. Thus it
appears that absolute terms are fundamental ; they are
the result of an immediate intellectual contact with
objects and of acts of abstraction based on this. Connotative terms, on the other hand, result from a combina-
tion of concepts, and are hence always composite terms.
Whilst absolute terms are susceptible of a real definition
(*definitio quid rei*) or of a definition answering the question
'What is this thing ?', connotative terms are susceptible
only of a nominal definition (*definitio quid nominis*),
answering the question 'What is meant by this term ?'
The nominal definition simply indicates the elements
which enter into the composition of a term.

The importance of this distinction can be seen if we
point out that according to Ockham the terms 'quantity'
and 'quantum' are synonymous and both are connotative.
For in his view a quantity is in reality identical with the
body, the colour, etc. that 'has' quantity. Hence
quantity directly signifies a body or colour, but connotes
that these subjects have parts distant from other parts.

For that reason it can be truly said 'This table is quantity'
or 'This table is quantitative' (which is the old sense of
quantum). Both propositions mean 'This table is something that has parts distant from each other'.

Terms of first and second imposition and intention. Ockham
further makes use of a distinction between terms of first
and second imposition and intention. By 'imposition'
is meant the act of imposing a name on an object, or
of assigning to a word the task of signifying ; 'intention'
means concept or mental term. By 'first' and 'second',
as used in this connexion, it is shown that conceptual
or mental language, and again spoken or written
language, consists of several levels. For we can *use* terms
(first level) or we can *speak about* terms (second level).
Let us first consider spoken or written language. On
certain words we have *imposed* the function of signifying.
Those words which do not signify parts or qualifications
of our spoken or written language as such are called
words of first imposition. On the other hand, those words
which signify parts or qualifications of our spoken or
written language are called *words of second imposition.*
Thus words like 'substantive', 'adjective', 'declension',
'conjugation', 'nominative case', etc., are words of second
imposition, in which the grammarian is interested. Words
like 'man', 'stone', 'white', 'intention', 'universal',
'species', etc., are words of first imposition. Hence words
of second imposition always signify words of first imposition.

The distinction between first and second intentions
concerns only concepts or mental terms, which, as we
said, are natural signs of their objects. First intentions
signify objects which are not 'intentions' or concepts ;
second intentions signify first intentions. Concepts like
'man', 'stone', 'white', etc. are *concepts of first intention* ;
concepts like 'universal', 'species', etc., are *concepts of
second intention.* Second intentions are predicated of first
intentions, but not *vice versa.*

Several distinct spheres or levels in the universe of discourse are reviewed by the logician. First, there is the level of objects which are not signs. Second, there is the level of those signs which signify first-level objects. Third, there is the level of those signs which signify the signs of the second level. This refers to the conceptual order. Concerning the order of spoken or written terms, there is first the level of anything that is not a spoken or written word ; practically, therefore, everything contained in the three levels mentioned above. Secondly, there is the level of those spoken or written words which signify the first-level objects ; these are first impositions. Thirdly, there is the level of those spoken or written words which signify the words of the second level ; these are words of second imposition.

Suppositio. The theory of *suppositio*, closely related to the distinctions just mentioned, is everywhere present in Ockham's philosophical and theological work. Though introduced by earlier logicians, the theory was refined and simplified by Ockham. After him it became quite common among all the scholastics.

The meaning of the term '*suppositio*' is intimately connected with that of the term 'signification'. Every categorematic term has signification, by its very nature if it is a concept, or by convention if it is a spoken or written word ; but when used in a proposition it does not always exercise its significative function. In the theory of *suppositio*, a term is said to have 'personal' *suppositio* when it is used to signify that of which it is (naturally or conventionally) a sign ; for in that case it acts for or 'impersonates' the object signified. However, terms themselves can become the subject of discourse, in which case they do not exercise a significative function in a proposition. Now, if a term which has become a subject of discourse is a concept and simply represents itself or is taken as such, then this term has 'simple' *suppositio*. For instance, in the proposition 'Man is a

species', it is being said that the *concept* 'man' is a species.
Hence what is represented here by 'the concept "man"',
or by the word associated with it, is not a *man* in reality,
but simply the concept itself. If a term which has become the subject of discourse is a spoken or written
word, then we have 'material' *suppositio*, as for instance
when we say : ' "Man" has three letters'. For it is
being stated that the *word* 'man' has three letters, but
not that *man*, i.e. a rational animal, has three letters.

This distinction is very important. A case in point is
the problem whether a real science, as for instance
physics, deals with physical objects of the outside world
or with propositions. Ockham explains that the term
'science' is a second intention, since it is predicated of
propositions or of a system of propositions. The propositions themselves, however, are composed, most of
them at least, of first intentions.

The theory of *suppositio* performs still another and
more important task. It provides the scholastics with
a logic of predication. This immediately becomes clear
when we turn to the distinctions which Ockham draws
between various types of personal *suppositio*. He explains
them by indicating the relations of such predicates as
'man' or 'white', etc., to their subjects, or, more precisely, to the individuals signified by the subjects.
Ockham considers a kind of atomic sentence, in which
individuals are denoted by the demonstrative pronouns
'this' or 'that' or by proper names. The relations
between these and other sentences are determined by
inferences. To make such an inference from a more
general proposition to an atomic proposition was called
'descent', the opposite process 'ascent'. Let us take for
instance the so-called 'determinate' *suppositio*. We get
this in a particular affirmative proposition such as 'Some
man is white'. Its atomic or singularised form is 'This
man is white'. The following inference (or, indeed,
equivalence) is valid : 'Some man is white, therefore

this man is white, or that man is white, or that man'
(and so on for every individual man).   Hence Ockham
defines determinate *suppositio* as that which allows the
descent from a proposition to a disjunction between the
singularised propositions derived from it.   Again, we
have a common, distributive, confused *suppositio*, when
a logical descent is possible from a universal proposition
to singularised propositions joined by the conjunction
'and', as in this instance : 'Every man is mortal ; therefore this man is mortal and that man is mortal' (and so
on for every individual man).

Finally the theory of *suppositio* is used by Ockham to
make clear and definite the notion of truth and falsity.
Ockham's definition of truth is in line with the Aristotelian view that a proposition is true when that which
is said to be is.   Ockham indeed is merely stating the
same thing as Aristotle, but with greater precision, when
he says that a proposition is true when subject and
predicate stand for (have *suppositio* for) the same thing.
For instance, the proposition 'Socrates is white' is true
if there really is one individual signified by the term
'Socrates' and also by the term 'white'.   Neither the
terms nor the notions associated with them are identical,
but both subject and predicate of the proposition stand
for the same object, which is signified by them.   The
proposition would be false if the individual signified by
'white' were not Socrates or if the individual signified
by 'Socrates' were not white.   The case is slightly more
complicated when the subject has material or simple
suppositio.   In material and simple *suppositio* a term has
no significative function, but simply stands for itself.
For instance, ' "Man" is a word' is true, if there really
is a word 'man' which the term 'word' stands for and
signifies.

Consequentiae.   Medieval logic did not regard the
syllogism as the only form of inference.   On the contrary, medieval logicians worked out a much more

general theory in which the syllogism appears only as a special type of inference : the general theory of *consequentiae*. A *consequentia* can be understood as a conditional proposition ; its antecedent and the consequent may be either simple or compound propositions. Ockham made himself a master in this branch of the subject. In fact, he himself collected quite a number of *consequentiae* which are well-known theorems of modern logic. Like most modern logicians, Ockham regarded as fundamental the *consequentiae* holding between unanalysed propositions (theorems of propositional calculus in modern logic).

Ockham's discussion of this subject is by no means as easy to follow as it would be if stated in modern logical symbolism. That Ockham, without the advantage of modern notation, was able to penetrate so deeply into these fundamental problems of logic, is a striking testimony to the power and clarity of his intellect. His *consequentiae* are not proved in any of the ways used in modern logic, though we do encounter attempts of this kind among the later scholastics ; they were formulated, it seems, merely by insight into logical relations.

Ockham certainly knew the so-called De Morgan laws (formulated by De Morgan in 1857). According to them, the contradictory opposite of a conjunctive proposition is equivalent to a disjunctive proposition in which each proposition is denied. In other words, he knew the law :

$$- (p \cdot q) \equiv (- p \vee - q)$$

And also the converse :

$$- (p \vee q) \equiv (- p \cdot - q)$$

Besides this there are many other theorems in the propositional calculus of modern logic which were known to Ockham. For convenience' sake we shall present

many of them here in modern symbolic form (the numbers are those given in the translation). We use the symbol of material implications ($\supset$) without maintaining that Ockham understood these *consequentiae* as material implications. On the contrary, he considered most of them to be strict implications. However, it seems that he had an idea of material implication, as in modern logic ; and in any case every strict implication is valid in material implication, though not vice versa.

(1) $(p \supset q) \supset - (p . - q)$

And also :

$(p . - q) \supset - (p \supset q)$

And again :

$[(p . q) \supset r] \supset - (p . q . - r)$

(2) $- p \supset (p \supset q)$

Likewise the destructive form of the conditional syllogism:

$[(p \supset q) . - q] \supset - p$

(3) $(p \supset q) \supset (- q \supset - p)$

Applied to a syllogism, as by Ockham, it will take this form :

$[(p . q) \supset r] \supset [- r \supset - (p . q)]$

or :

$[(p . q) \supset r] \supset [(- r . p) \supset -q)]$

The following are other syllogistic variations :

(4) $(p \supset q) \supset [(q \supset r) \supset (p \supset r)]$
(5) $(p \supset q) \supset [(r \supset p) \supset (r \supset q)]$
(6) $(p \supset q) \supset [(p . r) \supset (q . r)]$
(7) $(p \supset q) \supset [-(q . r) \supset - (p . r)]$

(8) This rule cannot be symbolised with ordinary means.

It states that from a proposition which is always true and never false, no proposition which may be either true or false can be inferred. And in rule (9) it is stated that a proposition which is always false (an impossible proposition) cannot be inferred from a proposition which may be either true or false ; since, if the latter proposition were true, falsity would follow from truth ; but that cannot be admitted.

(10) This rule simply states that from a proposition which is always false any proposition may follow. It could be symbolised in the form of the following theorem :

$$(p . - p) \supset r$$

We may substitute for r whatever we like. Soon after the time of Ockham the startling though formally true example was used : 'You are sitting and you are not sitting, therefore a stick is in the corner'. Ockham expressly states that the examples he gives are not formal *consequentiae* ; since he uses contingent propositions in the antecedent, it seems that he is referring to material implication. If this is true, then he has an idea of this still hotly disputed interpretation of a conditional proposition.

It would lead too far astray to go into further details. Let us only mention that Ockham has already some idea of a many-valued logic. In any case his logic is much richer and much more carefully developed than any modern textbook of neo-scholastic logic would lead us to suspect.

4. *Metaphysics*

It has been said that Ockham's basic ideas in logic and epistemology are opposed to the development of an ontological philosophy, i.e. of one that deals with being or reality in general. In other words, he may have a logic, even an excellent one, but he cannot have a

metaphysics. Ockham himself would have been sur-
prised at this insinuation. The best answer to it is
Ockham's own metaphysics, of which we shall now give
a general outline.

Metaphysics is a real science, or a science concerned
with real things, in the sense explained before. Its main
subject is the term 'being', which stands for (*supponit*)
beings. There is no 'being as such' in the universe outside the mind ; there are only *beings* (things, individuals
—whether accidents or substances): inanimate bodies,
plants, animals, human beings, angels, God ; and every
one of these individuals is conceived as *a* 'being' ; so
that of every one of them 'being' can be predicated.
Thus there is one concept which can be predicated about
everything that exists or can exist. The spoken or written
term 'being' is univocal. In fact, to deny this univocity
of the term 'being', i.e. to maintain that to the term
'being' there does not correspond one and the same
concept, predicable about any real thing, would, according to Ockham, entail agnosticism in regard to God.
Since we have no immediate or intuitive cognition of
God, and consequently no abstractive cognition such as
would immediately accompany or follow this ; and
since only cognitions of these two sorts are simple and
proper cognitions ; the only possibility left open is that
we should have a concept of God that is composed of
concepts abstracted from creatures. For instance, we
can abstract from creatures the notion of 'being' that is
predicable of every real thing : we can also abstract
from creatures the notion of 'first' that is predicable of
everything which is first in any respect. We can then
combine both concepts to form the composite concept
of 'first being' ; and this is a concept proper to God,
but not simple. If the elements of such concepts were
not predicable in exactly the same sense of God and
creatures there would be no link joining our experience
to the unexperienced, transcendent God.

However, and this is of equal importance, this uni-vocity of the term 'being', and of others used in meta-physics, does not imply that any reality is common to God and creatures. In fact, there is no common feature whatever in reality. There is something common only in the conceptual order. There is not even a real simi-larity between God and creature, neither in their sub-stantial being, nor in accidental being (since God has no accidents). There is, we could say, only a structural similarity that transcends any concrete content of the things conceived as 'beings', somewhat as a melody can be the same, though every note is different when played in a different key. Thus we can grasp in one concept things which are entirely dissimilar in their actual being : for the modes of infinity and finitude establish an infinite dissimilarity. Nevertheless God is a 'non-finite' (i.e. infinite) 'being', and a creature is a 'finite being', and every corresponding term in these expressions is univocal.

As we mentioned already, the term 'being' is the main subject of metaphysics. It is predicated of every indi-vidual or thing not as qualifying some other subject or thing, but in its own right. Being, therefore, is predicated in the manner of a 'quiddity', *in quid*. The term 'white' *qualifies* a subject, and therefore the scholastics say that it is predicated in the manner of a quality, or *in quale* ; the term 'whiteness', on the other hand, denotes or sig-nifies a thing, namely the real accident whiteness, and is said to be predicated in the manner of a 'quiddity', *in quid* ; i.e. it tells us *what thing* whiteness is. (Notice that *quid* in scholastic Latin has a much more restricted mean-ing than 'what' in English). The same is true *a fortiori* for the terms 'man', 'substance'. It is regrettable that this scholastic terminology is often misunderstood. The term '*in-quid* predication' has nothing to do with the recent controversy over essentialism and existentialism; it is concerned only with Aristotelian logic. This should be eminently clear in the case of the *in-quid* predication

of being ; for the term 'being' by its very meaning necessarily has reference to actual existence, since it denotes everything that exists or can exist in the universe. To introduce a distinction between 'being' and 'existing', 'essence' and 'existence', in a real thing is as meaningless for Duns Scotus (who calls it a fiction) as it is for Ockham. For, according to Ockham, the terms 'essence' and 'existence' both signify exactly the same individuals and the same reality. The difference between the terms is only grammatical. And Ockham is very sensitive to any encroachment of grammar on metaphysics.

Hence the terms 'being', 'thing', 'individual', and the abstract terms 'reality', 'essence', 'existence' denote exactly the same things in Ockham's metaphysics. Thus he can maintain that a creature is its own essence, and its own existence, and nevertheless allow for an ultimate difference between the being that is God and the being that is a creature. He draws other distinctions between God and creatures, no less radical than that supposed to hold between a being that is its own act of existence, and one that is not : e.g. that God is from Himself, and a creature is not from itself ; that God is infinite, a creature is finite ; that God is uncaused, a creature is caused, and so on.

Once Ockham's theory of univocity is established, the link is secured between creatures and God, and in consequence between ontology and natural theology, and also between natural theology and revealed theology. It is strange that Ockham should have been accused of having separated theology from philosophy. Really he made their common basis explicit. It is obvious that the Christian theologian would speak a language totally different from that of a pagan philosopher, were there not a common concept, at least of 'being', which they could both use. For, in fact, if there were no common concept, they could not even contradict each other. But it is also clear that we have no concept of God that is

both simple and at the same time proper to God. Not even the theologian has such a concept, for such a simple and proper concept is reserved to one who has an intuitive cognition of God or a special revelation from God.

On the proofs of God's existence. Ockham, therefore, has paved the way for a natural theology. He demonstrates that we *can* know something about God—little though it may be if we demand the utmost certainty. The question thus arises, *what* can we know about God with our unaided natural reason ?

We can know something about God either by way of demonstration (a concept explained earlier), or by way of a persuasive (probable or dialectical) argument. The latter argument does not proceed from evident premises ; but its premises are accepted by all, or at least by all acute and trained, minds. The conclusion may be *certain*, but it is not *evident*. Evidentness and certitude are by no means equivalent. We can be certain who our parents were, but the fact itself cannot be evident to us.

About God, there are only a few conclusions which can strictly be demonstrated. One is the truth that God exists. Ockham gives a proof for this truth in the *Ordinatio* and in his *Questions on Physics*, but he nowhere goes into a detailed presentation of it. In both places he starts with a criticism of the proof advanced by Duns Scotus, which in our opinion is the most powerful and most developed proof of this kind elaborated by any scholastic in the Middle Ages. Ockham, the logician, directs his criticism mainly against the idea of efficient causality used by Duns. Ockham does not deny that God is the first efficient cause, but he believes it is difficult to prove that in the order of efficient causes an infinite series of causes is impossible, so that a first efficient cause must be asserted. Ockham argues, however, that this difficulty does not arise if we consider conservation instead of origination. In a series of *efficient* or *producing*

causes we are not logically bound to postulate co-existence in time of all the causes belonging to the same series ; but in a series of *conserving* causes, where one thing maintains another in being, and the former is being maintained, and so on, it follows *ex hypothesi* that the whole series must be simultaneously existing. Hence an infinite series would, in this case, entail the actual co-existence of an infinity of separate beings, and that is considered to be impossible.

Ockham's criticism of Duns Scotus is directed, there-fore, against the actual form, but not against the main principle of his proof. Ockham also criticises, it is true, certain distinctions used by Duns, but this does not invalidate the general idea that there is at least one case where an infinite series is impossible, viz. a contempor-aneous infinity of separate beings, each conserving another. This idea of conservation used in Ockham's proof is distinctively Christian ; it is entirely foreign to Aristotelian thought, since Aristotle has no idea of creation, nor of any relation of efficient causality between God and the world. We only regret that Ockham did not elaborate this proof in detail and did not connect the idea of conservation with that of the essential tempor-ality in every creature, the idea which he so strongly defended against St Thomas Aquinas and Duns Scotus. For the idea of an '*Aevum*'—that is, of a created eternity —is rejected by Ockham. In this, to some extent, he follows St Bonaventure. For like the Seraphic Doctor, Ockham believed that it is impossible for a creature to possess the fullness of its being in one instant without any succession in its very being. What is produced must be in time ; if it were not, it could not be annihilated, nor would it be contingent.

According to Ockham, there are certain divine attri-butes that can be demonstrated, for instance that God is an intellectual nature. For it follows formally that if God is the highest being, God must have both intellect

and will. Ockham unfortunately does not enlarge on these demonstrations any more than he enlarges on those already mentioned. It is possible that he postponed them for treatment in his intended and promised exposition of Aristotle's *Metaphysics*, which he never found time to write. In any case, he seems to have been interested rather in showing how much it is *not* possible to demonstrate.

Thus, according to Ockham, we cannot *demonstrate* that there is only one God. The problem whether the unicity of God can be demonstrated or not was variously answered by the scholastic philosophers. Moses Maimonides, the great Jewish philosopher, denied the possibility. Duns Scotus tried hard to demonstrate it, but seems to have been left unsatisfied by all his demonstrations. For his part, Ockham denies the possibility; for, he says, the proof of God's existence does not carry us beyond the proposition 'God is a being not surpassed by anything else in His perfection'; and this by no means implies that God excels everything that is different from Him. God, it is true, will not be *excelled* by any being that equals His perfection; but neither will He excel it. There being no demonstrative argument in favour of God's unicity, Ockham falls back on a persuasive argument—one that he seems to have borrowed from Duns. It runs like this : Our proof of God's existence leads us to a being that exists of itself and hence exists necessarily. Suppose, now, that two gods exist. To say that two gods exist is to say that two gods of the same nature and of equal perfection may possibly exist—and that this involves no contradiction. If we can suppose that two gods exist, then there is no reason why we cannot suppose that three, four or even an infinity of such gods exist. But since, in God, that which is possible is also necessary; and since that which is necessary must exist; it would follow that by necessity an infinity of gods exist; but an infinity of separate beings is in-

admissible. And since an infinity of gods cannot exist, it follows that not even more than one God can exist and does exist, because of the contradiction that would be implied.

Similar arguments, probable or persuasive in the sense explained before, can be made for the truth that God knows things outside Himself, and that God is free as regards producing creatures. The same holds for God's infinity, for God's omnipotence (in the Christian sense), and for other attributes of God. In the discussion of these the logician is all the time at the elbow of the metaphysician and the theologian, ever reminding them that the requirements of a demonstration are exacting and difficult to fulfil. In a strictly scientific metaphysics Ockham wants only demonstrative conclusions ; he does not want convictions, well-founded as they may be. What the neo-scholastics would call physical or moral certitude, he leaves to apologetics. A Christian thinker is certainly equipped to see more clearly and farther than a pagan philosopher. However, he must not present his well-founded arguments as strict demonstrations ; for in so doing he would expose his faith to the danger of being ridiculed.

5. *On Creatures*

When dealing with philosophical problems concerning creatures Ockham never loses sight of the central idea that everything that is not God is radically contingent ; for to be created means to be entirely dependent on the free will of God. That our world is what it is is due to a free decision of God. To interpret this doctrine as meaning that God has ultimately an arbitrary will is to overlook Ockham's belief that God not only has a free will but is also infinitely wise and good. But His wisdom is a free wisdom, His goodness a free goodness ; He is bound only by the law of contradiction, if this means being bound at all.

Ockham accepts the system of the world commonly believed in by thinkers of the Middle Ages. The world is created in time—though with St Thomas Aquinas and Duns Scotus Ockham thinks that the beginning of the world in time cannot be demonstrated ; it is finite and has a certain order. Everything is created for man, and man is created for God. The earth is in the centre of the universe, surrounded by the spheres of the planets and stars. Another world like ours is possible. The material element in all bodies, both heavenly and earthly, is of the same nature. All created beings are divided into two groups, the spiritual and the material.

Every reality found in creatures can be reduced ultimately to two classes of categories : substances and qualities. Only these two categories signify or denote distinct entities ; all the other categories mentioned by Aristotle are connotative terms, which denote either a substance or a quality and connote something else. Thus 'quantity', for instance, is a term denoting either a substance or a quality ; what it connotes is that the substance or quality in question has parts distant from each other. 'Relation' denotes two entities (substances or qualities), and connotes that one of these entities is being compared with the other, and so on. So, too, for all the other categories.

Therefore place, surface, line, point, number, are not to be regarded as entities distinguishable from the bodies of which they are predicated. Likewise, time is not an entity separate from a being which exists in time or which has its being not all at once but successively. The same is true for motion, which is not an absolute entity distinct from the body in motion. In order to explain the cosmological facts—the spatio-temporal position and configuration of bodies, their number, their change and motion—Ockham needs only, in his cosmos, bodies that are distinguishable in virtue of their forms and qualities. Genuine changes are found only in substances and

qualities. But even in this simplified world, Ockham is still careful not to allow any other absolute entity to creep in which cannot be proved necessary for a full explanation of the facts. Thus he refuses to accept the theory that explains projectile motion by some quality given to a stone thrown into the air. It is sufficient to assume that the motion imparted by the hand to the stone remains until it is impeded. Hence he does not follow the old theory according to which the stone is kept in motion by the surrounding air, nor does he accept the 'impetus theory', according to which the projected object receives the 'quality' of impetus.

Ockham has left us only a few remarks on the nature of man. He is in line with the general tenets of the theologians. He follows the Franciscan school in holding a plurality of forms in a human being ; he believes that there is a real difference between ·the rational or intellective soul and the sensitive soul, and furthermore between the sensitive soul and the form of the body. It cannot be demonstrated (in the technical sense) that the rational soul is a form of the body ; we are assured of this by the teaching of the Church.

The rational soul is absolutely simple and is not distinct from its faculties, whether really (as St Thomas thought), or formally (as Duns Scotus thought). The activities of this one simple soul are distinguished into cognitive and appetitive functions, both of which can be stabilised by habits which as additional forms are accidental and really distinct forms of this soul. The liberty of the will can be evidently proved, since we do experience that we are the cause of free acts.

6. *Ethics*

Ockham's ethical theory is sometimes called positivistic ; and this is true in so far as the Venerable Inceptor maintains that a human act is good or moral, not because

it is in conformity with an eternal law which exists of itself and even governs the will of God, but simply because it is ordained and commanded by the will of God. Hence what God wills is good, what He forbids is bad. It is, by definition, an impossibility that God can ever order or command a bad thing. It follows that God's will is the ethical norm and must be obeyed by every creature. Once more, we have to remind the reader that God's will is identical with God's intellect, wisdom and love. The one living God, the omnipotent and merciful God, is the supreme rule of ethics. If, however, in a mental experiment we set aside all other attributes of God and view only God's power in itself, we may then admit the principle that God can do by this absolute power everything that does not contain a contradiction ; and in this sense, absolute and purely logical, it is true that God can command anything He pleases. For God is nobody's debtor, and He is only restricted—if this can be called a restriction—by the impossibility of what contains a contradiction. Hence God can command everything with this power, except not to obey Him. As soon as a human person knows that a certain command is the will of God, he is bound to obey. To do the will of God or, equivalently, to love God, is the supreme ethical rule.

However, it is well known that Ockham admitted that God can command by His absolute power that a person should hate Him or at least not love Him. It is important to note that this possibility is admitted in the purely ontological and logical realm. For in this realm there cannot be a contradiction, since it is a fact that creatures can command others to hate God; the command, therefore, is a reality, considered as a mental or spoken sentence, and every reality has God as its primary cause. In the ethical realm, however, an antinomy is encountered, the only real antinomy in Ockham's philosophy. If God commanded a creature to hate Him or simply

not to love Him, the creature would be obliged to obey,
but it could not obey since in obeying it would love
Him. Since the ethical laws are not propositions (which
alone are true or false and between which alone genuine
contradictions can occur), but are commands, their
ultimate source must be a will, and not any impersonal
thing of the ontological sphere, nor any proposition of
the logical sphere. Briefly, the command to hate God
is not a logical or ontological impossibility, but to fulfil
this command is an ethical impossibility.

For the rest, Ockham's ethics remain within the general
limits of scholastic teaching.

7. *Politics*

It now remains to say at least a few words about
Ockham's political ideas. His interest was not so much
focused on political theories in general, as on the special
problem of the relation between State and Church, or,
more concretely, the relation between the Papacy and
the Roman Empire of his days. It cannot be our task
to enter into a discussion of the purely ecclesiastical
controversies concerning the limits of the power of the
Pope within the Church, the rights of a general Council,
and so on—besides, there is little here that is definitely
established as to Ockham's teaching.

Ockham maintains, on the one hand, a clear distinction of spiritual and temporal power ; and nevertheless,
on the other, no severance but rather a co-ordination
of the two powers. The spiritual power is autonomous ;
it is directly from God and absolutely independent in
its own realm ; likewise the secular or temporal power
is from God through the people, who decide on or elect
their ruler, and it also is independent in its own realm
and governed only by natural law.

The ruler of a nation has been appointed by the people
either directly or indirectly through his ancestors ; how-

ever, he does not *owe* his power to the people but only
to God. Hence the people cannot arbitrarily take away
this power from him, but only in cases specified either
by positive or by natural law. A case for deposing a ruler
under natural law would be, for instance, if the ruler
proved to be unfit or even actually dangerous to the
common good.

It can be said that in general Ockham appears to
favour moderate opinions in regard to the hotly disputed
political questions of his time. He did not defend the
absolute power of the State or the Emperor, nor did he
follow the so-called 'curialists' in their exaggerations of
the power of the Pope.

Let us close this short sketch with the words in which
Ockham expressed his ideal of a commonwealth of all
nations : 'Therefore, he is not truly zealous for the
common good, who does not desire and work, as far as
he can in his station, for the whole world to be subject
to one monarch'.[1]

* * *

Ockham's philosophy had an enormous influence. But
it seems that he had few disciples. It is difficult to find
an 'Ockhamist' school in the same sense as we encounter
a Thomist or Scotist school. Ockham's teachings had,
rather, a stimulating effect. They awakened many
somewhat independent thinkers who were united at least
against the realism of the older scholastics. These
'*Nominales*' (in the mediaeval sense) constituted the *via
moderna*, which was not so much a school as a trend
of thought. It is still too early to pass judgment on this
great intellectual movement. One historical fact, however, seems to be quite securely established : it was the
physics of the *via moderna* which gave birth to modern
physics.

[1] *Breviloquium de potestate Papae*, LIB. IV, c. 13.

FOREWORD TO THE SECOND EDITION

Philotheus Boehner, o.f.m., never lived to see the fulfillment of two of his most cherished dreams: the publication of his *Ockham: Philosophical Writings* and the appearance of the critical edition of Ockham's *Opera Philosophica et Theologica* he initiated. His labors, however, inspired many, and both these visions have become realities. Furthermore, his numerous articles on Ockham and his thought were gathered together under the title *Collected Articles on Ockham*. This collection of his works still remains an outstanding commentary on much of *Ockham: Philosophical Writings*, reprinted here in this second edition, and a sturdy companion to the critical edition of Ockham's theological and philosophical works.

In the more than thirty years that have passed between the first and the second edition of *Ockham: Philosophical Writings*, significant changes have taken place in the history of medieval philosophical scholarship. The advent of Ockham's *Opera Philosophical et Theologica* has stimulated an immense amount of study of this great medieval philosopher and theologian. The time has arrived for the immense work of updating the bibliographies on Ockham done by Valens Heynck in 1950 and James P. Reilly in 1968, and this challenging task has recently been undertaken by Jan Beckmann of Fern Universität in Hagen, Federal Republic of Germany. For his bibliography see Beckmann, J. P., "Wilhelm von Ockham, Forschungsbericht 1955-1985," in Floistad, K. (ed.) *Chronicles of Medieval Philosophy*. Oslo, 1989.

Recent developments in Ockham scholarship have forced us to make a number of changes in the present edition of Boehner's text. It is evident that his bibliography needs updating, but the demands of space have set limits to this task. We

have, for the most part, tried to provide references to the most recent English books and articles on Ockham's philosophy, and we trust that Beckmann's much fuller bibliography will appear soon. We have noted the new editions of Ockham's Latin texts for his philosophical, theological, and political writings. The edition of the *Opera Politica* is still incomplete. For the political writings not contained in the three volumes which have appeared, we refer you to A. Stephen McGrade, *The Political Thought of William of Ockham*, 232-234. We have listed the major English translations which have appeared since the first edition of the present work; yet some care must be used with certain passages of these translations, since they may not be based on the critical Latin texts. Since we have had to limit the bibliography of secondary literature, we apologize to those who have labored so diligently on articles and works not cited. We have endeavored to deliver some indirect justice by listing bibliographical sources that are much more complete, especially the recent works of McGrade (1974), Adams (1987), Courtenay (1987), and Tachau (1988).

The appearance of the critical Latin edition of the *Opera Philosophica et Theologica* has also forced us to make a large number of changes in the Latin and English texts of Boehner's first edition. These alterations appear in the appendix. The appendix, first of all, provides the corrections for the *source* pages (i.e. 1, 17, 46, 63, 75, 79, 89, 96, 114, 127, and 136), providing the location where the texts are found in the new critical Latin edition. These entries give the title of the work, the volume of the *Opera Philosophica* (OP) or *Opera Theologica* (OT) where the work is found, and the page numbers where the selected Latin text may be located in the new edition. The appendix also contains corrections of the Latin text of Boehner's selections, and, where necessary, also corrections of the English translations—to bring them into conformity with the critical Latin text. We have not changed the Latin text in the cases where there is an insignificant inversion of word order. Nor have we altered the Latin text when the difference is either *ergo* or *igitur, quia* or *quod, postea* or *post,*

iste or *ille* (the latter in any of their gender or case endings).

In the reprinted Boehner texts we have indicated with a special sign the places where the Latin and English texts need adjustments. The symbol we have used is a line above the word or words where alterations occur. There are two special types of alterations which need further comment. We have indicated in some places that certain words, phrases, or paragraphs are found only in the second redaction of the *Scriptum in I Sententiarum*. The additions of this second redaction were made at different times and for different reasons, and information regarding these differences between the first or incomplete and the second or complete redaction can be found in *Opera Theologica* I, 19*-33*; II, 17*-18*; III, 6*-13* ; and IV, 9*-20*. The second type of alteration which needs further explanation is the alteration where we have used the <>sign. This indicates that the alteration is based on the conjecture of the editor(s) of the new edition. Sometimes a reader will see immediately that some conjecture was necessary. Frequently, however, if you consult the variant readings for the new edition, you will find the justification for the conjectures provided there.

The introductions to each volume of the *Opera Philosophica et Theologica* contain a vast amount of useful information about the works contained in the individual volumes. The footnotes in these critical editions also provide the reader with references to authors cited by Ockham or to contemporary philosophers and theologians with whom he agrees and disagrees. In correcting Boehner's text we have not corrected his references at the foot of the text. For this more detailed type of study we refer the reader to the places in the *Opera Philosophica et Theologica* indicated on the *source* pages.

We would like to thank Professor Raymond Klibansky, and Father Theo Maschke, o.f.m., Provincial of the Saxony Province of the Franciscan Order, to which Father Boehner belonged, for granting permission to print this revised edition. We also would like to thank Professors Edward P. Mahoney of

Duke University and Girard I. Etzkorn of The Franciscan Institute of St. Bonaventure University for their ever-genial help
and suggestions. We are also grateful to the Hackett Publishing Company, to Dan Kirklin, James Hullett, and Brian Rak
for their advice and assistance, and for the willingness of the
Hackett Publishing Company to reprint this bilingual selection of texts that surely will be of great use in any course on the
history of late medieval philosophy.

Boston College,   STEPHEN F. BROWN
October 1989

BIBLIOGRAPHICAL NOTE
BY STEPHEN F. BROWN

I. MODERN EDITIONS OF OCKHAM'S TEXTS

A. PHILOSOPHICAL WORKS

1. *Summa logicae* (Opera Philosophica I, edd. Ph. Boehner, Gedeon Gál et Stephanus Brown; St. Bonaventure, N.Y., 1974).
2. *Expositionis in libros artis logicae prooemium, Expositio in librum Porphyrii De praedicabilibus, Expositio in librum Praedicamentorum Aristotelis, Expositio in librum Perihermenias Aristotelis et Tractatus de praedestinatione et de praescientia Dei respectu futurorum contingentium* (Opera Philosophica II, edd. Ernestus A. Moody, Gedeon Gál, Angelus Gambatese, Stephanus Brown et Ph. Boehner; St. Bonaventure, N.Y., 1978).
3. *Expositio super libros Elenchorum* (Opera Philosophica III, ed. Franciscus del Punta; St. Bonaventure, N.Y., 1979).
4. *Expositio in libros Physicorum Aristotelis*—Prologus et libri I–III (Opera Philosophica IV, edd. Vladimirus Richter et Gerhardus Leibold; St. Bonaventure, N.Y., 1985).
5. *Expositio in libros Physicorum Aristotelis*—libri IV–VIII (Opera Philosophica V, edd. Gedeon Gál, Girardus I. Etzkorn, Romualdus Green, Rega Wood, Franciscus E. Kelley et Gerhardus Leibold; St. Bonaventure, N.Y., 1985).
6. *Brevis Summa libri Physicorum, Summula philosophiae naturalis, et Quaestiones in libros Physicorum Aristotelis* (Opera Philosophica VI, ed. Stephanus Brown; St. Bonaventure, N.Y., 1984).

B. THEOLOGICAL WORKS

1. *Scriptum in librum primum Sententiarum*—Prologus et dist. prima (Opera Theologica I, edd. Gedeon Gál et Stephanus Brown; St. Bonaventure, N.Y., 1967).

2. *Scriptum in librum primum Sententiarum*—Distinctiones II–III (Opera Theologica II, edd. Stephanus Brown et Gedeon Gál; St. Bonaventure, N.Y., 1970).

3. *Scriptum in librum primum Sententiarum*—Distinctiones IV–XVIII (Opera Theologica III, ed. Girardus I. Etzkorn; St. Bonaventure, N.Y., 1977).

4. *Scriptum in librum primum Sententiarum*—Distinctiones XIX–XLVIII (Opera Theologica IV, edd. Girardus I. Etzkorn et Franciscus E. Kelley; St. Bonaventure, N.Y., 1979).

5. *Quaestiones in librum secundum Sententiarum* (Opera Theologica V, edd. Gedeon Gál et Rega Wood; St. Bonaventure, N.Y., 1981).

6. *Quaestiones in librum tertium Sententiarum* (Opera Theologica VI, edd. Franciscus E. Kelley et Girardus I. Etzkorn; St. Bonaventure, N.Y., 1982).

7. *Quaestiones in librum quartum Sententiarum* (Opera Theologica VII, edd. Gedeon Gál, Rega Wood et Romualdus Green; St. Bonaventure, N.Y., 1984).

8. *Quaestiones variae* (Opera Theologica VIII, edd. Girardus I. Etzkorn, Franciscus E. Kelley et Josephus C. Wey; St. Bonaventure, N.Y., 1984).

9. *Quodlibeta Septem* (Opera Theologica IX, ed. Josephus C. Wey; St. Bonaventure, N.Y., 1980).

10. *Tractatus de quantitate* et *Tractatus de corpore Christi* (Opera Theologica X, ed. Carolus A. Grassi; St. Bonaventure, N.Y., 1986).

C. POLITICAL WORKS

1. *Octo quaestiones de potestate papae, An princeps pro suo succursu, scilicet guerrae, possit recipere bona ecclesiarum, etiam invito papa, Consultatio de causa matrimonali,* et *Opus nonaginta dierum,* cc. 1–6 (*Opera Politica* I, edd. J. G. Sikes, H. S. Offler, R. H. Snape et R. F. Bennett; Manchester, 1940).

2. *Opus nonaginta dierum,* cc. 7–124 (*Opera Politica* II, edd. R. F. Bennett, J. G. Sikes, et H. S. Offler; Manchester, 1963).

3. *Epistola ad fratres minores, Tractatus contra Ioannem,* et *Tractatus contra Benedictum* (*Opera Politica* III, ed. H. S. Offler; Manchester, 1956).

II. ENGLISH TRANSLATIONS

Adams, Marilyn McCord, and Kretzmann, Norman, *Predestination, God's Foreknowledge, and Future Contingents*. 2nd ed. Indianapolis & Cambridge, 1983.

Davies, Julian, *Ockham on Aristotle's Physics* (A Translation of Ockham's *Brevis Summa Libri Physicorum*). St. Bonaventure, N.Y., 1989

Freddoso, Alfred J., and Schuurman, Henry, *Ockham's Theory of Propositions: Part II of the "Summa logicae"*. Notre Dame, 1980.

Kluge, Eike-Henner W., "William of Ockham's Commentary on Porphyry" in *Franciscan Studies* 33 (1973), 171–254; 34 (1974), 306–382.

Loux, Michael J., *Ockham's Theory of Terms: Part I of the "Summa logicae"*. Notre Dame, 1974.

III. BIBLIOGRAPHIES AND BIBLIOGRAPHICAL SOURCES

Adams, Marilyn McCord, *William Ockham*. Notre Dame, 1987, v. 2, 1349–1369.

Brown, Stephen F., "Chronique: Etats-Unis d'Amérique" in *Bulletin de philosophie médiévale* 27 (1985), 194.

Courtenay, William J., *Schools and Scholars in Fourteenth-Century England*. Princeton, 1987, 386–413.

Ghisalberti, Alessandro, *Gugliemo di Ockham*. Milan, 1972, 285–301.

Heynck, Valens, "Ockham-Literatur 1919–1949" in *Franziskanische Studien* 32 (1950), 164–183.

McGrade, A. Stephen, *The Political Thought of William of Ockham*. Cambridge, 1974, 232–255.

Reilly, James P., "Ockham Bibliography: 1950–1967" in *Franciscan Studies* 28 (1968), 197–214.

Tachau, Katherine H., *Vision and Certitude in the Age of Ockham*. Leiden, New York, Copenhagen, and Cologne, 1988, 389–402.

IV. SELECT RECENT SECONDARY BIBLIOGRAPHY

Adams, Marilyn McCord, *William Ockham*. Notre Dame, 1987.

———, "The Structure of Ockham's Moral Theory" in *Franciscan Studies* 46 (1986), 1–35.

———, and Wood, Rega. "Is to Will It as Bad as to Do It: the Fourteenth-Century Debate" in *Franciscan Studies* 41 (1981), 5–60.

Alanen, Lilli, "Descartes, Duns Scotus and Ockham on Omnipotence and Possibility," in *Franciscan Studies* 45 (1985), 157–188.

Arnold, E., "Für Geschichte der Suppositionstheorie" in *Symposion: Jahrbuch für Philosophie* 3 (1952), 1–134.

Ashworth, E. J., "Inconsistency and Paradox in Medieval Disputations: A Development of Some Hints in Ockham," in *Franciscan Studies* 44 (1984), 129–139.

———, "Can I Speak More Clearly Than I Understand? A Problem of Religious Language in Henry of Ghent, Duns Scotus and Ockham" in *Historiographia Linguistica* 7 (1980), 29–38.

Baird, J., "La redéfinition Ockhamiste de la signification." in *Sprache und Erkenntnis im Mittelalter* (*Miscellanea Mediaevalia* 13.1, ed. A. Zimmermann), (Berlin, 1981), 451–458.

Bannach, Klaus, *Die Lehre von der doppelten Macht Gottes bei Wilhelm von Ockham*. Wiesbaden, 1975.

Beierle, John, "A Truth-Functional Non-modal Interpretation of Ockham's Theory of Consequences," in *Franciscan Studies* 44 (1984), 71–86.

Bertelloni, C. Francisco, "Ein Fehltritt im Ockhams Empirismus?" in *Franciscan Studies* 46 (1986), 227–241.

Bochenski, I. M., *A History of Formal Logic*. Notre Dame, 1961.

Boh, Ivan, "Propositional Attitudes in the Logic of Walter Burley and William Ockham" in *Franciscan Studies* 44 (1984), 31–59.

Boitani, Piero, and Torti, Anna, eds. *Intellectuals and Writers in Fourteenth-Century Europe*. Tübingen and Cambridge, 1986.

Boler, John, "Ockham on Evident Cognition" in *Franciscan Studies* 36 (1976), 85–98.

———, "Ockham on Intuitive Cognition" in *Journal of the History of Philosophy* 11 (1973), 95–106.

———, "Ockham's Cleaver" in *Franciscan Studies* 45 (1985), 119–144.

Bosley, Richard, "What Revision of Realism Could Meet Ockham's Critique?" in *Franciscan Studies* 45 (1985), 111–117.

Braakhuis, H.A.G., et al., eds. *English Logic and Semantics from the End of the Twelfth Century to the Time of Ockham and Burleigh.* 4th European Symposium on Medieval Logic and Semantics. Nijmegen, 1981.

Brown, Jerome V., "Abstraction and the Object of the Human Intellect according to Henry of Ghent" in *Vivarium* 11 (1973), 80–104.

Brown, Stephen, "A Modern Prologue to Ockham's Natural Philosophy" in *Sprache und Erkenntnis im Mittelalter* (Miscellanea Mediaevalia 13.1, ed. A. Zimmermann), (Berlin, 1981), 107–129.

―――, "Sources for Ockham's Prologue to the *Sentences*" in *Franciscan Studies* 26 (1966), 36–65; 27 (1967), 39–107.

―――, "Walter Burleigh's Treatise *De suppositionibus* and its Influence on William of Ockham" in *Franciscan Studies* 32 (1972), 15–64.

―――, "Walter Chatton's *Lectura* and William of Ockham's *Quaestiones in Libros Physicorum Aristotelis*" in *Essays Honoring Alan B. Wolter*. W. A. Frank and G. J. Etzkorn, eds. Franciscan Institute Publications, Theol. ser. 10 (St. Bonaventure, 1985), 81–115.

Buescher, G. N., *The Eucharistic Teaching of William of Ockham.* Washington, 1950.

Courtenay, William, *Adam Wodeham*. Leiden, 1978.

―――, *Schools and Scholars in Fourteenth-Century England.* Princeton, 1987.

Cova, Luciano, "L'unità della scienza teologica nella polemica di Walter Chatton con Guglielmo d'Ockham" in *Franciscan Studies* 45 (1985), 189–230.

Dales, Richard C., *The Scientific Achievement of the Middle Ages.* Philadelphia, 1973.

Dal Pra, M., "The Intuitive Knowledge of Non-Existents and the Problem of Late Medieval Skepticism" *New Scholasticism* 49 (1975), 410–430.

Day, Sebastian, *Intuitive Cognition. A Key to the Significance of the Later Scholastics*. St. Bonaventure, N.Y., 1947.

De Andrés, Teodoro, *El nominalismo de Guillermo de Ockham.* Madrid, 1969.

de Souza, José António, "As Idéias de Guilherme de Ockham sobre

a Independéncia do Poder imperial" in *Franciscan Studies* 46 (1986), 253–284.

Dettloff, W., *Die Entwicklung der Akzeptations- und Verdienstlehre von Duns Scotus bis Luther.* Münster i.W., 1963.

Dumont, Stephen D., "The Univocity of the Concept of Being in the Fourteenth Century: John Duns Scotus and William of Alnwick" in *Mediaeval Studies* 49 (1987), 1–75.

Eco, Umberto, "Signification and Detonation from Boethius to Ockham" in *Franciscan Studies* 44 (1984), 1–29.

Elie, H., *Le complexe significabile.* Paris, 1936.

Etzkorn, G. J., "John Reading on the Existence and Unicity of God, Efficient and Final Causality" in *Franciscan Studies* 41 (1981), 110–221.

———, "Walter Chatton and the Controversy on the Absolute Necessity of Grace" in *Franciscan Studies* 37 (1977), 32–65.

Fitzgerald, Michael, "An Interpretive Dilemma in Burlean Semantics" in *Franciscan Studies* 44 (1984), 181–192.

Fitzpatrick, N. A., "Walter Chatton on the Univocity of Being: A Reaction to Peter Aureoli and William Ockham" in *Franciscan Studies* 31 (1971), 88–177.

Freddosa, Alfred J., "A Symposium on Text Editing and Translating" in *Franciscan Studies* 46 (1986), 55–59.

Frettert, Lucan, *The Basis of Morality according to William Ockham.* Chicago, 1989.

Gál, Gedeon, "Gualteri de Chatton et Guillelmi de Ockham Controversia de Natura Conceptus Universalis" in *Franciscan Studies* 41 (1981), 110–221.

———, "William of Ockham died 'impenitent' in April 1347" in *Franciscan Studies* 42 (1982), 90–95.

Gelber, Hester, "I Cannot Tell a Lie: Hugh Lawton's Critique of Ockham on Mental Language" in *Franciscan Studies* 44 (1984), 141–179.

———, *Logic and the Trinity: A Clash of Values in Scholastic Thought,* 1300–1335. Ph.D. diss., University of Wisconsin, Madison, 1974.

Ghisalberti, Alessandro, *Gugliemo di Ockham.* Milan, 1972.

Gilbert, Neal W., "Ockham Wyclif, and the 'Via Moderna.' " in *Antiqui und Moderni: Traditionsbewußtsein und Fortschrittsbewußtsein im späten Mittelalter (Miscellanea Mediaevalia 9*, ed. A. Zimmermann), (Berlin, 1974), 85–125.

Goddu, A., *The Physics of William of Ockham.* Leiden, 1984.

———, "William of Ockham's Arguments for Action at a Distance" in *Franciscan Studies* 44 (1984), 227–244.

Gracia, Jorge (ed.), *Individuation in Scholasticism: The Later Middle Ages and the Counter-Reformation.* Munich-Vienna, 1990.

Grant, Edward, *Physical Science in the Middle Ages.* New York, 1971.

Gray, Christopher B., "Ockham on Trusts" in *Franciscan Studies* 46 (1986), 141–159.

Greive, H., "Zur Relationslehre Wilhelms von Ockham" in *Franziskanische Studien* 49 (1967), 248–258.

Habib, Nicholas, "A Medieval Perspective on the Meaningfulness of Fictitious Terms: A Study of John Buridan" in *Franciscan Studies* 45 (1985), 73–82.

Hamesse, Jacqueline, "Problèmes posés par les 'Reportationes' " in *Franciscan Studies* 46 (1986), 107–117.

Hay, Denys, *Europe in the Fourteenth and Fifteenth Centuries.* New York, 1966.

Henniger, M, "Henry of Harclay's Questions on Divine Prescience and Predestination" in *Franciscan Studies* 41 (1981), 250–335.

———, "Peter Aureoli and William of Ockham on Relations," in *Franciscan Studies* 45 (1985), 231–243.

Henry, D. P., *Medieval Logic and Metaphysics.* London, 1972.

———, "Ockham and the Formal Distinction" in *Franciscan Studies* 25 (1965), 285–292.

Hochstetter, E., *Studien zur Metaphysik und Erkenntnislehre Wilhelms von Ockham.* Berlin, 1927.

Hoffmann, F., *Die Schriften des Oxforder Kanzlers Johannes Lutterell. (Erfurter Theologische Studien 6)*, Leipzig, 1959.

———, *Die Theologische Methode des Oxforder Dominikanerlehrers Robert Holcot.* Münster i.W., 1972.

Hudson, A., and Wilks, M., eds. From *Ockham to Wyclif.* Studies in Church History, Subsidia 5. Oxford, 1987.

Iserloh, E., *Gnade und Eucharistie in der philosophischen Theologie des Wilhelm von Ockham*. Wiesbaden, 1956.

Jordan, Michael, "What's New in Ockham's Formal Distinction?" in *Franciscan Studies* 45 (1985), 97–100.

Kaluza, Z., and Vignaux, P., eds., *Logique, Ontologie, Théologie au XIVe Siècle: Preuve et raisons à l'Université de Paris*. Paris, 1984.

Karger, Elizabeth, "Modes of Personal Supposition: The Purpose and Usefulness of the Doctrine Within Ockham's Logic," in *Franciscan Studies* 44 (1984), 81–106.

Kennedy, L. A., "Philosophical Scepticism in England in the Mid-Fourteenth Century" in *Vivarium* 21 (1983), 35–57.

Kenny, A., *Wyclif*. Oxford, 1985.

Kent, Bonnie, "The Good Will According to Gerald Odonis, Duns Scotus, and William of Ockham" in *Franciscan Studies* 46 (1986), 119–139.

Klocker, Harry R., "Ockham and the Divine Freedom" in *Franciscan Studies* 45 (1985), 245–261.

———, "Two *Quodlibets* on Essence/Existence (Thomas Sutton and William of Ockham)" in *The Thomist* 46 (1982), 267–282.

Knudsen, C., *Walter Chattons Kritik an Wilhelm von Ockhams Wissenschaftslehre*. Bonn, 1976.

Knysh, George, "Biographical Rectifications concerning Ockham's Avignon Period" in *Franciscan Studies* 46 (1986), 61–91.

Kölmel, W. "Das Naturrecht bei Wilhelm von Ockham" in *Franziskanische Studien* 35 (1953), 39–85.

Kretzmann, Norman, Kenny, A., Pinborg, Jan, eds. *Cambridge History of Later Medieval Philosophy*. Cambridge, 1982.

———, ed., *Infinity and Continuity in Ancient and Medieval Thought*. Cornell, 1982.

———, "Ockham and the Creation of the Beginningless World" in *Franciscan Studies* 45 (1985), 1–31.

Lambertini, Roberto, "Ockham and Marsilius on an Ecclesiological Fallacy" in *Franciscan Studies* 46 (1986), 301–315.

Larre, Olga, "La filosofia natural de Guillermo de Ockham: La ontologia subyacente al movimiento de traslacion," in *Franciscan Studies* 44 (1984), 245–255.

Leff, Gordon, *William of Ockham*. Manchester, 1975.

Leibold, G., "Zu Interpretationsfragen der Universalienlehre Ockhams," in *Sprache und Erkenntnis im Mittelalter (Miscellanea Mediaevalia* 13.1, ed. A. Zimmermann), (Berlin, 1981), 459–464.

Lindberg, David C., *Roger Bacon's Philosophy of Nature*. Oxford, 1983.

————, ed. *Science in the Middle Ages*. Chicago, 1978.

Loux, M. J., "*Significatio and Suppositio*: Reflections on Ockham's Semantics" in *New Scholasticism* 53 (1979), 407–427.

McDonnell, Kevin, "Does William of Ockham Have a Theory of Natural Law?" in *Franciscan Studies* 34 (1974), 384–392.

McGrade, A. Stephen, "Ockham on the Birth of Individual Rights," in *Authority and Power: Studies in Medieval Laws and Government*. B. Tierney and P. Linehan, eds. (Cambridge, 1980), 149–165.

————, "Ockham on Enjoyment: Towards an Understanding of Fourteenth-Century Philosophy and Psychology" in *Review of Metaphysics* 34 (1981), 706–728.

————, *Political Thought of William of Ockham*, Cambridge, 1974.

————, "Plenty of Nothing: Ockham's Commitment to Real Possibilities" in *Franciscan Studies* 45 (1985), 145–156.

Mahoney, Edward P., "Sense, Intellect, and Imagination in Albert, Thomas, and Siger" in *Cambridge History of Later Medieval Philosophy*, 602–621.

Maier, Anneliese, *Ausgehendes Mittelalter; Gesammelte Aufsätze zur Geistesgeschichte des 14. Jahrhunderts*. 3 vols. Rome, 1964–1967.

————, *On the Threshold of Exact Science: Selected Writings of Anneliese Maier on Late Medieval Natural Philosophy*. ed and transl. S. D. Sargent. Philadelphia, 1982.

Maierù, A. ed., *English Logic in Italy in the 14th and 15th Centuries*. Naples, 1982.

————, *Terminologia logica della tarda scolastica*. Rome, 1972.

Marrone, Steven P., *Truth and Scientific Knowledge in the Thought of Henry of Ghent*. Cambridge, Mass., 1985.

Massobrio, Simona, "The Individuation of Matter in Ockham's Philosophy" in *Franciscan Studies* 44 (1984), 197–210.

Matteo, Anthony M., "Scotus and Ockham: A Dialogue on Universals" in *Franciscan Studies* 45 (1985), 83–96.

Matthews, Gareth, "A Note on Ockham's Theory of the Modes of Common Personal Supposition," in *Franciscan Studies* 44 (1984), 81–86.

Maurer, A., "William of Ockham on the Language of Reality," in *Sprache und Erkenntnis in Mittelalter (Miscellanea Mediaevalia* 13.2, ed. A. Zimmermann), (Berlin, 1981), 795–802.

————, "Ockham's Razor and Chatton's Anti-Razor" in *Mediaeval Studies* 46 (1984), 463–475.

Melloni, Alberto, "William of Ockham's Critique of Innocent IV" in *Franciscan Studies* 46 (1986), 161–203.

Miethke, Jürgen, "Marsilius und Ockham: Publikum und Leser ihrer politischen Schriften im späteren Mittelalter" in *Medioevo* 6 (1980), 543–567.

Miller, Richard H., "Buridan on Singular Concepts" in *Franciscan Studies* 45 (1985), 57–72.

Mohan, G. E., "The Prologue to Ockham's Exposition of the Physics of Aristotle" *Franciscan Studies* 5 (1945), 235–246.

Moody, E. A., *The Logic of William of Ockham*. New York, 1935.

————, *Studies in Medieval Philosophy, Science, and Logic*. Berkeley, 1975.

Murdoch, John, and Sylla, Edith, eds. *The Cultural Context of Medieval Learning*. Dordrecht, 1975.

————, "The Development of a Critical Temper: New Approaches and Modes of Analysis in Fourteenth-Century Philosophy, Science, and Theology" in *Medieval and Renaissance Studies*, 7, S. Wenzel, ed. (Chapel Hill, 1978), 51–79.

————, "*Scientia mediantibus vocibus*: Metalinguistic Analysis in Late Medieval Natural Philosophy" in *Sprache und Erkenntnis im Mittelalter (Miscellanea Mediaevalia* 13.1, ed. A. Zimmermann), (Berlin, 1981), 73–106.

————, and E. Synan. "Two Questions on the Continuum: Walter Chatton (?), o.f.m. and Adam Wodeham, o.f.m." in *Franciscan Studies* 26 (1966), 212–288.

Norena, C. P., "Ockham and Suarez on the Ontological Status of Universal Concepts" in *New Scholasticism* 55 (1981), 348–362.

Normore, Calvin and Edidin, A., "Ockham on Prophecy" in *International Journal of the Philosophy of Religion* 13 (1982), 179–189.

Nuchelmans, G., *Theories of the Proposition*. Amsterdam, 1973.

Oakley, John, "John XXII and Franciscan Innocence" in *Franciscan Studies* 46 (1986), 217–226.

Oberman, Heiko A., *The Harvest of Medieval Theology*. Cambridge, Mass., 1963.

_____, "Some Notes on the Theology of Nominalism with Attention to its Relation to the Renaissance" in *Harvard Theological Review* 53 (1960), 47–76.

Panaccio, Claude, "Propositionalism and Atomism in Ockham's Semantics" in *Franciscan Studies* 44 (1984), 61–70.

_____, "Guillaume d'Occam et les Pronoms demonstratifs" in *Sprache und Erkenntnis im Mittlalter (Miscellanea Mediaevalia* 13.1, ed. A. Zimmermann), (Berlin, 1981), 465–470.

_____, "Langage ordinaire et langage abstrait chez Guillaume d'Occam" in *Philosophiques* 3 (1974), 37–60.

Pelikan, Jaroslav, *"Determinatio ecclesiae"* and/or *"Communiter Omnes Doctores*: on Locating Ockham within the Orthodox Dogmatic Tradition" in *Franciscan Studies* 46 (1986), 37–45.

Perreiah, Alan, "Approaches to Supposition-Theory" in *New Scholasticism* 45 (1971), 381–408.

Pinborg, Jan et al., *Die Entwicklung der Sprachetheorie im Mittelalter*. Beiträge zur Geschichte der Philosophie und Theologie des Mittelalters, 42.2 Münster, i.W., 1967.

_____, *Logik und Semantik im Mittelalter*. Stuttgart, 1972.

Price, R., "William of Ockham and *Suppositio Personalis*" in *Franciscan Studies* 30 (1970), 131–140.

Randi, Eugenio, "Ockham, John XXII and the Absolute Power of God" in *Franciscan Studies* 46 (1986), 205–216.

Reilly, James P., "A Symposium on Text Editing and Translating" in *Franciscan Studies* 46 (1986), 47–55.

Richards, R. C., "Ockham and Skepticism" in *New Scholasticism* 42 (1968), 345–363.

Richter, V., "Ockham und Moderni in der Universalienfrage" in *Sprache und Erkenntnis im Mittelalter (Miscellanea Mediaevalia* 13.1, ed. A. Zimmermann), (Berlin, 1981), 471–475.

_____, "Zum incipit des Physikkommentars von Ockham" in *Philosophisches Jahrbuch* 81 (1974), 197–201.

————, "In Search of the Historical Ockham: Historical Literary Remarks on the Authenticity of Ockham's Writings" in *Franciscan Studies* 46 (1986), 93–105.

Robson, J. A., *Wyclif and the Oxford Schools*. Cambridge, 1961.

Rudavsky, T. ed., *Divine Omniscience and Omnipotence in Medieval Philosophy*. Dordrecht, 1985.

Ryan, John J., *The Nature, Structure and Function of the Church in William of Ockham*. Missoula, Montana, 1979.

————, "Evasion and Ambiguity: Ockham and Tierney's Ockham" in *Franciscan Studies* 46 (1986), 285–294.

————, *The Nature, Structure and Function of the Church in William of Ockham*. Missoula, Montana, 1979.

Scott, T.K., "Nicholas of Autrecourt, Buridan, and Ockhamism" *Journal of the History of Philosophy* 9 (1971), 15–41.

————, "Ockham on Evidence, Necessity, and Intuition" *Journal of the History of Philosophy* 7 (1969), 27–49.

Shapiro, H., *Motion, Time and Place According to William of Ockham*. St. Bonaventure, N.Y., 1957.

Siclari, A., "La 'Dialectica' di Giovanni di Damasco e la 'Summa Logicae' di Guglielmo di Occam" in *Sprache und Erkenntis im Mittelalter* (*Miscellanea Mediaevalia* 13.1, ed. A. Zimmermann), (Berlin, 1981), 476–487.

Spade, Paul V., "Ockham on Self-reference," *Notre Dame Journal on Formal Logic* 15 (1974), 298–300.

————, "Ockham's Distinctions between Absolute and Connotive Terms" in *Vivarium* 13 (1975), 55–76.

————, " A Defense of Burlean Dilemma" in *Franciscan Studies* 44 (1984), 193–196.

Steinmetz, D. C., "Luther and the Late Medieval Augustinians: Another Look" in *Concordia Theological Monthly* 44 (1973), 245–260.

Streveler, P., "Ockham and his Critics on: Intuitive Cognition" in *Franciscan Studies* 35 (1975), 223–236.

Stürner, Wolfgang, "Die Begründung der Iurisdictio temporalis bei Wilhelm von Ockham" in *Franciscan Studies* 46 (1986), 243–251.

Swiniarski, J., "A New Presentation on Ockham's Theory of Supposition with an Evaluation of Some Contemporary Criticisms" in *Franciscan Studies* 30 (1970), 181–217.

Sylla, Edith, "Medieval Concepts of the Latitude of Forms: The Oxford Calculators" in *Archives d'histoire doctrinale et littéraire du moyen âge* 40 (1973), 223–283.

———, "Walter Burley's *Tractatus primus*: Evidence concerning the Relations of Disputations and Written Works" in *Franciscan Studies* 44 (1984), 257–274.

Synan, Edward A., ed., *The Works of Richard Campsall*, v. 2. Toronto, 1982.

Tabbaroni, Andrea, "A Note on the Short Treatise Attributed to Ockham: The *Super terminos naturales*," in *Franciscan Studies* 44 (1984), 329–349.

Tachau, Katherine H., *Vision and Certitude in the Age of Ockham*. Leiden, New York, Copenhagen, Cologne, 1988.

Tierney, Brian, *Origins of Papal Infallibility, 1150–1350*. Leiden, 1972.

———, "Ockham's Infallibility and Ryan's Infallibility" in *Franciscan Studies* 46 (1986), 295–300.

———, and Linehan, P., "Ockham, the Conciliar Theory and the Canonists," *Journal of the History of Ideas* 15 (1954), 40–70.

Torrance, Thomas F., "Intuitive and Abstractive Knowledge: From Duns Scotus to John Calvin" in *De doctrina Ioannis Duns Scoti* (Studia Scholastico-Scotistica IV; Rome, 1968), 291–305.

Trapp, Damasus. "Augustinian Theology of the Fourteenth Century" in *Augustiniana* 6 (1956), 146–274.

Tweedale, Martin N., *John of Rodyngton on Knowledge, Science, and Theology*. Ph.D. diss., U.C.L.A., 1965.

Urban, Linwood, "William of Ockham's Theological Ethics" in *Franciscan Studies* 33 (1973), 310–350.

Vasoli, Cesare, "Polemiche occamiste" in *Rinascimento* 3 (1952), 119–141.

Vignaux, Paul, *Justification et prédestination au XIV siècle*. Paris, 1934.

———, "Nominalisme" in *Dictionnaire de théologie catholique* 11.1 (Paris, 1930), 717–784.

Vossenkühl, Wilhelm, "Ockham and the Cognition of Non-existents," in *Franciscan Studies* 45 (1985), 33–45.

Walsh, Katherine, *A Fourteenth-Century Scholar and Primate, Richard Fitzralph in Oxford, Avignon, and Armagh*. Oxford, 1981.

Webering, D., *Theory of Demonstration according to William Ockham*. St. Bonaventure, N.Y., 1953.

Weinberg, J., *Ockham, Descartes, and Hume*. Madison, 1977.

Weisheipl, James A., "Ockham and some Mertonians" in *Med. Stud.* 30 (1968), 163–213.

Wengert, R. G., "Necessity of the Past: What is Ockham's Model?" in *Franciscan Studies* 47 (1987), 234–256.

White, Graham, "Ockham's Real Distinction Between Form and Matter" in *Franciscan Studies* 44 (1984), 211–225.

Willing, Anthony, "Burdian and Ockham: The Logic of Knowing" in *Franciscan Studies* 45 (1985), 47–56.

Wippel, John F., *The Metaphysical Thought of Godfrey of Fontaines. A Study in Late Thirteenth-Century Philosophy*. Washington, D.C., (1981).

Wood, Rega, "Adam Wodeham on Sensory Illusions with an Edition of 'Lectura Secunda,' Prologus, Quaestio 3" in *Traditio* 38 (1982), 213–252.

Zimmermann, A., ed. *Sprache und Erkenntnis im Mittelalter (Miscellanea Mediaevalia* 13), Berlin, 1981.

I

ON THE NOTION
OF
KNOWLEDGE OR SCIENCE

Source :

Prologue to the *Expositio super viii libros Physicorum*   *2*

Prologus in Expositionem super viii libros Physicorum

Philosophos plurimos sapientiae titulo decoratos, qui tamquam luminaria fulgida splendore scientiae ignorantiae tenebratos caligine illustrant, aetas praeterita protulit et nutrivit. Inter alios autem philosophos peritissimus Aristoteles non parvae nec contemnendae doctrinae praeclarus apparuit, qui quasi lynceis oculis secretiora naturae rimatus philosophiae naturalis abscondita posteris revelavit.

Et quoniam quidem multi libros eiusdem conati sunt exponere, visum est mihi et multis studiose rogantibus, quid de eius intentione senserim, ad studentium utilitatem conscribere. Nec quisquam, nisi invidus, mihi debet esse molestus, si ea quae probabilia mihi videntur sine invidia communicem ; quia animo solummodo investigandi, non pertinacia contendendi nec in alicuius iniuriam, ad explanationem eorum quae Aristotelis sunt exquisita laboribus sine temeraria assertione procedam. Et sicut nonnumquam aliorum opiniones cum omni modestia sine malitia improbabo, ita paratus sum etiam sine impatientia, si aliquid dixero non consonum veritati, reprehendi. Caveat tamen corrector, ne in malis principiis consuetudo aut favor aut odium de correctore nonnumquam faciat perversorem, et advertat quod non possum me singulorum opinionibus, quae se mutuo reprobant, coaptare.

Sane, licet vir iste multa et magna divinitus adiutus invenerit, nonnullos tamen impeditus humanitus errores immiscuit veritati. Eapropter opiniones recitandas mihi nullus ascribat, cum non, quid iuxta veritatem catholi-

¹ Aristotle's *Physics*

Prologue to the Expositio super viii libros Physicorum

Past ages have begotten and reared many philosophers distinguished by the title 'sage'. Like shining lights they have illumined with the splendour of their knowledge those who were plunged in the dark night of ignorance. The most accomplished man to have appeared among them is Aristotle, outstanding as a man of no slight or insignificant learning. With the eyes of a lynx, as it were, he explored the deep secrets of nature and revealed to posterity the hidden truths of natural philosophy.

Since many have tried to explain his books, it seemed to me, and to many earnest enquirers, desirable that I should write down for the benefit of students what I thought to be the mind and intention of Aristotle. None but the envious should object to my desire to communicate ungrudgingly what I regard as probable opinions on this work [1] of the great philosopher. For my aim is investigation pure and simple, and not obstinate quarrelsomeness nor ill will ; and without any rash assertions I proceed to an explanation of what Aristotle's labours disclose. And just as at times, in all modesty and without malice, I shall disprove the opinions of others, so I am patiently ready to be corrected should I ever go against the truth. But let him who corrects me beware lest habitual adherence to bad principles, or bias, or hatred should make him sometimes pervert, instead of correct me. And he should also realise that I cannot accommodate myself to everybody's opinions when one opinion contradicts another.

Indeed, though the Philosopher has made, with God's help, many great discoveries, he has nevertheless, being human, mingled errors with the truth. Therefore, no-one

cam sentiam, sed quid istum Philosophum approbasse vel secundum sua principia, ut mihi videtur, approbare debuisse putem, referre proponam. De intentione alicuius diversa et adversa, cum ipse scripturae sacrae auctor non fuerit, sine periculo animae licitum est sentire ; nec in hoc error contrahit pravitatem. Quinimmo in exercitatione huius unicuique sine periculo liberum reservatur iudicium.

Expositurus itaque naturalem Aristotelis philosophiam a libro *Physicorum* incipiam, qui primus est.

Sed antequam ad expositionem textus accedam, aliqua praeambula, sicut in principio *Logicae* feci, praemittam. Et quia forte expositio super *Logicam* ad manus aliquorum non deveniet, qui tamen istam forte videbunt, idcirco aliqua ibidem dicta hic replicare addendo aliqua non pigebit.

Est ergo primo videndum, quid est scientia in generali, secundo aliquae distinctiones huius nominis 'scientia' sunt ponendae, tertio ex dicendis sunt aliquae conclusiones eliciendae, quarto de scientia naturali in speciali est videndum.

Circa primum dicendum est, quod scientia vel est quaedam qualitas existens subiective in anima, vel est collectio aliquarum talium qualitatum animam informantium. Et loquor tantum de scientia hominis.

Hoc probatur : Quia non minus est scientia, quae est habitus, talis qualitas quam actus scientiae ; sed actus scientiae est talis qualitas ; ergo et scientia, quae est habitus, est talis qualitas. Maior videtur manifesta. Minorem probo : Quia impossibile est contradictoria successive verificari de aliquo, nisi sit alicubi mutatio, scilicet acquisitio alicuius rei vel deperditio vel productio vel destructio vel motus localis ; sed nulla tali mutatione

may attribute to me these opinions that I am about to present, since I do not intend to express what I myself hold in accord with the Catholic faith, but only what I think the Philosopher has approved, or ought to have approved in accordance with his own principles. One may safely hold different and opposite opinions regarding the mind of an author, if he is not an author of Holy Scripture. And an error in this case is not a fault. Rather, in such a mental exercise, anybody may without risk retain freedom of judgment.

I am going to expound Aristotle's philosophy of nature, and I shall begin with his *Physics*, which comes first.

But before starting on an exposition of the text, I shall make a few preliminary remarks—as I have done at the beginning of the *Logic*. And lest perhaps the exposition of the *Logic* should not have come into the hands of some who will see the present work, it will not be amiss to repeat in part what was said there, with some additions.

First, then, we have to see what knowledge [1] in general is ; secondly, we have to lay down some distinctions concerning the term 'knowledge' ; thirdly, we have to draw a few conclusions from what is to be said ; and fourthly, we have to consider natural science in particular.

As to the first point, we must say that knowledge is a certain quality which exists in the soul as its subject, or a collection of several such qualities or forms of the soul. I am speaking here only of human knowledge.

This is proved as follows : Knowledge as a *habitus* ('habitual' knowledge) is no less such a quality than an act of knowledge is ; but an act of knowledge is such a quality ; therefore knowledge as a *habitus* is such a quality also. The major premise seems clear. I proceed to the proof of the minor : It is impossible that contradictory statements should successively be made true of something, unless there be some change somewhere, namely the acquisition or loss or production or destruc-

---

[1] Throughout, 'knowledge' and 'science' are both used for '*scientia*'.

existente in aliquo alio ab anima rationali potest anima aliquid intelligere, quod non prius intelligebat, per hoc quod vult intelligere aliquid quod non prius intellexit ; ergo anima habet aliquid quod prius non habuit. Sed illud non potest dari nisi intellectio vel volitio ; ergo volitio vel intellectio est aliqua talis qualitas. Sed qua ratione volitio est talis qualitas, eadem ratione et intellectio. Et per consequens eadem ratione habitus scientiae est talis qualitas, vel aggregans tales qualitates.

Praeterea : Potentia quae nihil habet, quod prius non habuit, non est magis habilis ad actum quam prius ; sed manifeste experimur, quod post multas cogitationes est aliquis habilior et pronior ad consimiles cogitationes nunc quam prius ; ergo aliquid habet nunc quod prius non habuit. Sed illud non potest poni nisi habitus ; ergo habitus est subiective in anima. Sed non potest esse aliquid tale subiective in anima, nisi sit qualitas ; ergo habitus est qualitas. Et per consequens, multo fortius, habitus qui est scientia est qualitas animae.

Circa secundum sciendum, quod 'scientia' multipliciter accipitur, et sunt variae distinctiones scientiae et non subordinatae.

Una est, quod 'scientia' uno modo est certa notitia alicuius veri. Et sic sciuntur aliqua per fidem tantum. Sicut dicimus, nos scire quod Roma est magna civitas, quam tamen non vidimus ; et similiter dico, quod scio istum esse patrem meum et istam esse matrem meam, et sic de aliis quae non sunt evidenter nota ; quia tamen eis sine omni dubitatione adhaeremus et sunt vera, dicimur scire illa.

Aliter accipitur 'scientia' pro evidenti notitia, quando scilicet aliquid dicitur sciri non tantum propter testimonium narrantium, sed si nullus narret hoc esse, ex

tion of something, or a local motion. But, though there be no change in anything but the rational soul, the soul is able to consider something it did not consider before, merely by willing to consider something it did not consider before. Therefore the soul now has something that it did not have before. But this something cannot be anything but either an act of intellection or a volition; therefore either an act of intellection or a volition is such a quality. However, for the same reason that a volition is such a quality, an act of intellection also is such a quality. And consequently, for the same reason the *habitus* of knowledge is also such a quality or a collection of such qualities.

Furthermore, a faculty that now has only what it had before and nothing else, is no more ready in its action now than it was before. Yet it is manifestly our experience that after many acts of thought a person is more fit and more inclined to have similar acts of thought than he was before. Therefore he now has something that he did not have before. But this something can be only a *habitus*. Therefore a *habitus* exists in the soul as in its subject. But only a quality can be in the soul as in its subject; therefore, a *habitus* is a quality. Hence *a fortiori*, the *habitus* which is knowledge is a quality in the soul.

As to the second point, we must realise that 'knowledge' is taken in many senses. Hence, there are different meanings of 'knowledge', and one is not subordinated to the other.

In one sense, knowledge is certain cognition of something that is true. In this sense, some truths are known only on trust; for instance, when we say we know that Rome is a big city, although we have not seen Rome. In the same way I say I know that this person is my father and this person is my mother. And so with many other things that are not ' evidently ' known. And yet because we adhere to these things without a shadow

notitia aliqua incomplexa terminorum aliquorum mediate vel immediate assentiremus ei. Sicut si nullus narraret mihi, quod paries est albus, ex hoc ipso quod video albedinem, quae est in pariete, scirem, quod paries est albus. Et ita est de aliis. Et isto modo scientia non est tantum necessariorum, immo etiam est aliquorum contingentium, sive sint contingentia ad utrumlibet sive alia.

Tertio modo dicitur 'scientia' notitia evidens alicuius necessarii. Et isto modo non sciuntur contingentia sed principia et conclusiones sequentes.

Quarto modo dicitur 'scientia' notitia evidens veri necessarii nata causari ex notitia evidenti praemissarum necessariarum applicatarum per discursum syllogisticum. Et isto modo distinguitur scientia ab intellectu, qui est habitus principiorum, et etiam a sapientia, sicut docet Philosophus vi⁰ *Ethicorum*.*

Alia distinctio scientiae est, quod aliquando 'scientia' accipitur pro notitia evidenti conclusionis, aliquando pro tota notitia demonstrationis.

Alia distinctio scientiae est, quod 'scientia' aliquando accipitur pro uno habitu secundum numerum non includentem plures habitus specie distinctos, aliquando accipitur pro collectione multorum habituum ordinem determinatum et certum habentium. Et isto secundo modo accipitur scientia frequenter a Philosopho. Et scientia isto modo comprehendit tamquam partes aliquo modo integrales habitus principiorum et conclusionum, notitias terminorum, reprobationes falsorum argumen-

---

* cap. iii sqq. (1139 sqq.)
[1] Here = 'science'   [2] Here = 'science' (ἐπιστήμη)

of doubt, and they are true, we are said to know them.

In another sense, 'knowledge' means an evident cognition, namely when we are said to know something not merely because someone has told us about it, but should assent to it, even if there were no-one to tell us about it, mediately or immediately on the basis of a non-complex cognition of certain terms. For instance, if no-one told me that the wall is white, I should still know that the wall is white, just by seeing whiteness on the wall. It is the same with other truths. In this sense we have knowledge not only of necessary facts, but also of some contingent facts, whether it is that their existence or non-existence is contingent, or whether they are contingent in any other sense.

In a third sense, 'knowledge' means an evident cognition of some necessary truth. In this sense, no contingent facts are known, but only first principles and the conclusions that follow from them.

In a fourth sense, 'knowledge'[1] means an evident cognition of some necessary truth caused by the evident cognition of necessary premises and a process of syllogistic reasoning. In this sense, knowledge is distinguished from understanding, which is the possession of first principles, and also from wisdom, according to the teaching of the Philosopher in the sixth book of the *Ethics*.

Another distinction is the following. Sometimes 'knowledge' means evident cognition of the conclusion alone, sometimes of the demonstration as a whole.

According to another distinction, knowledge is sometimes taken for a *habitus* numerically one, which does not include several specifically distinct *habitūs* ; sometimes it stands for a collection of several *habitūs* related according to a certain and determinate order. In this second sense, the Philosopher frequently uses the term 'knowledge'.[2] And in this same sense, a science somehow contains as integral parts the possession of first principles

torum et errorum et solutiones eorum. Et sic dicitur
metaphysica esse scientia et naturalis philosophia esse
scientia, et ita de aliis.

Tertio, ex istis eliciendae sunt aliquae conclusiones.
Prima est : Quod metaphysica, similiter mathematica
et philosophia naturalis, non est una scientia secundum
numerum illo modo, quo haec albedo est una numero
et iste calor et iste homo et iste asinus. Hanc probo :
Quia metaphysica comprehendit multas conclusiones,
circa quarum unam potest aliquis errare et ipsemet
eodem tempore aliam scire ; sicut per certam experientiam patet, quod idem primo addiscit unam conclusionem et postea aliam, et tamen aliquando prius erravit
circa utramque. Ex hoc arguo sic : Error circa A et
scientia circa A formaliter repugnant ; sed error circa A
et scientia circa B non repugnant formaliter, quia stant
simul ; ergo scientia circa A et scientia circa B non sunt
eiusdem rationis ; quia quando aliqua sunt eiusdem
rationis, quidquid formaliter contrariatur uni, contrariatur alteri. Sed si non sunt eiusdem rationis, et manifestum est quod neutrum est materia alterius nec forma,
ergo non faciunt unum numero per se : et per consequens comprehendens utrumque illorum non est unum
numero per se.

Praeterea : Metaphysica comprehendit tam notitiam
principiorum quam conclusionum, et similiter philosophia naturalis ; sed habitus principiorum et conclusionum distinguuntur : tum quia secundum Philosophum
i° *Posteriorum* * habitus principiorum est nobilior habitu
conclusionum, sed idem non est nobilius se ; tum quia
notitia principii est causa notitiae conclusionis ; idem

---

* cap. ii (71^b, 29 sqq.)

and conclusions, the concepts of terms, the rejection and refutations of sophistries and errors. In this sense, metaphysics is called a science and philosophy of nature a science, just as other sciences are so designated.

In the third place, from the preceding explanations some conclusions are to be drawn.

The first is that neither metaphysics nor philosophy of nature nor mathematics is numerically one piece of knowledge in the same way as this whiteness and this heat and this man and this donkey are each numerically one. Proof : Metaphysics contains many conclusions ; now a man may know one conclusion and yet the same man at the same time may be in error regarding another. For we know from experience that at times, when a man has been in error regarding several conclusions, he learns first one conclusion and after that another. From this I argue as follows : Error about the conclusion A and scientific knowledge of A are formally incompatible ; but error about A and scientific knowledge of B are not formally incompatible, since they coexist simultaneously. Therefore the notion of scientific knowledge of A and that of scientific knowledge of B are not the same notion ; for if the notions of things are the same, then whatever is formally incompatible with one is likewise formally incompatible with the other. But if the notion of these pieces of knowledge is not one and the same, then, since it is clear that they are not mutually related as matter and form, they do not of themselves constitute a numerical unity, and consequently whatever includes them both is not of itself a numerical unity.

Furthermore, metaphysics contains a cognition both of first principles and of conclusions, and the same is true for the philosophy of nature. But the possession of first principles is distinct from the possession of conclusions : First, because the Philosopher says in the first book of the *Posterior Analytics* that the possession (*habitus*) of first principles is nobler than the possession of con-

autem non est causa suiipsius. Ideo dicendum est, quod metaphysica non est una scientia numero, nec similiter philosophia naturalis. Sed philosophia naturalis est collectio multorum habituum, sicut dictum est. Nec est aliter una nisi sicut civitas dicitur una vel populus dicitur unus vel exercitus comprehendens homines et equos et caetera necessaria dicitur unus, vel sicut regnum dicitur unum, vel sicut universitas dicitur una, vel sicut mundus dicitur unus.

Secunda conclusio sequens est ista : Quod nulla scientia habet nisi duas causas proprie loquendo de causa, quia nullum accidens habet nisi tantum duas causas, scilicet finalem et efficientem : Quia secundum Philosophum, viii⁰ *Metaphysicae*,* accidens non habet materiam ex qua sed in qua ; nunc autem materia in qua non est causa illius cuius est materia in qua, sicut materia non est causa formae sed compositi ; ergo accidens non habet materiam. Sed si non habet causam materialem, non habet causam formalem. Ergo nullum accidens habet nisi tantum duas causas essentiales, scilicet finalem et efficientem. Sed omnis scientia, quae est una numero, est una qualitas numero, sicut dictum est ; ergo nulla talis scientia habet nisi tantum duas causas. Sed quando aliquid est aggregatum ex multis diversarum rationum, quorum nullum est materia alterius, si nullum illorum habet materiam, nec illud aggregatum habet materiam : ergo scientia, quae est collectio multorum talium habituum, non habet materiam, nec per consequens habet causam formalem.

Ideo dicendum est, quod, loquendo de virtute sermonis, nulla scientia habet nisi tantum duas causas essentiales, scilicet efficientem et finalem.

Sed quod dicitur, quod quaelibet scientia habet

* cap. iv (1044ᵇ, 8 sqq.)

clusions ; yet one and the same thing is not nobler than itself. Secondly, because the knowledge of the first principle is the cause of the conclusion ; yet one and the same thing is not the cause of itself. Hence we have to say that metaphysics is not a piece of knowledge which is numerically one. The same is true of the philosophy of nature, which is a collection of many *habitūs*, as we have said before. It is one in the same sense that a city, or a nation, or an army, which includes men and horses and other necessary things, or a kingdom, or a university, or the world, is said to be one.

The second conclusion that follows is this. Any scientific knowledge has only two causes, if we use the word 'cause' in its proper sense, since every accident has only two causes, namely a final and an efficient cause. For, according to the Philosopher in the eighth book of the *Metaphysics*, an accident has no matter *out of* which it is produced, but only a material principle *in* which it is produced. Now, the matter *in* which something is produced is not the cause of the thing whose material principle it is ; for matter is not the cause of form, but only of the compound [of matter and form]. Therefore an accident has no matter. But if an accident has no material cause, it also has no formal cause. Hence, any accident has only two essential causes, namely a final and an efficient cause. But each piece of knowledge that is numerically one is a quality that is numerically one, as has been said. Therefore any such piece of knowledge has only two causes. When, however, something is an aggregate of many heterogeneous things, and none of these is a material principle for another, it follows, that if none of these has matter, then the aggregate as a whole has no matter either. Therefore the knowledge that is a collection of many such *habitūs* has no matter, and in consequence no formal cause either.

For this reason we must maintain that, literally speaking, any knowledge has only two essential causes, namely,

causam materialem et formalem, si habeat veritatem,
est locutio impropria et metaphorica ; et tunc vocatur
'materia' illud, de quo est scientia. Sed iste est impro-
prius modus loquendi ; sic enim possem dicere, quod
color est materia visionis meae, et quod color est causa
materialis apprehensionis et sensationis. Similiter, forma
improprie vocatur distinctio partium scientiae ; sic enim
possem dicere, quod tres lineae sunt causa formalis
trianguli, et quod manus et pedes et caput et caetera
membra hominis sunt causa formalis hominis, quod non
est proprie dictum. Ideo, proprie loquendo, scientia non
habet nisi duas causas, quia non habet causam formalem
nec materialem : Quia, proprie loquendo, causa materialis est de essentia illius cuius est causa ; sed subiectum
scientiae non est de essentia scientiae, sicut patet manifeste. Similiter, proprie loquendo, causa materialis
recipit formam in se ; sed subiectum vel obiectum non
recipit in se scientiam nec aliquam partem scientiae, sed
solus intellectus recipit scientiam ; ergo obiectum vel
subiectum non est, proprie loquendo, causa materialis
scientiae ; et per consequens non habet causam formalem.

Tertia conclusio sequens est : Quod talis scientia una
unitate collectionis non habet unum subiectum, sed
secundum diversas partes habet subiecta diversa : Quia
subiectum scientiae non potest vocari nisi illud de quo
scitur aliquid ; sed in una scientia tali unitate sunt
multa de quibus alia sciuntur ; ergo talis scientia non
habet unum subiectum.

Propter quod sciendum, quod 'subiectum scientiae'
dupliciter accipitur : Uno modo pro illo, quod recipit

an efficient and a final cause. Hence, if the statement
that all knowledge has a material and formal cause be
true, it is so only in an improper and metaphorical sense.
For in this case 'matter' means that with which knowledge is concerned. Yet this is an improper mode of
speaking ; for in this way I could also say that colour
is the matter of vision and that the colour is the material
cause of perception and sensation. Likewise, it is only
in an improper sense that the distinction between the
parts of knowledge is called form ; for in this sense I
could also say that the three lines are the formal cause
of a triangle, and that the hands and the feet and the
other limbs of man are the formal cause of man, which
is not a proper way of speaking. Properly speaking,
therefore, knowledge has only two causes, since it lacks
a formal and a material cause. For, properly speaking,
the material cause belongs to the essence of that of which
it is a cause ; but the subject of knowledge does not
belong to the essence of knowledge as is manifestly
apparent. Again, properly speaking, a material cause
receives the form in itself ; but neither the subject nor
the object of knowledge receives in itself knowledge or
any part of knowledge, since only the intellect receives
knowledge. Therefore, properly speaking, neither the
object nor the subject is a material cause of knowledge.
Consequently knowledge has no formal cause either.

A third conclusion following from the preceding is this :
A science which has only a collective unity has not just
one subject ; rather it has different subjects according
to its different parts. For only that about which something is known can be called a subject of knowledge ;
yet, in a science that is only collectively one, there are
many things about which different things are scientifically known ; therefore, such a science has not just
one subject.

In order to explain this we must realise that the expression 'subject of knowledge' can be understood in

scientiam et habet scientiam in se subiective ; sicut
dicitur, quod corpus vel superficies est subiectum albedinis et ignis est subiectum caloris. Et isto modo
subiectum scientiae est ipsemet intellectus, quia quaelibet scientia talis est accidens intellectus. Alio modo
dicitur 'subiectum scientiae' illud, de quo scitur aliquid.
Et sic accipit Philosophus in libro Posteriorum* ; et sic
idem est subiectum conclusionis et scientiae, nec dicitur
subiectum, nisi quia est subiectum conclusionis. Et ideo,
quando sunt diversae conclusiones habentes diversa
subiecta illo modo quo logicus utitur hoc vocabulo 'subiectum', tunc illius scientiae, quae est aggregata ex
omnibus scientiis illarum conclusionum, non est aliquod
unum subiectum, sed diversarum partium sunt diversa
subiecta. Quando autem omnes conclusiones habent
idem subiectum, tunc totius aggregati est unum subiectum, illud scilicet, quod est subiectum omnium illarum
conclusionum.

Similiter sciendum, quod differentia est inter obiectum
scientiae et subiectum. Nam obiectum scientiae est tota
propositio nota, subiectum est pars illius propositionis,
scilicet terminus subiectus. Sicut scientiae, qua scio quod
omnis homo est susceptibilis disciplinae, obiectum est
tota propositio, sed subiectum est iste terminus 'homo'.

Ex istis patet, quod continere virtualiter totam notitiam conclusionum, vel esse primum ad quod omnia alia
referuntur, et multa alia huiusmodi quae attribuuntur
rationi subiecti, non sunt de ratione subiecti, quia subiectum non plus continet virtualiter habitum quam
praedicatum, nec omnia plus attribuuntur subiecto
quam alii. Et si aliquando hoc contingat, hoc accidit.

two different senses. In one sense it means that which receives knowledge and has the knowledge in it as in a subject, just as a body or a surface is the subject of whiteness, and fire the subject of heat. Understood in this sense, the subject of knowledge is the intellect itself, because any such knowledge is an accident of the intellect. Taken in the other sense, 'subject of knowledge' is said to be that about which something is known. It is thus that the Philosopher understands 'subject' in the *Posterior Analytics*. In this sense the subject of knowledge is the same thing as the subject of a conclusion, and it is called 'subject' only because it is the subject of a conclusion. If, therefore, there are different conclusions with different subjects—'subject' being taken in the sense in which the logician uses it—then that science which is an aggregate of all these scientifically known conclusions has not just some one subject, but the different parts have different subjects. Should all the conclusions, however, have the same subject, then the entire aggregate has but one subject, namely that which is the subject of all these conclusions.

We must also realise that there is a difference between the object and the subject of knowledge. For the object of knowledge is the whole proposition that is known ; the subject, however, is only a part of this proposition, namely the subject-term. For instance, the object of my knowledge that every man is educable is the entire proposition ; its subject, however, is the term 'man'.

From this it becomes clear that it is no part of the concept of 'a subject' that it should 'virtually' contain the whole knowledge of the conclusions, or be something which comes first, and to which everything else is referred. And the same holds good for many other such supposed implications of the concept 'subject'. For the subject no more 'virtually' contains a *habitus* than the predicate does, nor are all these things attributed more to the subject than to something else. And if this sometimes happens, it is only by accident.

Ex istis etiam patet, quod quaerere : Quid est subiectum logicae vel philosophiae naturalis vel metaphysicae vel mathematicae vel scientiae moralis ? nihil est quaerere, quia talis quaestio supponit, quod aliquid sit subiectum logicae et similiter philosophiae naturalis, quod est manifeste falsum ; quia nihil unum est subiectum totius, sed diversarum partium diversa sunt subiecta. Unde quaerere 'Quid est subiectum philosophiae naturalis ?' est simile quaestioni, qua quaereretur 'Quis est rex mundi ?' Quia sicut nullus est rex mundi, sed unus est rex unius regni et alter alterius, sic est de subiectis diversarum partium scientiae talis ; nec plus scientia, quae est talis collectio, habet unum subiectum, quam mundus habet unum regem vel quam unum regnum habet unum comitem.

Tamen pro dictis aliquorum auctorum, qui videntur assignare unum subiectum talium scientiarum, est sciendum, quod non intendunt, quod aliquid sit proprie subiectum primum totius, sed intendunt dicere, quod inter omnia subiecta diversarum partium est aliquod unum primum aliqua primitate, et aliquando unum est primum una primitate et aliud alia primitate. Sicut in metaphysica primum inter omnia subiecta primitate praedicationis est ens, sed primum primitate perfectionis est Deus ; similiter in philosophia naturali primum subiectum primitate praedicationis est substantia naturalis vel aliquid tale, et primum primitate perfectionis est homo vel corpus caeleste vel aliquid tale. Et hoc intendunt auctores per talia verba, et nihil aliud.

Quarto videndum est de scientia naturali magis in speciali, et videndum est, de quibus considerat, quomodo ab aliis scientiis distinguitur, sub qua parte philosophiae

From this it is clear that it is meaningless to ask 'What is the subject of logic or of the philosophy of nature, or of metaphysics, or of mathematics, or of ethics?' For such a question presupposes that something is *the* subject of logic, and likewise that something is *the* subject of the philosophy of nature. But that is manifestly false, because there is no one subject of the entire science, but the different parts have different subjects. Hence to ask 'What is *the* subject of the philosophy of nature?' is like asking 'Who is the king of the world?' Just as there is no-one who is the king of the world, but one man is king of one kingdom and another of another kingdom, so also with the subjects of the various parts of such a science. There is no more reason for a science, which is such a collection, to have one subject than for the world to have one king, or for one kingdom to have one count.

But since certain authors seem to assign one subject to such sciences, we must, in order to understand what they say, bear it in mind that they do not mean that something is properly speaking the first subject of the whole science. What they wish to say is that amongst all the subjects of the various parts there is one which is the first because of some priority. Sometimes one subject is first as regards one sort of priority, while another is first as regards another sort of priority. For instance, in metaphysics 'being' [*ens*] is the first subject of all as regards priority of predication, whereas the first subject as regards priority of perfection is 'God'. Likewise in the philosophy of nature the first subject as regards priority of predication is ' natural substance' or something of that kind, but the first as regards priority of perfection is 'man' or 'heavenly body' or something like that. This is what authors have in mind when they use such expressions, and nothing else.

In the fourth place, we must consider the science of nature more in detail. We have to see what it deals with, how it is distinguished from other sciences, under which

continetur, et de libro *Physicorum* in speciali.

Circa primum dicendum est, quod philosophia naturalis considerat de substantiis sensibilibus et compositis
ex materia et forma principaliter, secundario de aliquibus
substantiis separatis.

Ad cuius intellectum est sciendum, quod omnis scientia
est respectu complexi vel complexorum. Et sicut complexa sciuntur per scientiam ita incomplexa, ex quibus
complexa componuntur, sunt illa de quibus illa scientia
considerat. Nunc autem ita est, quod complexa, quae
sciuntur per scientiam naturalem, non componuntur ex
rebus sensibilibus nec ex substantiis, sed componuntur
ex intentionibus seu conceptibus animae communibus
talibus rebus. Et ideo, proprie loquendo, scientia
naturalis non est de rebus corruptibilibus et generabilibus
nec de substantiis naturalibus nec de rebus mobilibus,
quia tales res in nulla conclusione scita per scientiam
naturalem subiiciuntur vel praedicantur. Sed, proprie
loquendo, scientia naturalis est de intentionibus animae
communibus talibus rebus et supponentibus praecise pro
talibus rebus in multis propositionibus, quamvis in
aliquibus propositionibus, sicut in prosequendo patebit,
supponant tales conceptus pro seipsis. Et hoc est quod
dicit Philosophus, quod scientia non est de singularibus
sed est de universalibus supponentibus pro ipsis singularibus. Tamen, metaphorice et improprie loquendo,
dicitur scientia naturalis esse de corruptibilibus et de
mobilibus, quia est de illis terminis qui pro talibus
supponunt.

Et quod sic sit, ostendo : Nam accipio hanc propositionem : 'Omnis substantia sensibilis componitur ex
materia et forma '. Aut hic subiicitur res extra animam,
aut tantum intentio in anima, aut vox. Si res, et non
res communis, quia nulla talis est, sicut ostendetur et

part of philosophy it is contained ; and then we have
to consider the *Physics* in particular.

Concerning the first point, we must say that the
philosophy of nature deals primarily with sensible substances composed of matter and form, and in the second
place with certain separate substances.

In order to understand this, we must know that all
knowledge has to do with a proposition or propositions.
And just as the propositions [*complexa*] are known by
means of a science, so also the non-complex terms of
which they are composed are that subject matter which
is considered by a science. Now the fact is that the
propositions known by natural science are composed not
of sensible things or substances, but of mental contents
or concepts that are common to such things. Hence,
properly speaking, the science of nature is not about
corruptible and generable things nor about natural substances nor about movable things, for none of these
things is subject or predicate in any conclusion known
by natural science. Properly speaking, the science of
nature is about mental contents which are common to
such things, and which stand precisely for such things
in many propositions, though in some propositions these
concepts stand for themselves, as our further exposition
will show. This is what the Philosopher means when
he says that knowledge is not about singular things, but
about universals which stand for the individual things
themselves. Nevertheless, metaphorically and im-
properly speaking, the science of nature is said to be
about corruptible and movable things, since it is about
the terms that stand for these things.

I now prove this. For instance, I take the proposition
'Every sensible substance is composed of matter and
form'. The subject here is either a thing outside the
mind or a mental content or a word. If the subject is
a thing, it is certainly not a common thing, since such
a common thing does not exist, as will be shown later

6

alibi frequenter est ostensum, ergo subiicitur aliqua res
singularis ; et non magis una quam alia ; ergo vel
quaelibet subiicitur vel nulla ; et non quaelibet, quia
multae sunt quae non intelliguntur a sciente talem
propositionem, quia multae sunt de quibus numquam
cogitavit ; ergo nulla talis res subiicitur. Ergo subiicitur
intentio vel vox, et habetur propositum.

Et si dicatur, quod scientia realis est de rebus, ergo
cum Philosophia sit scientia realis, oportet quod sit de
rebus, et per consequens non est de intentionibus animae.

Similiter, per hoc distinguitur logica ab aliis scientiis,
quia logica est de intentionibus animae, aliae scientiae
non.

Ad primum istorum dicendum est, quod scientia realis
non est de rebus, sed est de intentionibus supponentibus
pro rebus, quia termini propositionum scitarum supponunt pro rebus. Unde in ista propositione scita, 'Omnis
ignis est calefactivus', subiicitur una intentio communis
omni igni et pro omni igne supponit, ideo dicitur
'notitia realis'.

Per idem ad secundum, quod logica per hoc distinguitur a scientiis realibus, quia scientiae reales sunt de
intentionibus, quia de universalibus supponentibus pro
rebus ; quia termini scientiarum realium, quamvis sint
intentiones, tamen supponunt pro rebus. Sed logica est
de intentionibus supponentibus pro intentionibus. Sicut
in ista propositione, 'Species praedicatur de pluribus
differentibus numero', subiicitur una intentio et non
supponit nisi pro intentionibus, et non pro rebus extra,

and as has been frequently shown elsewhere. Consequently, it is a singular thing. But there is no more reason why it should be this one singular thing than another. Therefore either every single thing is the subject or none of them are. But not every one of them is the subject, because there are many things unknown to him who knows such a proposition, since there are many things of which he has never thought. Consequently, none of these things is subject in the proposition. Therefore the subject of such a proposition is a mental content or a word ; which is our intended conclusion.

To this it could be objected : A real science is about things. Since philosophy, then, is a real science, it must be about real things. Consequently, it is not about mental contents.

Likewise, logic is distinguished from other sciences by the fact that logic is about mental contents ; whereas the other sciences are not.

To the first of these objections we have to say : A real science is not about things, but about mental contents standing for things ; for the terms of scientifically known propositions stand for things. Hence in the following scientifically known proposition, 'All fire is warming', the subject is a mental content common to every fire, and stands for every fire. This is the reason why the proposition is called real knowledge [that is, knowledge concerning real things].

The same answer applies to the second objection. Logic is distinguished from the real sciences in the following manner. The real sciences are about mental contents, since they are about contents which stand for things ; for even though they are mental contents, they still stand for things. Logic, on the other hand, is about mental contents that stand for mental contents. For instance, in this proposition, 'A species is predicated of numerically distinct things', the subject is a mental content which stands for mental contents only and not for

quia nulla res extra praedicatur de pluribus nisi forte vox vel scriptum ad placitum instituentium.

Est tamen sciendum, quod logica non negatur esse scientia realis, quasi non sit una res ; nam ita vera res est logica sicut scientia naturalis. Sed ideo negatur esse scientia realis, quia non est de intentionibus supponentibus pro rebus. Unde breviter, omnes auctoritates dicentes talem scientiam esse de talibus vel talibus rebus debent sic glossari : 'Hoc est de terminis supponentibus pro talibus rebus' ; sicut quod aliqua scientia dicitur esse de rebus generabilibus et corruptibilibus, hoc est, de terminis supponentibus in propositionibus scitis pro talibus rebus generabilibus et corruptibilibus.

Ex praedictis patet, quomodo de corruptibilibus et mobilibus potest esse una scientia. Nam talibus est unum commune, de quo necessario praedicantur propriae passiones. Sicut hoc commune 'corpus corruptibile' est commune omni rei corruptibili et de isto communi praedicantur necessario multa. Sic etiam de impossibilibus potest esse scientia ; nam hoc commune 'impossibile' est commune omnibus impossibilibus, et de isto communi pro impossibilibus aliquid vere praedicatur ; nam haec est vera : 'Omne impossibile repugnat necessario'. Et ita de hoc communi 'impossibile' aliquid necessario praedicatur et vere scitur. Et sic est de aliis. Nam de hoc communi 'ens per accidens' aliquid vere et necessario praedicatur, et ideo de hoc communi potest esse scientia. Et tamen de illo, de quo praedicatur hoc commune, non potest esse scientia, proprie loquendo, sed tantum loquendo improprie, quomodo dixi iam, quod de rebus generabilibus est scientia.

things outside the mind, for nothing outside the mind is predicated of many things, except, by convention, a spoken or written sign.

We should realise, however, that the reason why we deny logic to be a real science is not that it is not a thing, for logic is just as truly a thing as the science of nature is. We deny it to be a real science because it is not about mental contents that stand for real things. Briefly, then, all authorities stating that such a science is about such and such a thing, ought to be glossed in the following manner : 'This science is about terms which stand for such things'. For instance, to say that a science is about things that can be generated or corrupted means that it is about terms standing for such things in scientifically known propositions.

It is also clear from what has been said how a science of movable and corruptible things is possible. For there is one term common to such things, and of this term proper attributes [*passiones*] are necessarily predicated. The common term 'corruptible body', for instance, is a term common to every corruptible thing, and many attributes are necessarily predicated of it. In like manner there is also a science of impossibilities. For this common term 'impossibility' is common to all impossibilities, and of this common term there is something truly predicated, which holds for all impossibilities. For this is true : 'Any impossibility goes against a necessity'. Thus of this common term 'impossibility' something is necessarily predicated and genuinely known. And so it is with other terms. For of the common term 'accidental being' something is truly and necessarily predicated. Therefore a science about this common term is possible. And yet, properly speaking, there can be no science about the thing of which this common term is predicated. Only in an improper sense is a science of such a thing possible, as I have already explained when I said that there is a science of 'generable' things.

Et ideo multae distinctiones, quibus distinguitur, quod
res mobiles vel mutabiles possunt considerari sic vel sic,
et quod uno modo sunt mutabiles et alio modo immuta-
biles, et quod uno modo sunt contingentes, alio modo
necessariae, nihil valent ; nam eadem facilitate dicerem,
quod homo, si consideretur sic, est asinus ; si aliter, est
bos ; si tertio modo, est capra. Unde intelligendum,
quod consideratio mea vel tua nihil facit ad hoc quod
res sit mutabilis vel immutabilis, vel ad hoc quod sit
necessaria et incorruptibilis vel contingens, non plus
quam facit ad hoc quod tu sis albus vel niger, nec plus
quam facit ad hoc quod tu sis extra domum vel in domo.
Sed diversa suppositio terminorum bene facit ad hoc
quod de termino aliquod praedicatum vere praedicetur
vel vere negetur. Unde ad hoc quod haec sit vera,
'Res mutabilis est subiectum vel illud de quo scitur',
bene facit suppositio istius termini, non consideratio rei
extra. Nam si iste terminus 'res mutabilis' supponat
simpliciter pro se, tunc haec est vera 'Res mutabilis, (hoc
est, hoc commune "res mutabilis") est illud, de quo
aliquid scitur'. Si autem supponat personaliter, tunc
est falsa, quia quaelibet singularis est falsa. Et ita
diversa suppositio eiusdem termini bene facit ad hoc,
quod de eodem termino vere negetur aliquid et vere
affirmetur. Nam si in ista, 'Homo est species', 'homo'
supponat simpliciter, haec est vera ; et si in ista, 'Homo
non est species', idem terminus supponat personaliter,
illa est etiam vera. Sed quod illa res quae est extra
propter unam considerationem meam sit mutabilis et
propter aliam considerationem meam sit immutabilis,
est simpliciter falsum et asinine dictum. Sicut si vellem
dicere, quod Sortes propter unam considerationem meam

---

[1] See Introduction above, pp. xxxiv ff.

For this reason many distinctions are not valid, for instance that mobile or mutable things can be considered either in this or that way, and that they are mutable considered in one way but immutable in another, and that they are contingent in one way but necessary in another. For with the same ease I could say that a man considered in one way is an ass, considered in another way he is an ox, and considered in a third way he is a she-goat.

Therefore, we must understand that it does not depend on your consideration or mine whether a thing is mutable or immutable, contingent or necessary and incorruptible, any more than it does whether you are white or black, or whether you are inside or outside the house. On the other hand, it does certainly depend on the different *suppositio* [1] of the terms whether a predicate is truly predicated or truly denied of a term. Hence, in order that this proposition be true, 'The mutable thing is the subject or is that about which there is a science', what is important is not the consideration of the thing outside the mind but the *suppositio* of the term 'mutable thing'. For if it has simple *suppositio*, i.e. if it stands for itself, then our proposition is true : ' "Mutable thing" (i.e. this common term "mutable thing") is that about which something is scientifically known'. If, however, it has personal *suppositio*, then it is false, because every singular proposition of this kind is false. Hence, it is the different *suppositio* of the same term that causes something to be truly denied and truly affirmed of this term. For if, in the proposition ' Man is a species', 'man' has simple *suppositio*, the proposition is true ; and if, in the proposition 'Man is not a species', the same term has personal *suppositio*, then this proposition likewise is true. However, to say that a thing outside the mind is mutable according to one viewpoint and that it is immutable according to another, is simply false and asinine talk. Thus I could say for instance that Socrates is white from

est albus et propter aliam est niger. Tamen, si vellem
uti isto termino aequivoce, puta pro uno homine nigro
et pro uno alio homine albo, tunc ista, 'Sortes est albus',
est vera, si hoc nomen 'Sortes' accipiatur pro illo homine
albo, et haec, 'Sortes est niger', est vera, si accipiatur
pro alio homine nigro. Sicut est de ista, 'Omnis canis
est animal' ; quod si 'canis' stet pro animali latrabili
tantum, tunc est vera, si iste terminus 'canis' stet pro
caelesti sidere tantum, tunc est falsa.

Et sic distinguere propositiones est ars tradita a
Philosopho ; non autem dicere, quod eadem res secundum unam considerationem est asinus et eadem secundum aliam considerationem est capra. Nec umquam
talis modus loquendi a Philosopho invenitur ; et est
talis modus loquendi occasio multorum errorum in
simplicibus et inexpertis.

Circa secundum sciendum, quod ista scientia distinguitur ab aliis vel penes subiecta sua vel penes praedicata ; quia hic tam distinctio subiectorum quam
praedicatorum conclusorum de subiectis sufficit ad
distinctionem scientiarum. Tamen, qualiter hoc sit intelligendum, magis forte super *Metaphysicam* ostendetur.
Verumtamen sciendum est, quod aliqua eadem veritas
potest pertinere ad distinctas scientias, sicut alibi est
ostensum.

Circa tertium dicendum est, quod scientia pro maiori
parte est speculativa, quia illa scientia quae non est de
operibus nostris, est speculativa. Sed ista scientia est
huiusmodi, sicut manifeste patet ; ergo ista notitia est
speculativa. Verumtamen, si sit aliqua pars philosophiae
naturalis, quae sit de operibus nostris, circa quae eli-
cienda potest notitia illa dirigere, illa pars Scientiae
Naturalis erit practica, et non speculativa.

one viewpoint, but black from another. Of course, I could use the same term (i.e. 'Socrates') in an equivocal manner, and I could mean in the first case a white man and in the other another man who is black. In this case, of course, the proposition 'Socrates is white' is true, if this name 'Socrates' refers to the white man ; and the proposition 'Socrates is black' is also true, if it refers to the black man. As it is the same in the proposition 'Every dog is an animal' ; if 'dog' stands only for an animal which can bark, the proposition is true ; but if the term 'dog' stands only for a star in the heavens, it is false.

The method handed down by the Philosopher is to make distinctions concerning propositions in this way, and not to say that the same thing from one point of view is a donkey, and from another a she-goat. Nowhere do we find the Philosopher using such a manner of speech. It is just such a way of speaking that occasions many errors in the simple and uninitiated.

Concerning the second point, we must recognise that this science [philosophy of nature] is distinguished from other sciences either by its subjects or by its predicates. For here a distinction based either on the subjects or on the predicates of conclusions about the subjects suffices to distinguish sciences. Just how this has to be understood will be better explained, perhaps, when we shall deal with the exposition of the *Metaphysics*. In any case, we must recognise that the same truth may pertain to different sciences, as we have shown elsewhere.

Concerning the third point, we note that this is a theoretical science for the most part. For a science that does not treat of what we do is speculative. But this science is the kind that is not about what we do ; therefore it is speculative. But should there be some part of the philosophy of nature that provides a directive knowledge for the performance of actions, this part would be practical, not theoretical.

Circa quartum : Dicitur iste liber *Liber physicorum*, hoc est, liber naturalium secundum modum praeexpositum ; vel dicitur liber '*De physico auditu*', quia forte auditores istum librum audientes solam reportationem scripserunt. Sed de hoc non est magna cura.

Concerning the fourth point, this book is called the *Physics*, in other words, 'the book concerning the things of nature', in the sense explained above. It is also called the *Lectures on Physics*, perhaps because the audience listening to this book only took notes on it. This, however, is not of much consequence.

II

EPISTEMOLOGICAL
PROBLEMS

Sources :

1. Ostendam, quod intellectus noster, etiam pro statu isto, respectu eiusdem obiecti sub eadem ratione potest habere duas notitias incomplexas specie distinctas, quarum una potest dici intuitiva et alia abstractiva. . . .

Ad declarationem primae conclusionis primo praemittam aliquas distinctiones et conclusiones praeambulas, secundo probabo conclusionem principaliter intentam.

Est ergo prima distinctio ista : Quod inter actus intellectus sunt duo actus, quorum unus est apprehensivus : et est respectu cuiuslibet quod potest terminare actum potentiae intellectivae, sive sit complexum sive incomplexum, quia apprehendimus non tantum incomplexa sed et propositiones et demonstrationes et impossibilia et necessaria, et universaliter omnia quae respiciuntur a potentia intellectiva. Alius potest dici actus iudicativus, quo intellectus non tantum apprehendit obiectum, sed etiam illi assentit vel dissentit; et iste actus est tantum respectu complexi, quia nulli assentimus per intellectum nisi quod verum reputamus, nec dissentimus nisi quod falsum aestimamus. Et sic patet, quod respectu complexi potest esse duplex actus, scilicet actus apprehensivus et actus iudicativus.

Hoc probatur : Quia aliquis potest apprehendere aliquam propositionem, et tamen illi nec assentire nec dissentire, sicut patet de propositionibus neutris, quibus intellectus nec assentit nec dissentit, quia aliter non essent sibi neutrae.

Similiter : Laicus nesciens Latinum potest audire

[*The basis of immediate cognition*]

1. First I intend to show that our intellect, even in this life, can have two specifically distinct kinds of non-complex knowledge even when it is concerned with the same object under the same aspect. The one may be called intuitive, the other abstractive cognition. . . .

In order to explain this first conclusion, I shall present a few preliminary distinctions and conclusions ; after that I shall prove the conclusion which is principally intended.

The first distinction is between two acts of the intellect. The first act is an act of apprehension and relates to everything that can be the term of an act of the intellective power, whether this be something complex or non-complex. For we apprehend not only that which is non-complex, but also propositions and demonstrations, and impossibilities and necessities, and, in general, anything within the scope of the intellective power. The second act may be called an act of judgment, by which the intellect not only apprehends its object, but also gives its assent or disssent to it. This act has to do with a proposition [*complexum*] only. For our intellect does not assent to anything unless we believe it to be true, nor does it dissent from anything unless we believe it to be false. It is clear, therefore, that in reference to a proposition, a twofold act is possible, namely an act of apprehension and an act of judgment.

Proof : It is possible that someone apprehends a proposition, but nevertheless gives neither assent nor dissent to it ; this is clearly true, for instance, of indifferent propositions, to which the intellect gives neither assent nor dissent, because otherwise they would not be indifferent for it.

Likewise, a layman who does not know Latin may

multas propositiones in Latino, quibus nec assentit nec dissentit, et certum est, quod intellectus potest assentire alicui propositioni et dissentire alteri ; ergo etc.

Secunda distinctio est : Quod, sicut respectu complexi est duplex actus, sic respectu complexi est duplex habitus correspondens, scilicet unus inclinans ad actum apprehensivum et alius inclinans ad actum iudicativum.

Ista distinctio patet : Quia aliquis post multas apprehensiones alicuius propositionis, quae est neutra, magis sentit se inclinatum ad apprehendendum et cogitandum de illa propositione quam prius ; ergo habet habitum inclinantem ad actus apprehensivos. Quod autem sit habitus inclinans ad actus iudicativos, patet per Philosophum vi° *Ethicorum,** ubi ponit intellectum, scientiam etc.

Prima conclusio praeambula est ista : Quod actus iudicativus respectu alicuius complexi praesupponit actum apprehensivum respectu eiusdem. . . .

Ex istis sequitur secunda conclusio : Quod omnis actus iudicativus praesupponit in eadem potentia notitiam incomplexam terminorum : quia praesupponit actum apprehensivum, et actus apprehensivus respectu alicuius complexi praesupponit notitiam incomplexam terminorum. . . .

Tertia conclusio est : Quod nullus actus partis sensitivae est causa immediata et proxima, nec partialis nec totalis, alicuius actus iudicativi ipsius intellectus.

Haec conclusio potest persuaderi : Quia qua ratione ad aliquem actum iudicativum sufficiunt illa quae sunt in intellectu tamquam causae proximae et immediatae, et ad omnem actum iudicativum ; sed respectu alicuius actus iudicativi sufficiunt ea quae sunt in intellectu,

* *Cf.* cap. iii–viii

hear many propositions in this language to which he
gives neither assent nor dissent. On the other hand, it
is certain that the intellect can give its assent to one
proposition and its dissent to another proposition. Therefore, apprehension and judgment are distinct.

The second distinction is, that just as in regard to a
proposition there can be a twofold act, so also there can
be two corresponding *habitūs* ; the one inclines the
intellect towards an act of apprehension ; the other
towards an act of judgment.

This distinction is manifest. For after someone has
frequently apprehended an indifferent proposition, he
finds himself more inclined to apprehend and think
about this proposition than he was before. Therefore
he has now a *habitus* inclining him towards acts of apprehension. The fact that there is also a *habitus* inclining
one towards acts of judgment is clear from the statement
of the Philosopher in the sixth book of the *Ethics*, where
he affirms the existence of [the several *habitūs* of] understanding, knowledge, etc.

First preliminary conclusion : The act of judgment
in reference to a proposition (*complexum*) presupposes
an act of apprehending the same proposition. . . .

Second conclusion, following from the preceding
discussion [here omitted]. Every act of judgment presupposes in the same faculty a non-complex cognition
of the terms ; for it presupposes an act of apprehension,
and the act of apprehending a proposition presupposes
non-complex cognition of the terms. . . .

Third conclusion : No act of the sensitive part of the
soul is either partially or totally the immediate and
proximate cause of the intellect's own act of judgment.

A persuasive argument can be adduced for this conclusion. If we assume that contents of the intellect
suffice as proximate and immediate causes to produce
some act of judgment, then they suffice to produce every
such act. Now contents of the intellect suffice for some

scilicet respectu conclusionis, quia si sit in intellectu
actus sciendi praemissas, statim scitur conclusio omni
alio circumscripto : ergo ad omnem actum iudicativum
sufficiunt ea quae sunt in intellectu tamquam causae
proximae.

Praeterea : Ex quo causae quae sunt in parte intellectiva sufficere possunt, frustra ponuntur aliae causae.

His praemissis probo primo primam conclusionem sic :
Omnis notitia incomplexa aliquorum terminorum, quae
potest esse causa notitiae evidentis respectu propositionis
compositae ex illis terminis, distinguitur secundum
speciem a notitia incomplexa illorum quae, quantumcumque intendatur, non potest esse causa notitiae
evidentis respectu propositionis eiusdem. Hoc patet :
Quia illa quae sunt eiusdem rationis et aeque perfecta
possunt in eodem passo aequaliter disposito habere
effectus eiusdem rationis, vii° *Topicorum* * ; sed certum
est, quod intellectus potest habere notitiam incomplexam,
tam de Sorte quam de albedine, cuius virtute non potest
evidenter cognoscere, an sit albus vel non, sicut per
experientiam patet ; et praeter istam potest habere
notitiam incomplexam, virtute cuius potest evidenter
cognoscere, quod Sortes est albus, si est albus. Ergo
de istis potest habere duas notitias incomplexas, quarum
una potest esse causa notitiae evidentis illius propositionis contingentis, et alia, quantumcumque intendatur,
non ; ergo specie distinguuntur. . . .

Secundo arguo principaliter sic : Omne intelligibile,
quod est a solo intellectu apprehensibile et nullo modo
sensibile, cuius aliqua notitia incomplexa sufficit ad
notitiam evidentem alicuius veritatis contingentis de eo,
et aliqua notitia incomplexa eiusdem non sufficit, potest
cognosci ab intellectu duabus cognitionibus specie dis-

* cap. i (152ᵃ, 2 sq.)

act of judgment, namely a conclusion ; because when the knowledge of the premises is in the intellect, the conclusion is immediately known without the help of anything else. Therefore contents of the intellect suffice as the proximate cause of every act of judgment.

Furthermore, since the causes existing in the intellective part can be sufficient, the assumption of other causes is superfluous.

Given these premises I shall prove the main conclusion as follows. Any non-complex cognition of terms that can cause evident cognition of a proposition composed of these terms, is specifically distinct from a non-complex cognition which, no matter how, intense it is, cannot cause evident cognition of the same proposition. This is manifest. For things of the same kind that are equally perfect can produce effects of the same kind in the same object when this is equally disposed to receive the effect. This the Philosopher shows in the seventh book of the *Topics*. Now it is certain, as experience teaches, that the intellect can have a non-complex cognition of both Socrates and whiteness, on the strength of which it cannot know evidently whether Socrates is white or not. But besides this knowledge, the intellect can have another cognition by which it is able to know evidently that Socrates is white, if he is white. Hence the intellect can have two non-complex cognitions of these things : the one cognition can cause evident knowledge of this contingent proposition ; and the other cannot, no matter how intense it is. Therefore these two cognitions are specifically distinct. . . .

The second main proof : Whenever an intelligible thing can be known only by intellect and in no way by sense, if there can be one non-complex cognition of the thing that suffices for evident knowledge of a contingent truth and another that does not suffice, then the two cognitions are specifically distinct. But acts of intellect,

tinctis ; sed intellectiones, affectiones, delectationes, tristitiae et huiusmodi sunt intelligibiles et nullo modo sensibiles, et aliqua notitia incomplexa earum sufficit ad notitiam evidentem, utrum sint vel non sint, et utrum sint in tali subiecto vel non, et aliqua notitia earundem non sufficit ; ergo etc. Minor, quantum ad primam partem, patet : Quia quilibet experitur in se quod intelligit, diligit, delectatur, tristatur ; et ista notitia, cum sit respectu contingentis, non potest accipi ex propositionibus necessariis ; ergo oportet quod accipiatur vel a notitia incomplexa terminorum vel rerum importatarum, vel ab aliqua contingente quae accipitur a notitia incomplexa terminorum vel rerum, vel erit processus in infinitum in talibus contingentibus. Tertium est impossibile, quia est ponere statum in talibus. Si detur secundum, vel ergo illa contingens habet aliquem terminum, qui potest accipi ab aliquo sensibili, vel nullum. Primum non potest dari, quia nulla est propositio de aliquo sensibili, ex qua sequatur necessario dilectionem esse in voluntate, sicut alias patebit ; et per consequens nulla est talis propositio contingens, virtute cuius potest evidenter cognosci, quod iste diligit. Si detur secundum, habetur propositum, quod sola notitia incomplexa terminorum mere intelligibilium sufficit ad notitiam evidentem talis veritatis contingentis. Si detur primum, habetur propositum. Secunda pars illius minoris patet : Quia non est inconveniens, quod aliquis de aliquo intelligibili ignoret, utrum sit vel non sit, et tamen quod habeat notitiam incomplexam de illo non plus quam de aliquo sensibili. Unde si intellectus primo videret dilectionem

emotions, pleasures, griefs and the like, can be apprehended only by the intellect and not by the sense-faculty.
Now some non-complex knowledge of them suffices for
evident knowledge of whether they exist or not, and
whether or not they exist in such and such a subject.
Yet not all non-complex knowledge of them suffices for
this ; therefore, etc. The first part of the minor premise
is shown thus : Everyone experiences in himself that he
understands, loves, is pleased, is sad. Since such knowledge concerns contingent facts, it cannot be obtained
from necessary propositions. Therefore, either (1) it
must be obtained from a non-complex knowledge of the
terms, or the things for which the terms stand, or (2)
from a contingent proposition obtained from non-
complex cognition of the terms or things, or (3) we can
go on *in infinitum* with such contingent propositions. The
third case is impossible, since there must be an end in
the series of such propositions. If the second case is
assumed, then the contingent proposition either contains
some term which can be obtained from a sensible object,
or it does not. The first alternative cannot be admitted ;
for there is no proposition about a sensible thing from
which it would necessarily follow that love is occurring
in the will, as will be made clear elsewhere, and consequently there is no contingent proposition in virtue
of which it is evidently knowable that this man loves.
If the second alternative is conceded, we have the result
we wanted : that a non-complex knowledge of purely
intelligible terms is sufficient for evident knowledge of
such a contingent truth. The second part of the minor
premise is shown thus : There is no inconsistency in the
supposition that someone does not know whether a
certain intelligible thing exists or does not exist, and
has nevertheless a non-complex cognition of it ; this is
no more inconsistent than the corresponding supposition
about a certain sensible thing. If, therefore, someone's
intellect should directly perceive another person's love

alterius et esset ita certus de dilectione alterius sicut de
dilectione propria, non esset inconveniens quin post
dilectionem eandem intelligeret et tamen ignoraret
ipsam esse, quamvis esset, sicut est de aliquo sensibili
primo viso et post intellecto.

Ista secunda ratio probat, quod intellectui est possibilis
talis duplex cognitio, et hoc respectu mere intelligibilis.
Prima autem ratio probat, quod de facto pro statu isto
intellectus habet talem duplicem cognitionem, etiam
respectu sensibilium. . . .

Dico igitur, quantum ad istum articulum, quod
respectu incomplexi potest esse duplex notitia, quarum
una potest vocari 'abstractiva' et alia 'intuitiva'. Utrum
autem alii velint vocare talem notitiam incomplexam
intuitivam, non curo, quia hoc solum intendo principaliter probare, quod de eadem re potest intellectus
habere duplicem notitiam incomplexam specie distinctam.

Sciendum tamen, quod 'notitia abstractiva' potest
accipi dupliciter : Uno modo quia est respectu alicuius
abstractiva multis singularibus, et sic cognitio abstractiva
non est aliud quam cognitio alicuius universalis abstrahibi-
lis a multis, de quo dicetur post. Et si universale sit vera
qualitas existens subiective in anima, sicut potest teneri
probabiliter, concedendum esset, quod illud universale
potest intuitive videri, et quod eadem notitia est intuitiva
et abstractiva, isto modo accipiendo 'notitiam abstractivam' ; et sic non distinguuntur ex opposito. Aliter
accipitur 'cognitio abstractiva', secundum quod abstrahit
ab existentia et non existentia et ab aliis conditionibus
quae contingenter accidunt rei vel praedicantur de re.

and he were thus as certain of this other person's love as of his own love, then there would not be any difficulty about supposing that later on he could still think of this love and nevertheless not know whether it continued to exist, even though it did still exist ; just as may happen with some sensible thing which is first seen and then thought of.

This second argument proves that it is possible for the intellect to have this twofold cognition and to have it about purely intelligible facts, whereas the first proves that our intellect actually has this twofold cognition in the present life, and has it even as regards sensible facts. . . .

I maintain, therefore, . . . that there are two ways of knowing something non-complex. The one can be called 'abstractive cognition', the other 'intuitive cognition'. But I am not concerned whether others wish to call this non-complex cognition 'intuitive cognition' or not. For what I intended to prove in the first instance was just that our intellect can have two specifically different non-complex cognitions of the same thing.

We must realise, however, that the term 'abstractive cognition' can be taken in two senses. In one sense it means cognition that relates to something abstracted from many singulars ; and in this sense abstractive cognition is nothing else but cognition of a universal which can be abstracted from many things. We shall speak about this later. If such a universal is a true quality existing in the mind as its subject—which is a probable opinion—then it must be conceded that such a universal can be intuitively known and that the same knowledge is intuitive and also abstractive, according to this first meaning of 'abstractive'. And in this sense 'intuitive' and 'abstractive' are not contrasted.

Abstractive cognition in the second sense abstracts from existence and non-existence and from all the other conditions which contingently belong to or are predi-

Non quod aliquid cognoscatur per notitiam intuitivam, quod non cognoscitur per notitiam abstractivam, sed idem totaliter et sub omni eadem ratione cognoscitur per utramque notitiam. Sed distinguuntur per istum modum : Quia notitia intuitiva rei est talis notitia, virtute cuius potest sciri, utrum res sit vel non, ita quod, si res sit, statim intellectus iudicat eam esse et evidenter cognoscit eam esse, nisi forte impediatur propter imperfectionem illius notitiae. Et eodem modo, si esset perfecta talis notitia, per potentiam divinam conservata de re non existente, virtute illius notitiae incomplexae evidenter cognosceret illam rem non esse.

Similiter notitia intuitiva est talis, quod quando aliquae res cognoscuntur, quarum una inhaeret alteri, vel una distat loco ab altera, vel alio modo se habet ad alteram, statim virtute illius notitiae incomplexae illarum rerum scitur, si res inhaeret vel non inhaeret, si distat vel non distat, et sic de aliis veritatibus contingentibus, nisi illa notitia sit nimis remissa vel sit aliquod aliud impedimentum. Sicut si Sortes in rei veritate sit albus, illa notitia Sortis et albedinis, virtute cuius potest evidenter cognosci quod Sortes est albus, dicitur notitia intuitiva. Et universaliter; omnis notitia incomplexa termini vel terminorum seu rei vel rerum, virtute cuius potest evidenter cognosci aliqua veritas contingens, maxime de praesenti, est notitia intuitiva.

Notitia autem abstractiva est illa, virtute cuius de re contingente non potest sciri evidenter, utrum sit vel non sit. Et per istum modum notitia abstractiva abstrahit ab existentia et non-existentia, quia nec per ipsam potest

cated of a thing. This does not mean that something may be known by intuitive cognition which is not known by abstractive cognition ; rather, the same thing is known fully, and under the same aspect, by either cognition. But they are distinguished in the following manner. Intuitive cognition of a thing is cognition that enables us to know whether the thing exists or does not exist, in such a way that, if the thing exists, then the intellect immediately judges that it exists and evidently knows that it exists, unless the judgment happens to be impeded through the imperfection of this cognition. And in the same way, if the divine power were to conserve a perfect intuitive cognition of a thing no longer existent, in virtue of this non-complex knowledge the intellect would know evidently that this thing does not exist.

Then, too, intuitive cognition is such that when one thing known by means of it inheres as an accident in another, or is locally distant from the other, or stands in some other relation to the other, then non-complex cognition of these things gives us an immediate knowledge whether a certain thing inheres or does not inhere in another, or whether it is distant from it or not, and so for other contingent truths ; unless this cognition is too weak, or there be other impediments. For instance, if Socrates is in reality white, then knowledge of Socrates and of whiteness is called intuitive cognition, when it can be evidently known in virtue of such knowledge that Socrates is white. Generally speaking, any non-complex cognition of one or more terms or things, is an intuitive cognition, if it enables us to know a contingent truth, especially about present facts.

Abstractive cognition, on the other hand, is that knowledge by which it cannot be evidently known whether a contingent fact exists or does not exist. In this way abstractive cognition abstracts from existence and non-existence ; because, in opposition to intuitive

evidenter sciri de re existente quod existit, nec de non
existente quod non existit, per oppositum ad notitiam
intuitivam.

Similiter, per notitiam abstractivam nulla veritas contingens, maxime de praesenti, potest evidenter cognosci,
sicut de facto patet, quod quando cognoscitur Sortes et
albedo sua in absentia, virtute illius notitiae incomplexae
nec potest sciri, quod Sortes est vel non est, vel quod est
albus vel non est albus, vel quod distat a tali loco vel
non, et sic de aliis veritatibus contingentibus. Et tamen
certum est, quod istae veritates possunt evidenter
cognosci. Et omnis notitia complexa terminorum vel
rerum significatarum ultimate reducitur ad notitiam
incomplexam terminorum. Ergo isti termini vel res una
alia notitia possunt cognosci quam sit illa, virtute cuius
non possunt cognosci tales veritates contingentes. Et illa
erit intuitiva. Et ista est notitia, a qua incipit notitia
experimentalis : quia universaliter ille, qui potest
accipere experimentum de aliqua veritate contingente et
mediante illa de veritate necessaria, habet aliquam
notitiam incomplexam de aliquo termino vel re, quam
non habet ille, qui non potest sic experiri. Et ideo,
sicut secundum Philosophum i⁰ *Metaphysicae* * et ii⁰
Posteriorum† scientia istorum sensibilium quae accipitur
per experientiam, de qua ipse loquitur, incipit a sensu,
id est a notitia intuitiva sensitiva istorum sensibilium,
ita universaliter notitia scientifica istorum pure intelligibilium accepta per experientiam incipit a notitia intuitiva intellectiva istorum intelligibilium.

Est tamen advertendum, quod aliquando propter
imperfectionem notitiae intuitivae, quia scilicet est valde

---

* cap. i (980ᵃ, 29 sq.) † cap. xix (100ᵃ, 4 sqq.)

cognition, it does not enable us to know the existence of what does exist or the non-existence of what does not exist.

Likewise, through abstractive cognition no contingent truth, in particular none relating to the present, can be evidently known. This is clear from the fact that when Socrates and his whiteness are known in his absence, this non-complex knowledge does not enable us to know whether Socrates exists or does not exist, or whether he is white or is not white, and the same for other contingent truths. But yet it is certain that these truths can be evidently known. And any complex knowledge of terms, or of things signified by terms, is ultimately reduced to non-complex knowledge of terms. Hence these terms or things can be known by a cognition which is different from that which cannot give us knowledge of such contingent truths ; and this will be intuitive cognition. And it is from this that empirical knowledge begins ; for, generally speaking, he who is enabled by observation to know a contingent truth and, by means of this, a necessary truth, has non-complex knowledge of some term or thing which another who is unable to make this observation cannot have. And therefore, just as the knowledge of sensible facts that is obtained from experience (as the Philosopher says in the first book of the *Metaphysics* and in the second book of the *Posterior Analytics*) begins with the senses, i.e. from a sense-intuition of these sensible facts, so in general the scientific knowledge of these purely intelligible facts of experience begins with an intellective intuition of these intelligible facts.

Still, it is to be noted that at times it may happen that no contingent truths, or only a few, can be known about a thing that we know intuitively, owing to the imperfec-

imperfecta et obscura vel propter aliqua impedimenta
ex parte obiecti vel propter aliqua alia impedimenta,
potest contingere, quod vel nullae vel paucae veritates
contingentes de re sic intuitive cognita possunt cognosci.

2. *Utrum cognitio intuitiva possit esse de obiecto non-existente?*

Quod non : Quia contradictio est, quod visio sit et
nihil videatur ; ergo contradictio est, quod visio sit et
obiectum visum non sit.

Contra : Visio est qualitas absoluta distincta ab obiecto;
ergo potest sine contradictione fieri sine obiecto.

In ista quaestione pono duas conclusiones. Prima est,
quod cognitio intuitiva potest esse per potentiam divinam
de obiecto non existente. Quod probo primo per articulum fidei 'Credo in Deum Patrem omnipotentem' quem
sic intelligo : quod quidlibet est divinae potentiae attribuendum quod non includit manifestam contradictionem; sed istud fieri a Deo non includit contradictionem;
ergo etc.

Praeterea : In illo articulo fundatur illa propositio
famosa theologorum : 'Quidquid Deus producit mediantibus causis secundis potest immediate sine illis producere et conservare'. Ex ista propositione arguo sic :
Omnem effectum quem potest Deus mediante causa
secunda potest immediate per se ; sed in notitiam
intuitivam corporalem potest mediante obiecto ; ergo

tion of the intuitive cognition (it being very imperfect or very obscure), or because of some impediment on the part of the object, or some other impediment.

[*Intuitive cognition of non-existing things*]

2. *Whether intuitive cognition can be had of an object that does not exist?*

It cannot : For it is a contradiction that there should be an act of seeing and nothing be seen ; therefore it is a contradiction that there should be an act of seeing but the seen object not exist.

On the contrary : Vision is a non-relative quality distinct from the object ; without contradiction, therefore, it can occur without an object.

On this question I lay down two conclusions. First : Intuitive cognition of a non-existent object is possible by the divine power. I prove this first by the article of faith 'I believe in God the Father almighty', which I understand in the following sense : Anything is to be attributed to the divine power, when it does not contain a manifest contradiction. But that this [i.e. cognition of a non-existent object] should be produced by the power of God, does not contain a contradiction ; therefore, etc.

Again, on this article is based the famous maxim of the theologians : 'Whatever God can produce by means of secondary causes, He can directly produce and preserve without them'. From this maxim I argue thus. Every effect which God can produce by means of a secondary cause He can produce directly on His own account. God can produce intuitive sense cognition by means

potest in eam immediate per se.

Praeterea : Omnis res absoluta distincta loco et subiecto ab alia re absoluta potest per divinam potentiam existere alia re absoluta destructa ; sed visio stellae in caelo, tam sensitiva quam intellectiva, est huiusmodi ; ergo etc.

Et si dicis, quod secundum istam rationem sequitur, quod Deus posset videri intuitive et beatifice non exhibita sua praesentia actuali in ratione obiecti actualiter praesentis ipsi intellectui, quod falsum est et erroneum : Respondeo, quod hic non est aliqua habitudo, arguendo quod quia Deus potest facere talem visionem sine obiecto creato, a quo non dependet nisi tamquam a causa secunda, ergo Deus potest videri intuitive et beatifice non exhibita sua praesentia actuali in ratione obiecti actualiter praesentis ipsi intellectui, a quo obiecto dependet illa visio sicut a causa prima. Nam quamvis secundum doctores Deus potest facere effectus proprios causarum secundarum sine illis causis secundis, non tamen potest aliquem effectum facere sine causa prima. Unde sicut non est possibile, quod color causet effective visionem suam in oculo nisi sit actualiter praesens, ita non est possibile, quod Deus causet visionem in intellectu nisi exhibita sua actuali praesentia.

Secunda conclusio est : Quod naturaliter cognitio intuitiva non potest causari nec conservari obiecto non existente. Cuius ratio est, quia effectus realis non potest causari nec produci de non esse in esse ab illo quod nihil est ; et per consequens, naturaliter loquendo, requirit tam causam producentem quam conservantem existere.

Et si dicis : Si quis videat solem et post intret obscurum

of an object ; hence He can produce it directly on His own account.

Furthermore, every non-relative reality that differs in its place and its subject [of inherence] from another non-relative reality can still exist by virtue of the divine power when the other non-relative reality is destroyed. But seeing a star in the sky, whether by sense or by intellect, is such a reality ; therefore, etc.

You may object that according to this argument it follows that there could be an intuitive and beatific vision of God without His actual presence as an object actually present to the intellect ; which is false and erroneous. I answer that there is no logical connexion in the following way of arguing : 'Because God can make such an act of seeing without a created object (on which this act depends only as a secondary cause), therefore, there can be an intuitive and beatific vision of God without His actual presence as an object actually present to the intellect (an object on which this is dependent as its first cause)'. For though, according to the Doctors, God can make the proper effects of secondary causes without these secondary causes, nevertheless He cannot make any effect without its first cause. For this reason, just as it is not possible that a colour should, as efficient cause, cause itself to be seen in the eye unless it is actually present, so in like manner it is not possible that God should cause an act of seeing Him in the intellect unless His actual presence is given.

Second conclusion : So far as natural causes are in question, an intuitive cognition cannot be caused or preserved if the object does not exist. The reason is this. A real effect cannot be caused, or brought from nothing into being, by that which is nothing. Hence, if we are speaking of the natural mode of causation, it requires for its existence both a productive and a preservative cause.

You may object : 'If someone sees the sun and then

locum, apparet sibi quod videat solem in eodem situ et eadem magnitudine ; ergo visio solis remanet ipso absente ; et eadem ratione remaneret ipso non existente : Respondeo : non manet visio solis, sed manet aliqua qualitas, puta lux impressa oculo, et illa qualitas videtur. Et si intellectus formet talem propositionem, 'Lux videtur in eodem situ, etc.', et sibi assentiat, decipitur propter illam qualitatem impressam visam.

Ad argumentum principale dico, quod contradictio est, quod visio sit et quod illud quod videtur non sit in effectu nec esse possit. Ideo contradictio est, quod chimaera videatur intuitive. Sed non est contradictio, quod illud quod videtur nihil sit in actu extra suam causam, dummodo possit esse in effectu, vel aliquando fuit in rerum natura. Et sic est in proposito. Unde Deus ab aeterno vidit omnes res factibiles, et tamen tunc nihil fuerunt.

3. *Utrum primum cognitum ab intellectu primitate generationis sit singulare?*

Quod non : Quia universale est primum et proprium obiectum intellectus ; ergo primo cognoscitur primitate generationis.

Contra : Idem omnino est obiectum sensus et intellectus ; sed singulare est primum obiectum sensus tali primitate ; ergo etc.

Hic primo dandus est intellectus quaestionis, secundo ad quaestionem.

enters a dark room, it appears to him that he sees the sun in the same place and of the same size. Hence a sight of the sun remains, when the sun is absent ; and for the same reason would remain, even if it did not exist'. To this I answer : 'No sight of the sun does remain ; but there does remain a quality, viz. the light-impression in the eye, and it is this quality that is seen. And if the intellect formulates such a proposition as "Light is seen at the same place, etc." and gives its assent to it, it is deceived by this quality or impression which it sees'.

To the main argument I answer : It is a contradiction that an act of seeing should exist while that which is seen neither exists nor can exist in reality. Hence it is a contradiction that a chimera should be intuitively seen. But it is no contradiction that what is seen should be nothing actually existing outside its cause, provided only that it can exist in reality or has once been in the universe. And so it is in our case. It was thus that God from all eternity saw all things that could be made, and nevertheless they were then nothing.

[*The primacy of cognition of singular things*]

3. *Whether the singular is the first thing known, as regards the origin of cognition ?*

It is not the first thing known : for the universal is the first and proper object of the intellect ; and is, therefore, the first thing known, as regards the origin of cognition.

On the contrary : Both intellect and sense have the very same object ; but if we are speaking of the origin of cognition, a singular thing is the first object of the sense faculty ; therefore, etc.

Answer : We must first clarify the meaning of the question, and then answer it.

Circa primum sciendum, quod hic accipitur 'singulare' non pro omni illo, quod est unum numero, quia sic quaelibet res est singularis, sed accipitur pro re, quae est una numero et non est signum naturale vel voluntarium sive ad placitum commune multis, quomodo dictio scripta, conceptus et vox prolata significativa non sunt singularia, sed tantum res quae non est commune signum.

Secundo sciendum, quod non intelligitur ista quaestio de qualibet cognitione singularis, quia quaecumque cognitio universalis sic est cognitio singularis, quia nihil per talem cognitionem cognoscitur nisi singulare et singularia, tamen illa est cognitio communis. Sed intelligitur quaestio de cognitione propria et simplici singularis.

Circa secundum : Supposito quod quaestio intelligitur de cognitione propria singularis dico tunc primo : Quod singulare praedicto modo acceptum cognitione sibi propria et simplici est primo cognitum.

Quod probatur sic : Quia res extra animam, quae non est signum, tali cognitione primo intelligitur ; sed omnis res extra animam est singularis ; ergo etc.

Praeterea : Obiectum praecedit actum proprium et primum primitate generationis ; nihil autem praecedit actum talem nisi singulare ; ergo est.

Secundo dico : Quod cognitio simplex, propria singulari et prima tali primitate est cognitio intuitiva. Quod autem illa cognitio sit prima, patet : quia cognitio singularis abstractiva praesupponit intuitivam respectu eiusdem obiecti, et non econverso. Quod autem sit propria singulari, patet : quia immediate causatur a re

Concerning the first point we have to realise that here 'singular thing' does not mean everything that is numerically one ; for, in this sense, *everything* is singular. Instead we take 'singular thing' here for a thing which not only is numerically one, but in addition is not a natural or conventional sign belonging in common to many things signified. In this sense neither a written expression nor a concept nor a significant oral utterance, but only a thing which is not a common sign, is a singular thing.

Secondly, we should know that our question does not refer indiscriminately to any cognition of a singular thing. For in a sense every universal cognition is a cognition of a singular thing, since such a universal cognition gives us knowledge only of a singular thing or singular things. Our question rather refers to a proper and simple cognition of a singular thing.

On the second point : Granted that the question is taken to be about proper cognition of a singular thing, I maintain in the first place that a singular thing, taken in the above sense, is what is first known, in a cognition that is simple and proper to this singular thing.

This conclusion is proved in the following manner : What is first known by such cognition is an extra-mental thing which is not a sign ; but everything outside the mind is singular ; therefore, etc.

Furthermore, the object precedes the act which is proper to it and that comes first in order of origination ; but only a singular thing precedes such an act ; therefore, etc.

Secondly, I maintain that this cognition which is simple, proper to a singular thing, and the first to be acquired, is an intuitive cognition. That such a cognition is first, is clear ; for abstractive cognition of a singular thing presupposes an intuitive cognition of the same object, and not vice versa. The fact that it is proper to one singular thing is likewise clear ; for it is

singulari vel nata est causari, et non est nata causari ab
alia re singulari, etiam eiusdem speciei ; ergo etc.

Tertio dico : Quod cognitio prima abstractiva primitate generationis et simplex non est cognitio propria
singulari, sed est cognitio communis aliquando, immo
semper. Primum patet : quia non habetur cognitio
propria simplex de aliquo singulari pro tempore pro quo
non potest haberi cognitio eius specifica ; sed quandoque
ita est, sicut patet de veniente a remotis, quod causat
talem sensationem, virtute cuius possum tantum iudicare,
quod illud visum est ens. Manifestum est, quod in illo
casu cognitio abstractiva, quam habeo primo primitate
generationis, est cognitio entis et nullius inferioris, et
per consequens non est conceptus specificus nec est conceptus proprius singularis. Secundum patet : quia nulla
cognitio abstractiva simplex est plus similitudo unius rei
singularis quam alterius respectu sibi simillimi nec
causatur a re nec nata est causari ; ergo nulla talis est
propria singulari, sed quaelibet est universalis.

Sed hic sunt aliqua dubia. Primum est, quia videtur
quod cognitio intuitiva non sit propria, quia quaecumque
intuitiva demonstratur, aequaliter assimilatur uni singulari sicut alteri simillimo, et aequaliter repraesentat unum
sicut alterum ; ergo non plus videtur esse cognitio unius
quam alterius.

Secundum dubium est, quia si cognitio prima abstractiva sit aliquando cognitio et conceptus entis, sicut dicis
de veniente a remotis, ergo eodem modo prima intuitiva
in eodem casu erit cognitio communis entis, quia impossibile est, quod eiusdem rei sint plures conceptus

immediately caused, or is of such a nature as to be so caused, by this singular thing ; it cannot naturally be caused by another singular thing, even of the same species.

Thirdly, I maintain that the abstractive cognition which is simple and comes first in order of origination is not proper to a singular thing, but is sometimes, indeed always, a cognition common to many. The first part of this thesis is shown thus : We have no proper and simple cognition of a singular thing, as long as we can get no specific knowledge of it. Now this is sometimes the case, for instance, when somebody, approaching from a distance, causes in me a sense-perception with the help of which I can judge only that what I see is an existent. In this case it is clear that my first abstractive cognition (first, that is, in order of origination) is the cognition of existence, and of nothing less general ; consequently it is not a specific concept nor a concept proper to a singular thing. The second part of the thesis is likewise clear. For no simple abstractive cognition is more a likeness of one singular thing than of another thing very similar to this thing, nor is such cognition caused by a thing or of such nature as to be caused by a thing ; therefore no such cognition is proper to a singular thing, but every such cognition is universal.

But here some doubts arise.

First : It seems that intuitive cognition is not proper knowledge. For any assigned intuitive cognition will have no more likeness to one singular thing than to another very similar one, and will represent the one as much as the other. Therefore it does not seem to be a cognition of one rather than the other.

Second doubt : If the first abstractive cognition is at times a cognition or concept of existence, as you hold in the instance of a man coming from afar, then the first intuitive cognition in such a case will also be cognition of existence in general, since it is impossible to have

simplices proprii ; sed de uno veniente a remotis possum
habere unam visionem, per quam tantum iudico illud
esse ens, aliam, per quam iudico illud esse animal, tertiam, per quam iudico illud esse hominem, quartam,
per quam iudico illud esse Sortem ; sed illae visiones
sunt alterius rationis ; ergo omnes illae non possunt esse
cognitiones propriae illius singularis visi.

Tertium est, quia videtur quod prima abstractiva sit
propria, maxime quando obiectum est debito modo
approximatum : quia per primam abstractivam possum
recordari de eadem re prius visa, quod non posset fieri
nisi haberem abstractivam propriam.

Quartum dubium est, quia videtur secundum iam
dicta, quod conceptus generis potest abstrahi ab uno
individuo, puta conceptus 'animalis', sicut patet de
veniente a remotis, quando habeo talem visionem, per
quam iudico illud visum esse animal.

Ad primum istorum dico, quod intuitiva est propria
cognitio singularis, non propter maiorem assimilationem
uni quam alteri, sed quia naturaliter ab uno et non ab
altero causatur nec potest ab altero causari.

Si dicis 'Potest causari a solo Deo', verum est. Sed
semper nata est talis visio causari ab uno obiecto creato
et non ab alio. Et si causatur naturaliter, causatur ab
uno et non ab alio, nec potest causari. Unde propter
similitudinem non plus dicitur intuitiva propria cognitio
singularis quam abstractiva prima, sed solum propter
causalitatem, nec alia causa potest assignari.

Ad secundum dubium dico, quod aliquando illae
visiones sunt eiusdem speciei et solum differunt sicut

several simple concepts of the same thing. Nevertheless, in the case of one coming from afar, I can have one look from which I judge that this is an existent, another from which I judge that this is an animal, a third one from which I judge that this is a man, and a fourth one from which I judge that this is Socrates. Yet these various looks are different in kind ; therefore, it is not possible that all of them are proper to the singular thing seen.

Third doubt : It seems that the firŝt abstractive cognition is a proper one, especially when the object is sufficiently close, because by the first abstractive cognition I can recall the same thing as I saw before. But this could not happen, unless my abstractive cognition were proper to the thing.

Fourth doubt : According to what has been said it seems possible that the concept of a genus could be abstracted from one individual, let us say, the concept 'animal' ; as is clear from the case of one coming from a distance, when I see enough to judge that what I am seeing is an animal.

To the first doubt, I say that we have a cognition proper to one singular thing, not on account of a greater likeness to one than to another, but because this intuitive cognition is naturally caused only by the one and not by the other, and cannot be caused by the other.

If you say that it may be caused by God alone, I admit that this is true. Nevertheless, where created things are concerned, it is always of the nature of such a look to be caused by one object and not by another ; and if it is naturally caused, it can be caused only by the one object and not by the other. Therefore the reason why intuitive cognition, rather than the first abstractive cognition, is said to be proper to the singular thing, is not similarity, but only causality ; no other reason can be assigned.

To the second doubt, I say that sometimes such looks are of the same species and differ only as the more or

magis perfectum et minus perfectum in eadem specie,
puta si videatur aliquod ex partibus eiusdem rationis,
in quo non essent plura accidentia sensibilia, a visu,
tunc per approximationem illius visibilis, puta albi,
intenditur visio et fit clarior ; et secundum hoc potest
causari diversum et diversum iudicium, quod tale visum
est ens vel corpus vel color vel albedo etc.

Si dicis : 'Illa differunt specie quae non possunt
causare effectum eiusdem speciei ; sed visio clara et
obscura sunt huiusmodi ; igitur etc.' : Respondeo et
dico, quod quantumcumque causae auctae et intensae,
si non possunt causare effectum eiusdem speciei, differunt
specie, et aliter non. Nunc autem illa visio aucta et
intensa potest in omnem effectum in quem potest visio
clara, et per consequens sunt eiusdem speciei. Aliquando
tamen visio clara et obscura sunt alterius speciei, puta
quando diversa obiecta videntur, puta si videatur scutum
diversis coloribus coloratum secundum minorem et
maiorem approximationem ; sed illae visiones non sunt
eiusdem obiecti sed diversorum.

Ad tertium dico, quod videndo aliquid habeo aliquam
cognitionem abstractivam propriam ; sed illa non erit
simplex, sed composita ex simplicibus. Et ista notitia
composita est principium recordationis, quia per hoc
recordor de Sorte, quia vidi eum sic figuratum, coloratum, talis longitudinis et talis latitudinis et in tali loco,
et per illud compositum recordor me vidisse Sortem.
Sed circumscribas omnes conceptus simplices praeter
unum, non plus recordaris de Sorte per illum quam de
alio homine sibi simillimo ; bene possum recordari me
vidisse, sed utrum sit Sortes vel Plato, nescio. Et ideo
cognitio abstractiva simplex non est propria singulari :
sed composita bene potest esse propria.

Ad quartum dico, quod conceptus generis numquam

less perfect differ within the same species. For instance, if we saw something composed only of homogeneous parts, where no more than one accident, let us say whiteness, is visible, then as this thing approaches, our vision becomes stronger and clearer, and accordingly different judgments are possible, viz. that what we see is an existent, or a body, or a colour, or whiteness, etc.

You object, perhaps : 'Things which cannot cause the same specific effect differ specifically. But clear and obscure vision cannot ; therefore, etc.' I answer : 'If certain causes, no matter how much they are intensified and increased, cannot cause an effect specifically the same, then they are specifically different ; otherwise not. But this vision, if increased and intensified, can produce every effect that clear vision can. Consequently obscure and clear vision are of the same kind'. Sometimes, however, clear and obscure vision are specifically different : for instance, if different objects are seen, as when something like a many-coloured shield is viewed from a greater or lesser distance. But these views are not of the same object but of different objects.

To the third doubt, I say that when I see something, I do have a proper abstractive cognition ; only it will not be a simple cognition, but one composed of simple cognitions. This composite knowledge is the basis of recollection ; for I recall Socrates because I have seen him with such a figure, colour, height and width, and in such a place, and by putting these together I recall having once seen Socrates. But if you leave out all simple concepts except one, you cannot by means of this have memory relating to Socrates rather than any other man who is very similar to him ; I can well recall having seen someone, but whether it was Socrates or Plato, I do not know. Therefore a simple abstractive cognition is not proper to a singular thing ; however, a composite cognition may well be proper to one.

To the fourth doubt I answer : 'The concept of a

abstrahitur ab uno individuo. Et ad illud de veniente
a remotis dico, quod iudico illud esse animal, quia prius
habeo conceptum animalis, qui conceptus est genus, et
ideo per illum conceptum ducor in notitiam recorda-
tivam. Unde si prius non haberem conceptum generis
animalis, nihil iudicarem nisi quod illud visum est
aliquid.

Et si quaeras : Quae notitia abstractiva primo habetur mediante intuitiva ? Respondeo : 'Aliquando conceptus entis tantum, aliquando conceptus generis, aliquando conceptus speciei specialissimae, secundum quod
obiectum est magis vel minus remotum'. Semper tamen
imprimitur conceptus entis, quia quando obiectum est
debito modo approximatum, simul causatur a re extra
singulari conceptus specificus et conceptus entis.

Ad principale dico, quod universale est obiectum
primum primitate adaequationis, non autem primitate
generationis.

De universali

4. Cum non sufficiat logico tam generalis notitia terminorum, sed oportet cognoscere magis in speciali terminos,
ideo postquam de divisionibus generalibus terminorum
tractatum est, de quibusdam contentis sub aliquibus
illarum divisionum prosequendum est.

Est autem primo tractandum de terminis secundae
intentionis, secundo de terminis primae intentionis.
Dictum est autem, quod termini secundae intentionis
sunt tales 'universale', 'genus', 'species', etc. Ideo de
illis, quae ponuntur quinque universalia, est modo
dicendum. Primo tamen dicendum est de hoc communi

---

[1] See Introduction above, p. xxxiii

genus is never abstracted from only one individual'.
Concerning the instance of a man coming from a distance,
I say that I judge him to be an animal, since I am
already in the possession of the concept 'animal', a concept that is a genus ; and therefore, by means of this
concept I am led to recognition. Hence, if I did not
already possess the concept of the genus 'animal', I
would judge only that this which is seen is something.

If you ask, which abstractive cognition is first obtained
by the help of intuitive cognition, I answer : 'Sometimes
only the concept 'existent', sometimes the concept of a
genus, sometimes the concept of the ultimate species ;
but it all depends on whether the object is more or less
remote'. However, we always get an impression of the
concept 'existent', because if the object is sufficiently
close, a concept of the species and the concept 'existent'
are simultaneously caused by the extra-mental singular
thing.

To the principal objection I answer : A universal is
the first object in the order of adequacy [i.e. of adequacy as object of the intellect], but not in the order
of origin of cognition.

The problem of universals

4. A general knowledge of terms is not sufficient for the
logician ; he must also know terms more in detail.
Therefore, having dealt with the general divisions of
terms [in the previous chapters of the *Summa logicae*],
we must turn to some of the things that come under
members of this division.

First we have to treat terms of second intention [1] ;
secondly, terms of first intention. It has been said that
terms of second intention are those like 'universal',
'genus', 'species', etc. Hence we must say something
about those which are set up as the five predicables.
But first we must speak of the general term 'universal,'

'universale', quod praedicatur de omni universali, et de 'singulari' opposito sibi.

Est autem primo sciendum, quod 'singulare' dupliciter accipitur. Uno modo hoc nomen 'singulare' significat omne illud quod est unum et non plura. Et isto modo tenentes quod universale est quaedam qualitas mentis praedicabilis de pluribus, non tamen pro se sed pro illis pluribus, dicere habent, quod quodlibet universale est vere et realiter singulare : quia sicut quaelibet vox, quantumcumque communis per institutionem, est vere et realiter singularis et una numero, quia est una et non plures, ita intentio animae significans plures res extra est vere et realiter singularis et una numero, quia est una et non plures, quamvis significet plures res. Aliter accipitur hoc nomen 'singulare' pro illo, quod est unum et non plura nec est natum esse signum plurium. Et sic accipiendo 'singulare', nullum universale est singulare, quia quodlibet universale natum est esse signum plurium et natum est praedicari de pluribus. Unde vocando universale aliquid quod non est unum numero, quam acceptionem multi attribuunt universali, dico quod nihil est universale, nisi forte abuteris isto vocabulo dicendo populum esse unum universale, quia non est unum sed multa ; sed illud puerile esset.

Dicendum est igitur, quod quodlibet universale est una res singularis, et ideo non est universale nisi per significationem, quia est signum plurium. Et hoc est quod dicit Avicenna v° *Metaphysicae* * : 'Una forma apud intellectum est relata ad multitudinem, et secundum hunc respectum est universale, quoniam ipsum est intentio in intellectu, cuius comparatio non variatur ad quodcumque acceperis'. Et sequitur : 'Haec forma, quamvis in comparatione individuorum sit universalis,

* v. i ; ed. Venet. (1508), fol. 87r^b

which is predicated of every universal, and of the term 'singular', which is opposed to it.

First we must realise that 'singular' is taken in two senses. In one sense the name 'singular' signifies whatever is one thing and not several. If it is so understood, then those who hold that a universal is a certain quality of the mind predicable of many things (but standing for these many things, not for itself) have to say that every universal is truly and really a singular. For just as every word, no matter how common it may be by convention, is truly and really singular and numerically one, since it is one thing and not many, so likewise the mental content that signifies several things outside is truly and really singular and numerically one, since it is one thing and not many things, though it signifies several things.

In another sense the name 'singular' is taken for that which is one and not several things and is not of such a nature as to be the sign of several things. If 'singular' is understood in this sense, then no universal is singular, since every universal is of such a nature as to be a sign of, and to be predicated of, several things. Hence, if a universal is that which is not numerically one—a meaning attributed by many to 'universal'—then I say that nothing is a universal, unless perhaps you wish to abuse this word by saying that a population is a universal, since it is not one but many. But that would be childish.

Hence we have to say that every universal is one singular thing. Therefore nothing is universal except by signification, by being a sign of several things. This is what Avicenna says in the fifth book of the *Metaphysics* : 'One form in the intellect has reference to a multitude, and in this sense it is a universal, since the universal is a content in the intellect which is equally related to anything you take'. And later on : 'This form, though universal in reference to individuals, is nevertheless individual in reference to the particular mind in which

tamen in comparatione animae singularis in qua imprimitur, est individua ; ipsa enim est una ex formis
quae sunt in intellectu'. Vult dicere, quod universale
est una intentio singularis ipsius animae nata praedicari
de pluribus, ita quod propter hoc quod est nata praedicari
de pluribus, non pro se sed pro illis pluribus, ipsa dicitur
universalis ; propter hoc autem quod est una forma
existens realiter in intellectu, dicitur singularis. Et ita
singulare primo modo dictum praedicatur de universali,
non tamen secundo modo dictum, ad modum quo
dicimus quod sol est causa universalis, et tamen vere est
res particularis et singularis, et per consequens vere est
causa singularis et particularis. Dicitur enim sol causa
universalis, quia est causa plurium, scilicet omnium
istorum inferiorum generabilium et corruptibilium ;
dicitur autem causa particularis, quia est una causa et
non plures causae. Sic intentio animae dicitur universalis, quia est signum praedicabile de pluribus ; dicitur
autem singularis, quia est una res et non plures res.

Verumtamen sciendum, quod universale duplex est :
Quoddam est universale naturaliter, quod scilicet naturaliter est signum praedicabile de pluribus ad modum
proportionaliter, quo fumus naturaliter significat ignem
et gemitus infirmi dolorem et risus interiorem laetitiam :
et tale universale non est nisi intentio animae, ita quod
nulla substantia extra animam nec aliquod accidens
extra animam est tale universale. Et de tali universali
loquar in sequentibus capitulis. Aliud est universale per
voluntariam institutionem. Et sic vox prolata, quae est
vere una qualitas, est universalis, quia scilicet est signum
voluntarie institutum ad significandum plura. Unde
sicut vox dicitur communis, ita potest dici universalis ;
sed hoc non habet ex natura rei, sed ex placito instituentium tantum.

it is impressed, for it is one of the forms in the intellect'. He wishes to say here that the universal is one particular content of the mind itself, of such a nature as to be predicated of several things ; therefore, it is by the very fact that it is of such a nature as to be predicated of several things (standing not for itself, but for those many things), that it is called a 'universal'. By the fact, however, that it is one form really existing in the intellect, it is called a 'singular'. Hence 'singular' in the first sense is predicated of the universal, but not 'singular' in the second sense. In like manner, we say that the sun is a universal cause, and nevertheless it is in truth a particular and singular thing, and consequently a singular and particular cause. For the sun is called 'universal cause', because it is the cause of many things, namely of all that can be generated and corrupted here below. It is, on the other hand, called 'particular cause', because it is one cause and not several causes. Likewise the content of the soul is called 'universal', because it is a sign predicable of many ; on the other hand, it is called 'singular', because it is one thing and not many things.

It must, however, be understood that there are two sorts of universal. There is one sort which is naturally universal ; in other words, is a sign naturally predicable of many things, in much the same way as smoke naturally signifies fire, or a groan the pain of a sick man, or laughter an inner joy. Such a universal is nothing other than a content of the mind ; and therefore no substance outside the mind and no accident outside the mind is such a universal. It is only of such a universal that I shall speak in the chapters that follow.

The other sort of universal is so by convention. In this way, an uttered word, which is really a single quality, is universal ; for it is a conventional sign meant to signify many things. Therefore, just as the word is said to be common, so it can be said to be universal. But it is not so by nature, only by convention.

Quod universale non est res extra

5. Et quia non sufficit ista narrare, nisi manifesta ratione probentur, ideo pro praedictis aliquas rationes adducam necnon et auctoritatibus confirmabo.

Quod enim nullum universale sit aliqua substantia extra animam existens, evidenter probari potest.

Primo quidem sic : Nullum universale est substantia singularis et una numero. Si enim diceretur quod sic, sequeretur quod Sortes esset aliquod universale, quia non maior ratio, quod unum universale sit substantia singularis quam alia ; nulla igitur substantia singularis est aliquod universale, sed omnis substantia est una numero et singularis ; quia omnis res vel est una res et non plures, vel est plures res. Si est una et non plures, est una numero ; hoc enim ab omnibus vocatur unum numero. Si autem aliqua substantia est plures res, vel est plures res singulares vel plures res universales. Si primum detur, sequitur, quod aliqua substantia esset plures substantiae singulares, et per consequens eadem ratione aliqua substantia esset plures homines ; et tunc, quamvis universale distingueretur a particulari uno, non tamen distingueretur a particularibus. Si autem aliqua substantia esset plures res universales, accipio unam istarum rerum universalium et quaero : aut est una res et non plures, aut est plures res. Si primum detur, sequitur quod est singularis ; si secundum detur, quaero : aut est plures res singulares, aut plures res universales, et ita vel erit processus in infinitum, vel stabitur quod nulla substantia est universalis ita quod non singularis. Ex quo relinquitur, quod nulla substantia est universalis.

Item, si aliquod universale esset substantia una existens

A universal is not a thing outside the mind

5. Since it is not sufficient merely to assert this without proving it by manifest reasoning, I shall advance a few reasons for what has been said above and I shall confirm by arguments from authority.

That a universal is not a substance existing outside the mind can in the first place be evidently proved as follows : No universal is a substance that is single and numerically one. For if that were supposed, it would follow that Socrates is a universal, since there is no stronger reason for one singular substance to be a universal than for another ; therefore no singular substance is a universal, but every substance is numerically one and singular. For everything is either one thing and not many, or it is many things. If it is one and not many, it is numerically one. If, however, a substance is many things, it is either many singular things or many universal things. On the first supposition it follows that a substance would be several singular substances ; for the same reason, then, some substance would be several men ; and thus, although a universal would be distinguished from one particular thing, it would yet not be distinguished from particular things. If, however, a substance were several universal things, let us take one of these universal things and ask 'Is this one thing and not many, or is it many things ?' If the first alternative is granted, then it follows that it is singular ; if the second is granted, we have to ask again 'Is it many singular or many universal things ?' And thus either this will go on *in infinitum*, or we must take the stand that no substance is universal in such a way that it is not singular. Hence, the only remaining alternative is that no substance is universal.

Furthermore, if a universal were one substance exist-

in substantiis singularibus ab eis distincta, sequeretur quod posset esse sine eis, quia omnis res prior naturaliter alia potest esse sine ea per divinam potentiam ; sed consequens est absurdum.

Item, si illa opinio esset vera, nullum individuum posset creari ; sed aliquid individui praeexisteret, quia non totum caperet esse de nihilo, si universale quod est in eo prius fuit in alio. Propter idem etiam sequitur, quod Deus non posset unum individuum substantiae annihilare, nisi cetera individua destrueret : Quia si annihilaret aliquod individuum, destrueret totum quod est de essentia individui, et per consequens destrueret illud universale quod est in eo et in aliis, et per consequens alia non manent, cum non possint manere sine parte sua, quale ponitur illud universale.

Item, tale universale non posset poni aliquid totaliter extra essentiam individui, igitur esset de essentia individui, et per consequens individuum componeretur ex universalibus, et ita individuum non esset magis singulare quam universale.

Item, sequitur quod aliquid de essentia Christi esset miserum et damnatum : Quia illa natura communis existens realiter in Christo realiter existit in Iuda et est damnata ; igitur in Christo et in damnato, quia in Iuda. Hoc autem absurdum est.

Aliae autem rationes multae possent adduci, quas causa brevitatis pertranseo.

Et eandem conclusionem confirmo per auctoritates. . . .

Ex quibus aliisque multis patet, quod universale est intentio animae nata praedicari de multis. Quod ratione

ing in singular things and distinct from them, it would follow that it could exist apart from them ; for every thing naturally prior to another thing can exist apart from it by the power of God. But this consequence is absurd.

Furthermore, if that opinion were true, no individual could be created, but something of the individual would pre-exist ; for it would not get its entire being from nothing, if the universal in it has existed before in another individual. For the same reason it would follow that God could not annihilate one individual of a substance, if He did not destroy the other individuals. For if He annihilated one individual, He would destroy the whole of the essence of the individual, and consequently he would destroy that universal which is in it and in others ; consequently, the other individuals do not remain, since they cannot remain without a part of themselves, such as the universal is held to be.

Furthermore, we could not assume such a universal to be something entirely extrinsic to the essence of an individual ; therefore, it would be of the essence of the individual, and consequently the individual would be composed of universals ; and thus the individual would not be more singular than universal.

Furthermore, it follows that something of the essence of Christ would be miserable and damned ; since that common nature which really exists in Christ, really exists in Judas also and is damned. Therefore, something is both in Christ and in one who is damned, namely in Judas. That, however, is absurd.

Still other reasons could be advanced which I pass over for the sake of brevity.

The same conclusion I will now confirm by authorities. . . .

From these and many other texts it is clear that a universal is a mental content of such nature as to be predicated of many things. This can also be confirmed

etiam confirmari potest. Nam omne universale secundum omnes est de multis praedicabile ; sed sola intentio animae vel signum voluntarie institutum natum est praedicari et non substantia aliqua ; ergo sola intentio animae vel signum voluntarie institutum est universale. Sed nunc non utor 'universali' pro signo voluntarie instituto, sed pro illo quod naturaliter est universale. Quod autem substantia non sit nata praedicari patet : Quia si sic, sequitur, quod propositio componeretur ex substantiis particularibus, et per consequens subiectum esset Romae et praedicatum in Anglia, quod absurdum est.

Item, propositio non est nisi in mente vel in voce vel in scripto ; ergo partes eius non sunt nisi in mente vel in voce vel in scripto ; huiusmodi autem non sunt substantiae particulares. Constat igitur, quod nulla propositio ex substantiis componi potest; componitur autem propositio ex universalibus ; universalia igitur non sunt substantiae ullo modo.

Opinio Scoti de universali et reprobatio eius

6. Quamvis multis sit perspicuum, quod universale non sit aliqua substantia extra animam existens in individuis distincta realiter ab eis, videtur tamen aliquibus quod universale est aliquo modo extra animam in individuis, non quidem distinctum realiter ab eis, sed tantum distinctum formaliter ab eisdem. Unde dicunt, quod in Sorte est natura humana, quae contrahitur ad Sortem per unam differentiam individualem, quae ab illa natura non distinguitur realiter sed formaliter. Unde non sunt duae res, una tamen non est formaliter alia.

Sed ista opinio omnino improbabilis mihi videtur. Probo : Quia in creaturis numquam potest esse aliqua distinctio qualiscumque extra animam, nisi ubi res

by reason.   All agree that every universal is predicable
of things.   But only a mental content or conventional
sign, not a substance, is of such nature as to be predicated.
Consequently, only a mental content or a conventional
sign is a universal.   However, at present I am not using
'universal' for a conventional sign, but for that which is
naturally a universal.   Moreover, it is clear that no
substance is of such nature as to be predicated ; for if
that were true, it would follow that a proposition would
be composed of particular substances, and consequently
that the subject could be in Rome and the predicate in
England.   That is absurd.

Furthermore, a proposition is either in the mind or in
spoken or written words.   Consequently, its parts are
either in the mind or in speech or in writing.   Such
things, however, are not particular substances.   Therefore, it is established that no proposition can be composed of substances ; but a proposition is composed of
universals ; hence universals are in no way substances.

Scotus's opinion on universals and its refutation

6. Although it is clear to many that a universal is not a
   substance existing outside the mind in individuals and
   really distinct from them, still some are of the opinion that
   a universal does in some manner exist outside the mind
   in individuals, although not really but only formally
   distinct from them.   Hence they say that in Socrates
   there is human nature, which is ' contracted to ' Socrates
   by an individual difference which is not really but only
   formally distinct from this nature.   Hence the nature
   and the individual difference are not two things, although
   the one is not formally the other.

   However, this opinion appears to me wholly untenable.   Proof : In creatures no extra-mental distinction
   of any kind is possible except where distinct things

distinctae sunt. Si ergo inter istam naturam et istam differentiam sit qualiscumque distinctio, oportet quod sint res realiter distinctae. Assumptum probo per formam syllogisticam sic : Ista n̄atūrā est distincta formaliter ab ista natura ; haec differentia individualis est distincta formaliter ab hac natura ; ergo haec differentia individualis non est haec natura.

Item, eadem res non est communis et propria ; sed secundum eos differentia individualis est propria, universale autem est commune ; ergo differentia individualis non est communis ; ergo nullum universale et differentia individualis sunt eadem res.

Item, eidem rei creatae non possunt convenire opposita ; commune autem et proprium sunt opposita ; ergo eadem res non est communis et propria ; quod tamen sequitur, si differentia individualis et natura communis essent eadem res.

Item, si natura communis esset eadem realiter cum differentia individuali, ergo tot essent realiter naturae communes, quot sunt differentiae individuales, et per consequens nullum eorum esset commune, sed quodlibet esset proprium differentiae, cui est eadem realiter.

Item, quaelibet res seipsa vel per aliquid sibi intrinsecum distinguitur a quocumque distinguitur ; sed alia est humanitas Sortis et alia Platonis ; ergo seipsis distinguuntur, non ergo per differentias additas.

Item, secundum sententiam Aristotelis, quaecumque differunt specie, differunt numero ; sed natura hominis ēt asini specie distinguuntur seipsis ; ergo seipsis distinguuntur numero ; ergo seipsa quaelibet illarum est una numero.

Item, illud quod per nullam potentiam potest competere pluribus, per nullam potentiam est praedicabile de

exist. If, therefore, some kind of distinction exists between this nature and this difference, it is necessary that they be really distinct things. I prove the minor premise in syllogistic form as follows : This nature is not formally distinct from itself ; this individual difference is formally distinct from this nature ; therefore this individual difference is not this nature.

Furthermore, the same thing is not common and proper ; however, according to them, the individual is proper, but the universal is common ; therefore the individual difference is not common ; consequently no universal is the same thing as the individual difference.

Furthermore, opposites cannot belong to the same created thing ; 'common' and 'proper' are opposites ; therefore the same thing is not common and proper, as would follow if individual difference and common nature were the same thing.

Furthermore, if common nature were really the same as the individual difference, then there would be in reality as many common natures as there are individual differences, and hence none of them would be common, but each one would be proper to the difference with which it is really identical.

Furthermore, everything which is distinguished from something else is distinguished either of itself or by some thing intrinsic to itself ; but the humanity of Plato is one thing and the humanity of Socrates another ; therefore they are distinguished of themselves ; therefore *not* by having differences added to them.

Furthermore, according to Aristotle, things specifically different are also numerically different ; but the nature of a man and the nature of a donkey are of themselves specifically different ; therefore, of themselves, they are numerically different ; consequently, each of these natures is on its own account numerically one.

Furthermore, what no power can cause to belong to several things no power can make predicable of several

pluribus ; sed talis natura, si sit eadem realiter cum
differentia individuali, per nullam potentiam potest convenire pluribus, quia nullo modo potest competere alteri
individuo ; ergo per nullam potentiam potest esse praedicabile de pluribus, et per consequens per nullam
potentiam potest esse universale.

Item, accipio illam differentiam individualem et
naturam quam contrahit, et quaero : aut inter ea est
maior distinctio quam inter duo individua, aut minor?
Non maior, quia non differunt realiter ; individua autem
differunt realiter. Nec minor, quia tunc essent eiusdem
rationis, sicut duo individua sunt eiusdem rationis ; et
per consequens, si unum est de se unum numero, et
reliquum erit de se unum numero.

Item, quaero : aut natura est differentia individualis,
aut non? Si sic, arguo syllogistice sic : Haec differentia
individualis est propria et non communis ; haec differentia individualis est natura ; ergo natura est propria
et non communis, quod est intentum. Similiter arguo
syllogistice sic : Haec differentia individualis non est
distincta formaliter a differentia individuali ; haec
differentia individualis est natura ; ergo natura non est
distincta formaliter a differentia individuali. Si autem
detur, quod haec differentia individualis non est natura,
habetur propositum ; nam sequitur : Differentia individualis non est natura, ergo differentia individualis non
est realiter natura, quia ex opposito consequentis sequitur
oppositum antecedentis, sic arguendo : Differentia individualis est realiter natura, ergo differentia individualis
est natura. Consequentia patet : quia a determinabili
sumpto cum determinatione non distrahente nec mi-

things ; now no power can make such a nature, if it is really the same as the individual difference, belong to several things, because in no manner can [something really identified with one individual] belong to another individual ; therefore, no power can make it predicable of several things, and consequently no power can make it universal.

Furthermore, I take this individual difference and the nature that it 'contracts' and ask 'Is the distinction greater or less than between two individuals ?' It is not greater, since they do not differ really ; whereas individuals do differ really. Nor is it less, for then the two things said to be distinct would fall under the same concept, just as two individuals fall under the same concept. Consequently, if the one is numerically one on its own account, the other will also be so on its own account.

Furthermore, I ask 'Is the nature the individual difference, or is it not ?' If it is, then I shall argue in syllogistic form as follows : This individual difference is proper and not common, this individual difference is the nature ; consequently the nature is proper and not common, which is what we intended to prove. Likewise I argue in syllogistic form as follows : This individual difference is not formally distinct from this individual difference ; this individual difference is the nature ; therefore, this nature is not formally distinct from the individual difference. If, however, the other alternative is granted, namely 'This individual difference is not the nature', our thesis is admitted, since this therefore follows : The individual difference is not the nature, therefore the individual difference is not really the nature. For from the opposite of the consequent the opposite of the antecedent follows, by this argument : The individual difference is really the nature, therefore the individual difference is the nature. The inference is clear, since it is a valid inference to argue from a determinable as qualified by a determination which does not

nuente ad determinabile per se sumptum est consequentia
bona. 'Realiter' autem non est determinatio distrahens
nec diminuens. Ergo sequitur : Differentia individualis
est realiter natura, ergo differentia individualis est natura.

Dicendum est ergo, quod in creaturis nulla est talis
distinctio formalis ; sed quaecumque in creaturis sunt
distincta, realiter sunt distincta et sunt res distinctae, si
utrumque illorum sit vera res. Unde sicut in creaturis
tales modi arguendi numquam negari debent : Hoc est
A, hoc est B, ergo B est A, nec tales : Hoc non est A,
hoc est B, ergo B non est A, ita numquam debent negari
in creaturis, quin, quandocumque contradictoria verificantur de aliquibus, illa sunt distincta, nisi aliqua
determinatio vel aliquod syncategorema sit causa talis
verificationis, quod in propositio poni non debet.

Et ideo debemus dicere cum Philosopho, quod in substantia particulari nihil est substantiale penitus, nisi
forma particularis et materia particularis vel aliquod
compositum ex talibus. Et ideo non est imaginandum,
quod in Sorte sit humanitas vel natura humana distincta
a Sorte quocumque modo, cui addatur una differentia
individualis contrahens illam naturam. Sed quidquid
imaginabile substantiale existens in Sorte, vel est materia
particularis vel forma particularis vel aliquod compositum ex his. Et ideo omnis essentia et quidditas et quidquid est substantiae, si sit realiter extra animam, vel est
simpliciter absolute materia vel forma vel compositum
ex his vel substantia immaterialis abstracta secundum
doctrinam Peripateticorum.

[1] [This saving clause means that e.g., we cannot infer validly :
A dead man is in animate, *ergo* some man is inanimate.—TR.]

cancel or diminish it,[1] to the determinable without the qualification. 'Really', however, is not a cancelling or diminishing determination, hence this follows : The individual difference is really the nature, therefore the individual difference is the nature.

Therefore it must be said that in creatures there is no such formal distinction ; but whatever in creatures is distinct, is really distinct, and constitutes a distinct thing, if each of the two things distinguished is truly a thing. Just as in creatures we must never deny the validity of such modes of arguing as 'This is *A*, this is *B*, consequently a *B* is *A*', or 'This is not *A*, this is *B*, consequently a *B* is not *A*', so also as regards creatures whenever contradictory predicates are true of certain things, we must not deny that the things are distinct ; unless of course some determination or some syncategorematic term should be what causes this to be true, as should not be assumed in our present case.

Therefore we must say with the Philosopher that in a particular substance nothing whatsoever is substantial except the particular form and the particular matter or a compound of matter and form. Hence we must not imagine that in Socrates we have human nature or humanity distinct in any way from Socrates, to which is added an individual difference that 'contracts' this nature. But any imaginable substantial reality that exists in Socrates is either the particular matter or the particular form or a compound of the two. Therefore every essence and quiddity and everything substantial, if it really exists outside the mind, is either simply and absolutely matter or form, or a compound of them, or it is a separate immaterial substance, according to the teachings of the Peripatetics.

7. *Ideo potest aliter dici. $\overline{\text{Et dico}}$,† quod universale non
est aliquid reale habens esse subiectivum, nec in anima
nec extra animam, sed tantum habet esse obiectivum in
anima, et est quoddam fictum habens esse tale in esse
obiectivo, quale habet res extra in esse subiectivo. Et
$\overline{\text{dico}}$ ‡ per istum modum : Quod intellectus videns aliquam rem extra animam fingit consimilem rem in mente,
ita quod si haberet virtutem productivam, sicut habet
virtutem fictivam, talem rem in esse subiectivo numero
distinctam a priori produceret extra ; et esset consimi-
liter proportionaliter, sicut est de artifice. Sicut enim
artifex videns domum vel aedificium aliquod extra fingit
in anima sua consimilem domum et postea consimilem
producit extra et est solo numero distincta a priori, ita
in proposito illud fictum in mente ex visione alicuius rei
extra esset unum exemplar ; ita enim, sicut domus ficta,
si fingens haberet virtutem productivam realem, est
exemplar ipsi artifici, ita illud fictum esset exemplar
respectu sic fingentis. Et illud potest vocari universale,
quia est exemplar et indifferenter respiciens omnia singularia extra ; et propter istam similitudinem in esse
obiectivo potest supponere pro rebus quae habent consimile esse extra intellectum. Et ita isto modo universale
non est per generationem sed per abstractionem, quae
non est nisi fictio quaedam.

---

* *Prima redactio* : *mutationes secundae redactionis inveniuntur in notis.*
† Et dico probabiliter *Sec. red.*
‡ Et dico hoc *Sec. red.*

[1] Ockham's first opinion, later abandoned

[*A universal is a thought-object* [1]]

7. Another theory [different from those opinions concerning
the nature of universals previously criticised by Ockham]
could be advanced. I maintain that a universal is not
something real that exists in a subject [of inherence],
either inside or outside the mind, but that it has being
only as a thought-object in the mind. It is a kind
of mental picture which as a thought-object has a being
similar to that which the thing outside the mind has in
its real existence. What I mean is this : The intellect,
seeing a thing outside the mind, forms in the mind a
picture resembling it, in such a way that if the mind had
the power to produce as it has the power to picture,
it would produce by this act a real outside thing which
would be only numerically distinct from the former real
thing. The case would be similar, analogously speaking,
to the activity of an artist. For just as the artist who
sees a house or building outside the mind first pictures
in the mind a similar house and later produces a similar
house in reality which is only numerically distinct from
the first, so in our case the picture in the mind that we
get from seeing something outside would act as a pattern.
For just as the imagined house would be a pattern for
the architect, if he who imagines it had the power to
produce it in reality, so likewise the other picture would
be a pattern for him who forms it. And this can be
called a universal, because it is a pattern and relates
indifferently to all the singular things outside the mind.
Because of the similarity between its being as a thought-
object and the being of like things outside the mind, it
can stand for such things. And in this way a universal
is not the result of generation, but of abstraction, which
is only a kind of mental picturing.

Primo ostendam,* quod est aliquid in anima habens tantum esse obiectivum sine esse subiectivo.

Hoc primo patet : Quia secundum philosophos ens primaria divisione dividitur in ens in anima et extra animam ; et ens extra animam dividitur in decem praedicamenta. Tunc quaero : Quomodo hic accipitur 'ens in anima' ? Aut pro illo quod tantum habet esse obiectivum, et habetur propositum. Aut pro illo quod habet esse subiectivum, et hoc non est possibile : quia illud quod habet verum esse subiectivum in anima continetur sub ente, quod praecise dividitur in decem praedicamenta, quia sub qualitate ; intellectio enim et universaliter omne accidens informans animam est vera qualitas sicut calor vel albedo, et ita non continetur sub illo membro, quod dividitur contra ens quod dividitur in decem praedicamenta.

Praeterea : Figmenta habent esse in anima, et non subiectivum, quia tunc essent verae res, et ita chimaera et hircocervus et huiusmodi essent verae res ; ergo sunt aliqua quae tantum habent esse obiectivum.

Similiter : Propositiones, syllogismi et huiusmodi, de quibus est Logica, non habent esse subiectivum, ergo tantum habent esse obiectivum, ita quod eorum esse est eorum cognosci ; ergo sunt talia entia habentia tantum esse obiectivum.

Similiter : Artificialia in mente artificis non videntur habere esse subiectivum, sicut nec creaturae in mente divina ante creationem.

Similiter : Respectus rationis communiter ponuntur a doctoribus. Tunc quaero : Aut tantum habent esse subiectivum, et tunc erunt verae res et reales ; aut tantum esse obiectivum, et habetur propositum.

---

* Igitur faciam aliqua argumenta ad probandum *Sec. red.*

I shall first show that something exists in the mind whose being is that of an object of thought only, without inhering in the mind as an independent subject.

This is clear from the following : According to the philosophers, existence is primarily divided into existence in the mind and existence outside the mind, the latter being subdivided into the ten categories. If this is admitted, then I ask 'What is understood here by "existence in the mind"?' It means either existence as a thought-object, and then we have our intended thesis, or it means existence as in a subject. The latter, however, is not possible ; for, whatever exists truly in the mind as a subject, is contained under existence that is divided into the ten categories, since it falls under quality. For an act of intellect, and indeed in general every accident or form of the mind, is a true quality, like heat or whiteness, and hence does not fall under the division of existence that is set over against existence in the ten categories. [Consequently the main distinction of the philosophers would be futile.]

Furthermore, fictions have being in the mind, but they do not exist independently, because in that case they would be real things and so a chimera and a goat-stag and so on would be real things. So some things exist only as thought-objects.

Likewise, propositions, syllogisms, and other similar objects of logic do not exist independently ; therefore they exist only as thought-objects, so that their being consists in being known. Consequently, there are beings which exist only as thought-objects.

Again, works of art do not seem to inhere in the mind of the craftsman as independent subjects any more than the creatures did in the divine mind before creation.

Likewise, conceptual relations are commonly admitted by the [scholastic] doctors. If this is conceded, then I ask 'Do they exist only in a subject ?' In that case they will be genuine things and real relations. Or do they

Similiter : Secundum istos aliter opinantes 'ens' dicit conceptum univocum et tamen nullam aliam rem.

Similiter : Omnes quasi distinguunt intentiones secundas ab intentionibus primis, non vocando intentiones secundas aliquales reales qualitates in anima ; ergo cum non sint realiter extra, non possunt esse nisi obiective in anima.*

Secundo dico,† quod illud fictum est illud, quod primo et immediate denominatur ab intentione universalitatis et habet rationem obiecti, et est illud quod immediate terminat actum intelligendi, quando nullum singulare intelligitur, quod quidem, quoniam est tale in esse obiectivo quale est singulare in esse subiectivo, ideo ex natura sua potest supponere pro ipsis singularibus, quorum est aliquo modo similitudo. . . .

Dico ergo,‡ quod sicut vox est universalis et genus et species, sed tantum per institutionem, ita conceptus sic fictus et abstractus a rebus singularibus praecognitis est universalis ex natura sua. . . .

8. Alia posset esse opinio, quod passio animae est ipse actus intelligendi. Et quia ista opinio videtur mihi probabilior de omnibus opinionibus, quae ponunt istas passiones animae esse subiective et realiter in anima tamquam verae qualitates ipsius, ideo circa istam opinionem primo ponam modum ponendi probabiliorem. . . .

Dico ergo, quod qui vult tenere praedictam opinionem,

* probabiliter *add. Sec. red.*   † Diceret ista opinio *Sec. red.*
‡ Posset ergo dici *Sec. red.*
[1] Second opinion, finally held by Ockham

exist only as thought-objects? In that case we have our intended thesis.

Again, according to those who think differently, the term 'being' means a univocal concept, and nevertheless does not mean a distinct reality.

Likewise, practically all men distinguish second intentions from first intentions, and they do not call the second intentions real qualities of the mind. Since they are not in reality outside the mind, they can only exist as thought-objects in the mind.

Secondly, I maintain that this mental picture is what is primarily and immediately meant by the concept 'universal', and has the nature of a thought-object, and is that which is the immediate term of an act of intellection having no singular object. This mental picture, in the manner of being that a thought-object has, is just whatever the corresponding singular is, in the manner of being proper to a subject ; and so by its very nature it can stand for the singulars of which it is in a way a likeness. . . .

I maintain, therefore, that just as a spoken word is universal and is a genus or a species, but only by convention, in the same way the concept thus mentally fashioned and abstracted from singular things previously known is universal by its nature. . . .

[A universal is an act of the intellect [1]]

8. There could be another opinion, according to which a concept is the same as the act of knowing. This opinion appears to me to be the more probable one among all the opinions which assume that these concepts really exist in the soul as a subject, like true qualities of the soul ; so I shall first explain this opinion in its more probable form.

I maintain, then, that somebody wishing to hold this

potest supponere quod intellectus apprehendens rem
singularem elicit unam cognitionem in se, quae est
tantum illius singularis, quae vocatur passio animae,
potens ex natura sua supponere pro illa re singulari, ita
quod sicut ex institutione haec vox 'Sortes' supponit pro
illa re quam significat, ita quod audiens istam vocem
'Sortes currit' non concipit ex ea, quod haec vox 'Sortes',
quam audit, currit, sed quod res significata per illam
vocem currit, ita qui videret vel intelligeret aliquid
affirmari de illa intellectione singularis rei, non conciperet
illam intellectionem esse talem vel talem, sed conciperet
ipsam rem, cuius est, esse talem vel talem, ita quod, sicut
vox ex institutione supponit pro illa re, ita ipsa intellectio
ex natura sua sine omni institutione supponit pro re,
cuius est.

Sed praeter istam intellectionem illius rei singularis
format sibi intellectus alias intellectiones, quae non
magis sunt istius rei quam alterius.   Sicut haec vox
'homo' non magis significat Sortem quam Platonem, ideo
non magis supponit pro Sorte quam Platone, ita esset
de tali intellectione, quod non magis intelligitur per eam
Sortes quam Plato et sic de omnibus aliis hominibus.   Et
ita etiam esset aliqua intellectio, per quam non magis
intelligeretur hoc animal quam illud animal, et sic de
aliis.

Breviter igitur, ipsae intellectiones animae vocantur
passiones animae, et supponunt ex natura sua pro ipsis
rebus extra vel pro aliis rebus in anima, sicut voces
supponunt pro rebus ex institutione. . . .

. . . Tali intellectione confusa intelliguntur res singulares extra. Sicut habere intellectionem hominis confusam
non est aliud quam habere unam cognitionem, qua non
magis intelligitur unus homo quam alius, et tamen quod
tali cognitione magis cognoscitur sive intelligitur homo

opinion may assume that the intellect apprehending a singular thing performs within itself a cognition of this singular only. This cognition is called a state of mind, and it is capable of standing for this singular thing by its very nature. Hence, just as the spoken word 'Socrates' stands by convention for the thing it signifies, so that one who hears this utterance, 'Socrates is running', does not conceive that this word, 'Socrates', which he hears, is running, but rather that the thing signified by this word is running ; so likewise one who knew or understood that something was affirmatively predicated of this cognition of a singular thing would not think that the cognition was such and such, but would conceive that the thing to which the cognition refers is such and such. Hence, just as the spoken word stands by convention for a thing, so the act of intellect, by its very nature, and without any convention, stands for the thing to which it refers.

Beside this intellectual grasp of a singular thing the intellect also forms other acts which do not refer more to one thing than to another. For instance, just as the spoken word 'man' does not signify Socrates more than Plato, and hence does not stand more for Socrates than Plato, so it would be with an act of intellect which does not relate to Socrates any more than to Plato or any other man. And in like manner there would be also a knowledge whereby this animal is not more known than that animal ; and so with other notions.

To sum up : The mind's own intellectual acts are called states of mind. By their nature they stand for the actual things outside the mind or for other things in the mind, just as the spoken words stand for them by convention. . . .

. . . By such a common or confused intellection, singular things outside the mind are known. For instance, to say that we have a confused intellection of man, means that we have a cognition by which we do not understand one man rather than another, but that by such a cognition we have cognition of a man

quam asinus. Et hoc non est aliud quam quod talis
cognitio aliquo modo assimilationis magis assimilatur
homini quam asino, et non magis isti homini quam illi.
Et secundum istud videtur consequenter dicendum, quod
tali cognitione confusa possunt infinita cognosci. Nec
magis videtur hoc esse inopinabile quam quod eadem
dilectione vel desiderio possunt infinita diligi vel deside-
rari. Sed hoc secundum non videtur inopinabile ; nam
potest aliquis diligere omnes partes alicuius continui,
quae sunt infinitae, vel potest appetere quod omnes
partes continui durent in esse ; et cum non appeteretur
esse tali appetitu nisi aliqua pars continui, et non magis
una quam alia, oportet quod omnes appetantur, quae
tamen sunt infinitae. Similiter potest aliquis appetere
esse omnibus hominibus, qui possunt esse, qui tamen
sunt infiniti, quia infiniti possunt generari. Sic igitur
posset dici, quod eadem cognitio potest esse infinitorum,
non tamen erit cognitio propria alicui illorum ; nec illa
cognitione potest unum discerni ab alio, et hoc propter
aliquam similitudinem specialem istius cognitionis ad
individua illa et non ad alia.

rather than a donkey. And this amounts to saying that such a cognition, by some kind of assimilation, bears a greater resemblance to a man than to a donkey, but does not resemble one man rather than another. In consequence of the aforesaid, it seems necessary to say that an infinity of objects can be known by such a confused cognition. Still this seems no more untenable than that an infinity of objects can be liked or desired by the same act of liking or desiring. Yet the latter does not seem to be untenable. For a man may like all the parts of a continuous thing, which are infinite in number, or he may desire that all these parts remain in existence. Now in such a case, what $\overline{\text{was}}$ desired would simply be a part of the continuous thing, but not one part rather than another; therefore all parts must be desired; these parts, however, are infinite in number. Likewise, somebody can desire the existence of all men who can exist. Now these are infinite in number, since an infinity of men can be generated.

And so it could be said that one and the same cognition refers to an infinite number of singulars without being a cognition proper to any one of them, and this is so because of some specific likeness between these individuals that does not exist between others. However, no singular thing can be distinguished from another by such a cognition.

III

LOGICAL PROBLEMS

Sources :

De terminis

1. Omnes logicae tractatores intendunt astruere quod argumenta ex propositionibus, et propositiones ex terminis componuntur. Unde terminus aliud non est quam pars propinqua propositionis. Definiens enim 'terminum' Aristoteles i⁰ *Priorum* * dicit : Terminum voco, in quem resolvitur propositio, ut praedicatum $\overline{vel}$ de quo praedicatur, vel apposito vel diviso esse vel non esse.

Sed quamvis omnis terminus sit pars propositionis vel esse possit, non omnes termini tamen eiusdem sunt naturae ; et ideo ad perfectam notitiam terminorum habendam oportet aliquas $\overline{distinctiones}$ terminorum praecognoscere. Est autem sciendum, quod sicut secundum $\overline{Boethium}$ i⁰ *Perihermenias* : † triplex est oratio, scilicet scripta, prolata, et concepta tantum habens esse in intellectu, sic triplex est terminus, scilicet scriptus, prolatus et conceptus. Terminus scriptus est pars propositionis scriptae in aliquo corpore quae oculo corporali videtur vel videri potest. Terminus prolatus est pars propositionis ab ore prolatae et natae audiri aure corporali. Terminus conceptus est intentio seu passio animae aliquid naturaliter significans vel consignificans, nata esse pars propositionis mentalis et pro eodem nata supponere. Unde isti termini concepti et propositiones ex eis compositae sunt illa verba mentalia, quae beatus Augustinus xv⁰ *De Trinitate* ‡ dicit nullius esse linguae, quae tantum in mente manent et exterius proferri non possunt, quamvis voces tamquam signa eis subordinata pronuntientur exterius.

* cap. i (24ᵇ, 16 sq.)
† *In librum De interpretatione,* ed. ii, LIB. I (Migne *PL*, TOM. LXIV, col. 413 D)
‡ cap xxvii. 1 (Migne *PL*, TOM. XLII, col. 1097)

On terms [in general]

1. All those who deal with logic try to establish that arguments are composed of propositions, and propositions of terms. Hence a term is simply one of the parts into which a proposition is directly divided. Aristotle defines 'terms' in the first book of the *Prior Analytics* by saying : 'I call a term that into which a proposition is resolved (viz. the predicate, or that of which something is predicated) when it is affirmed or denied that something *is* or *is not* something'.

Although every term is or can be a part of a proposition, yet not all terms are of the same kind. Hence to obtain a perfect knowledge of them, we must first get acquainted with some distinctions between terms.

According to Boethius in the first book of the *De interpretatione*, language is threefold : written, spoken and conceptual. The last named exists only in the intellect. Correspondingly the term is threefold, viz. the written, the spoken and the conceptual term. A written term is part of a proposition written on some material, and is or can be seen with the bodily eye. A spoken term is part of a proposition uttered with the mouth and able to be heard with the bodily ear. A conceptual term is a mental content or impression which naturally possesses signification or consignification, and which is suited to be part of a mental proposition and to stand for that which it signifies.

These conceptual terms and the propositions formed by them are those mental words which St Augustine says in the fifteenth book of *De Trinitate* do not belong to any language ; they remain only in the mind and cannot be uttered exteriorly. Nevertheless vocal words which are signs subordinated to these can be exteriorly uttered.

Dico autem voces esse signa subordinata conceptibus seu intentionibus animae, non quia proprie accipiendo hoc vocabulum 'signa' ipsae v̄ōcēs significent ipsos conceptus animae primo et proprie, sed quia voces imponuntur ad significandum illa eadem, quae per conceptus mentis significantur, ita quod conceptus primo naturaliter aliquid significat, et secundario vox significat illud idem, in tantum quod voce instituta ad significandum aliquod significatum per conceptum mentis, si conceptus ille mutaret significatum suum, eo ipso ipsa vox sine nova institutione suum significatum permutaret. Et pro tanto dicit Philosophus,* quod voces sunt earum, quae sunt in anima, passionum notae. Sic etiam intendit Boethius,† quando dicit voces significare conceptus ; et universaliter omnes auctores dicentes quod omnes voces significant passiones vel sunt notae earum, non aliud intendunt nisi quod voces sunt signa secundario significantia illa quae per passiones animae primario importantur, quamvis aliquae voces primario importent passiones animae vel conceptus, quae tamen secundario important alias animae intentiones, sicut inferius ostendetur.

Et sicut dictum est de vocibus respectu passionum seu intentionum seu conceptuum, eodem modo proportionaliter quantum ad hoc tenendum est de his quae sunt in scripto respectu vocum.

Inter istos autem terminos aliquae differentiae reperiuntur. Una est quod conceptus sive passio animae naturaliter significat quidquid significat ; terminus autem prolatus vel scriptus nihil significat nisi secundum voluntariam institutionem. Ex quo sequitur alia differentia, videlicet quod terminus prolatus vel scriptus ad placitum potest mutare suum significatum, terminus

---

* *Perihermenias*, cap. i (16ᵃ, 3 sq.)
† *In librum De interpretatione*, ed. i (Migne *PL*, TOM. LXIV, col. 301 sq.)

I say vocal words are signs subordinated to mental concepts or contents. By this I do not mean that if the word 'sign' is taken in its proper meaning, spoken words are properly and primarily signs of mental concepts ; I rather mean that words are applied in order to signify the very same things which are signified by mental concepts. Hence the concept signifies something primarily and naturally, whilst the word signifies the same thing secondarily. This holds to such an extent that a word conventionally signifying an object signified by a mental concept would immediately, and without any new convention, come to signify another object, simply because the concept came to signify another object. This is what is meant by the Philosopher when he says 'Words are signs of the impressions in the soul'. Boethius also has the same in mind when he says that words signify concepts. Generally speaking, all authors who maintain that all words signify, or are signs of, impressions in the mind, only mean that words are signs which signify secondarily what the impressions of the mind import primarily. Nevertheless, some words may also primarily signify impressions of the mind, or concepts ; these may in turn signify secondarily other intentions of the mind, as will be shown later.

What has been said about words in regard to impressions or contents or concepts holds likewise analogously for written words in reference to spoken words.

Certain differences are to be found among these [three] sorts of terms. One is the following : A concept or mental impression signifies naturally whatever it does signify ; a spoken or written term, on the other hand, does not signify anything except by free convention.

From this follows another difference. We can change the designation of the spoken or written term at will, but the designation of the conceptual term is not to be changed at anybody's will.

autem conceptus non mutat suum significatum ad placitum cuiuscumque.

Propter tamen protervos est sciendum, quod 'signum' dupliciter accipitur : Uno modo pro omni illo quod apprehensum aliquid aliud in cognitionem facit venire, quamvis non faciat mentem venire in primam eius, sicut alibi est ostensum, sed in actualem post habitualem eiusdem. Et sic vox naturaliter significat, sicut quilibet effectus significat saltem suam causam ; sic etiam circulus significat vinum in taberna. Sed tam generaliter non loquor hic de 'signo'. Aliter accipitur 'signum' pro illo, quod aliquid facit in cognitionem venire et natum est pro illo supponere vel tali addi in propositione, cuiusmodi sunt syncategoremata et verba et illae partes orationis, quae finitam significationem non habent, vel quod natum est componi ex talibus, cuiusmodi est oratio. Et sic accipiendo hoc vocabulum 'signum', vox nullius est signum naturale.

De termino stricte sumpto

2. Est autem sciendum, quod hoc nomen 'terminus' tripliciter accipitur : Uno modo vocatur terminus omne illud, quod potest esse copula vel extremum propositionis categoricae, videlicet subiectum vel praedicatum, vel determinatio extremi vel verbi. Et isto modo etiam una propositio potest esse terminus, sicut potest esse pars propositionis ; haec enim est vera : ' "Homo est animal", est propositio vera', in qua haec tota propositio : 'Homo est animal', est subiectum, et 'propositio vera' est praedicatum.

Aliter accipitur hoc nomen 'terminus' secundum quod distinguitur contra orationem. Et sic omne incomplexum vocatur terminus, et sic de termino in praecedenti capitulo sum locutus.

For the sake of quibblers, however, it should be noted that 'sign' can assume two meanings. In one sense it means anything which, when apprehended, makes us know something else ; but it does not make us know something for the first time, as has been shown elsewhere ; it only makes us know something actually which we already know habitually. In this manner, a word is a natural sign, and indeed any effect is a sign at least of its cause. And in this way also a barrel-hoop signifies the wine in the inn. Here, however, I am not speaking of 'sign' in such a general meaning. In another sense, 'sign' means that which makes us know something else, and either is able itself to stand for it, or can be added in a proposition to what is able to stand for something—such are the syncategorematic words and the verbs and other parts of a proposition which have no definite signification—or is such as to be composed of things of this sort, e.g. a sentence. If 'sign' is taken in this sense, then a word is not a natural sign of anything.

The various meanings of 'term'

2. The noun 'term' has three meanings. In one sense, 'term' is the name of everything that can be the copula or one of the extremes in a categorical proposition, namely the subject or the predicate, or any qualification of the subject or predicate or of the verb. In this sense, even a proposition can be a term, as it can be part of a proposition. For it is true to say : ' "Man is an animal" is a true proposition'. In this case, the entire proposition 'Man is an animal' is the subject and 'true proposition' is the predicate.

In another sense, the noun 'term' is contrasted with a sentence. Then, every non-complex expression is called a 'term'. (It was in this sense that I used 'term' in the preceding chapter.)

Tertio modo accipitur praecise pro illo quod significative sumptum potest esse subiectum vel praedicatum
propositionis. Et isto modo nullum verbum nec coniunctio nec adverbium nec praepositio nec interiectio est
terminus. Multa etiam nomina non sunt termini,
scilicet nomina syncategorematica, quia talia, quamvis
possint esse extrema propositionum, si sumantur materialiter vel simpliciter, tamen quando sumuntur significative, non possunt esse extrema propositionum. Unde
ista oratio : ' "Legit" est verbum', congrua est et vera, si
hoc verbum 'legit' sumeretur materialiter ; si autem
significative sumeretur, non intelligibilis esset. Similiter
est de talibus : ' "Omnis " est nomen', ' "Olim " est
adverbium', ' "Si" est coniunctio', ' "Ab" est praepositio'.
Et isto modo accipit Philosophus 'terminum', quando
definit terminum i° Priorum.*

Non solum autem unum incomplexum potest esse ter-
nimus sic accepto 'termino', sed etiam compositum ex
duobus incomplexis, scilicet compositum ex adiectivo et
substantivo, et compositum ex participio et adverbio vel
praepositione cum suo casuali potest esse terminus, sicut
potest esse subiectum vel praedicatum propositionis. In
ista enim propositione : 'Homo albus est homo', nec
'homo' nec 'albus' est subiectum, sed hoc totum 'homo
albus'. Similiter hic : 'Currens velociter est homo', nec
'currens' nec 'velociter' est subiectum, sed hoc totum
'currens velociter'.

Est autem sciendum, quod non tantum nomen acceptum in recto potest esse terminus, sed etiam casus obliquus
potest esse terminus, quia potest esse subiectum propositionis et etiam praedicatum. Verumtamen obliquus

---

* cap. i (24^b, 16 sq.)

[1] Ockham refers to such words as 'all' (*omnis*) which would be
classed under the heading of 'nouns' in medieval grammar (as *nomina
adiectiva*).

Thirdly, 'term' in its precise meaning designates everything that in its significative function can be either subject or predicate of a proposition. In this sense a verb or a conjunction or an adverb or a proposition or an interjection is not a term. Even many nouns will not be terms, viz. the syncategorematic nouns[1]; although they may be extremes of a proposition when taken in material or simple *suppositio*, nevertheless, when taken in their significative function, they cannot be extremes of a proposition. For instance, the sentence ' "Reads" is a verb' makes sense and is true if the verb 'reads' is taken in material supposition.[2] If, however, it were taken in its significative function, the sentence would be unintelligible. The same holds for the following propositions : ' "All" is a noun', ' "once" is an adverb', ' "If" is a conjunction', ' "From" is a preposition'. It is in this [last] sense that the Philosopher understands 'term' when he defines it in the first book of the *Prior Analytics*.

Not only can one simple expression be a term in this sense, but also a composite of two such simple expressions, viz. of an adjective and a substantive, and of a participle and an adverb, or of a preposition with its grammatical case, since such a compound, too, can be subject or predicate of a proposition. For in the proposition 'A white man is a man', neither 'man' nor 'white' is the subject, but only the whole expression 'white man'. Likewise in the proposition '[The one] running swiftly is a man', neither '[the one] running' nor 'swiftly' is the subject but the entire expression '[the one] running swiftly'.

Yet not only the noun in the nominative case may be a term, but also a noun in another case, because such a noun can be subject and also predicate of a proposition.

[1] Lest it seem that Ockham labours the point of this paragraph unduly, the reader should recollect that in those days there were no quotation marks.

non potest esse subiectum respectu cuiuscumque verbi.
Non enim bene dicitur : 'Hominis videt asinum', quamvis bene dicatur : 'Hominis est asinus'. Quomodo autem
et respectu quorum verborum potest obliquus esse
subiectum, et respectu quorum non, ad grammaticum
pertinet, cuius est constructiones vocum considerare.

De divisione termini in categorematicum
et syncategorematicum

3. Adhuc aliter dividitur terminus tam vocalis quam mentalis, quia terminorum quidam sunt categorematici,
quidam syncategorematici. Termini categorematici
finitam et certam habent significationem. Sicut hoc
nomen 'homo' significat omnes homines, et hoc nomen
'animal' omnia animalia, et hoc nomen 'albedo' omnes
albedines.

Termini autem syncategorematici, cuiusmodi sunt
tales : 'omnis', 'nullus', 'aliquid', 'totus', 'praeter',
'tantum', 'inquantum' et huiusmodi, non habent finitam
significationem et certam, nec significant aliquas res
distinctas a rebus significatis per categoremata. Immo
sicut in algorismo cifra per se posita nihil significat, sed
addita alteri figurae facit eam significare, ita syncategorema proprie loquendo nihil significat, sed magis
additum alteri facit. ipsum significare aliquid, sive facit
ipsum pro aliquo vel aliquibus aliquo modo determinato
supponere, vel aliud officium circa categorema exercet.
Unde hoc syncategorema 'omnis' non habet aliquod certum significatum, sed additum 'homini' facit ipsum stare
seu supponere actualiter sive confuse et distributive pro
omnibus hominibus ; additum autem 'lapidi' facit ipsum
stare pro omnibus lapidibus, et additum 'albedini' facit
ipsum stare pro omnibus albedinibus. Et sicut est de

However, a noun which is not in the nominative case cannot be subject in reference to *any* verb. For it is not correct to say 'The man's sees a donkey', although it is correct to say, 'The man's is a donkey'. How a noun in an oblique case may be subject and which verbs can or cannot have such a subject are questions for the grammarian to decide, for his task it is to study the constructions of words.

Division into Categorematic and Syncategorematic terms

3. There is still another distinction holding both between vocal, and between mental, terms. Some are categorematic, others syncategorematic, terms. Categorematic terms have a definite and fixed signification, as for instance the word 'man' (since it signifies all men) and the word 'animal' (since it signifies all animals), and the word 'whiteness' (since it signifies all occurrences of whiteness). Syncategorematic terms, on the other hand, as 'every', 'none', 'some', 'whole', 'besides', 'only', 'in so far as', and the like, do not have a fixed and definite meaning, nor do they signify things distinct from the things signified by categorematic terms. Rather, just as, in the system of numbers, zero standing alone does not signify anything, but when added to another number gives it a new signification ; so likewise a syncategorematic term does not signify anything, properly speaking ; but when added to another term, it makes it signify something or makes it stand for some thing or things in a definite manner, or has some other function with regard to a categorematic term. Thus the syncategorematic word 'every' does not signify any fixed thing, but when added to 'man' it makes the term 'man' stand for all men actually, or with confused distributive *suppositio*. When added, however, to 'stone', it makes the term 'stone' stand for all stones ; and when added to 'whiteness', it makes it stand for all occurrences of

isto syncategoremate 'omnis', ita proportionaliter de aliis
est tenendum, quamvis distinctis syncategorematibus
distincta officia conveniant, sicut de aliquibus inferius
ostendetur.

Et si proterviatur, quod haec dictio 'omnis' est significativa, ergo aliquid significat : Dicendum est, quod
non ideo dicitur significativa, quia aliquid determinate
significat, sed quia facit aliquid significare vel supponere
vel stare pro aliquo, sicut declaratum est. Et sicut hoc
nomen 'omnis' nihil determinate et finite significat
secundum modum loquendi Boethii, sic dicendum est
de omnibus syncategorematibus, et universaliter de
coniunctionibus et praepositionibus.

De quibusdam autem adverbiis aliter est : quia quaedam eorum determinate significant illa, quae significant
nomina categorematica, quamvis alio modo significandi
important.

De differentia inter nomina connotativa et absoluta

4. Postquam de nominibus concretis et abstractis est discus-
sum, nunc de alia divisione nominum, quibus scholastici
frequenter utuntur, est dicendum.

Unde sciendum, quod nominum quaedam sunt mere
absoluta, quaedam sunt connotativa. Nomina mere
absoluta sunt illa quae non significant aliquid principaliter et aliud vel idem secundario ; sed quidquid
significatur per idem nomen, aeque primo significatur.
Sicut patet de hoc nomine 'animal', quod non significat
nisi boves et asinos et homines et sic de aliis animalibus,
et non significat unum primo et aliud secundario, ita
quod oporteat aliquid significari in recto et aliud in
obliquo, nec in definitione exprimente quid nominis
oportet ponere talia distincta in diversis casibus vel
aliquod verbum adiectivum. Immo proprie loquendo

whiteness. As with this syncategorematic word 'every', so with others, although the different syncategorematic words have different tasks, as will be shown further below.

Should some quibbler say that the word 'every' is significant and consequently it signifies something, we answer that it is called significant, not because it signifies something determinately but only because it makes something else signify or represent or stand for something, as we explained before. And just as we say that the noun [1] 'every' does not signify anything in a determinate and limited way, to use Boethius's way of speaking, we must maintain the same of all syncategorematic words and all conjunctions and prepositions.

It is, however, different with some adverbs, because certain of them determinately signify the same things which categorematic words signify, though they do so in a different mode of signification.

On the difference between connotative and absolute terms

4. Having discussed concrete and abstract terms, we must now speak of another division of names frequently used by the teachers of philosophy.

Certain names are purely absolute, others are connotative. Purely absolute names are those which do not signify one thing principally, and another or even the same thing secondarily ; but everything alike that is signified by the same absolute name, is signified primarily. For instance, the name 'animal' just signifies oxen, donkeys and also all other animals ; it does not signify one thing primarily and another secondarily, in such a way that something has to be expressed in the nominative case and something else in an oblique case ; nor is there any need to have nouns in different cases, or participles, in the definitions which express the meaning of 'animal'. On the contrary, properly speaking, such names have no definitions expressing the meaning of the

talia nomina non habent definitionem exprimentem quid
nominis, quia proprie loquendo unius nominis habentis
definitionem exprimentem quid nominis est una definitio
explicans quid nominis, sic scilicet, quod talis nominis
non sunt diversae orationes exprimentes quid nominis
habentes partes distinctas, quarum aliqua significat
aliquid, quod non eodem modo importatur per aliam
partem alterius orationis.   Sed talia, quantum ad quid
nominis, possunt aliquo modo pluribus orationibus non
easdem res secundum suas partes significantibus explicari ;
et ideo nulla earum est proprie definitio exprimens quid
nominis.   Verbi gratia : 'Angelus' est nomen mere
absolutum si non sit nomen officii sed tantum substantiae,
et istius nominis non est aliqua una definitio exprimens
quid nominis ; nam unus explicat, quid hoc nomen
significat, sic dicendo : 'Intelligo per "angelum" aliquam
substantiam abstractam a materia' ; alius sic : 'Angelus
est substantia intellectualis et incorruptibilis'; alius sic :
'Angelus est substantia simplex non componens cum
alio'.   Et ita bene explicat unus, quid significat hoc
nomen, sicut alius.   Et tamen aliquis terminus positus
in una oratione significat aliquid, quod non significatur
eodem modo per terminum positum in altera oratione.
Et ideo nulla earum est proprie definitio exprimens quid
nominis.   Et ita est de multis nominibus mere absolutis,
quod stricte loquendo nullum eorum habet definitionem
exprimentem quid nominis.   Talia autem nomina sunt
huiusmodi : 'homo', 'animal', 'capra', 'lapis', 'arbor',
'ignis', 'terra', 'aqua', 'caelum', 'albedo', 'nigredo',
'calor', 'dulcedo', 'odor', 'sapor' et huiusmodi.

Nomen autem connotativum est illud, quod significat
aliquid primario et aliquid secundario.   Et tale nomen
proprie habet definitionem exprimentem quid nominis,

term. For, strictly speaking, a name that has a definition expressing the meaning of the name, has only one such definition, and consequently no two sentences which express the meaning of such terms are so different in their parts that some part in the first sentence signifies something that is not signified by any corresponding part in the second. The meaning of absolute names, however, may be explained in some manner by several sentences, whose respective parts do not signify the same things. Therefore, properly speaking, none of these is a definition explaining the meaning of the name. For instance, 'angel' is a purely absolute name, at least if it means the substance and not the office of an angel. This name has not some one definition expressing the meaning of the term. For someone may explain the signification of the name by saying : 'I understand by "angel" a substance which exists without matter' ; another thus : 'An angel is an intellectual and incorruptible substance' ; again another thus : 'An angel is a simple substance which does not enter into any composition with anything else'. And what is signified by this name is explained just as well by the one as by the other definition. Nevertheless, not every term in each of these sentences signifies something that is signified in the same manner by a similar term in each of the other sentences. For this reason, none is, strictly speaking, a definition expressing the meaning of the name. And so it is with many names that are purely absolute. Strictly speaking, none of them has a definition expressing the meaning of the names. Names like the following are of this kind : 'man', 'animal', 'goat', 'stone', 'tree', 'fire', 'earth', 'water', 'sky', 'whiteness', 'blackness', 'heat', 'sweetness', 'odour', 'taste', and so on.

A connotative name, however, is that which signifies something primarily and something else secondarily. Such a name has, properly speaking, a definition

et frequenter oportet ponere unum terminum illius
definitionis in recto et aliud in obliquo, sicut est de hoc
nomine 'album' ; nam habet definitionem exprimentem
quid nominis, in qua una dictio ponitur in recto et alia
in obliquo. Unde si quaeras, quid significat hoc nomen
'album', dices quod ista oratio tota : 'Aliquid informa-
tum albedine', vel : 'Aliquid habens albedinem'. Et
patet quod una pars orationis istius ponitur in recto et
alia in obliquo. Potest etiam aliquando aliquod verbum
cadere in definitione exprimente quid nominis. Sicut
si quaeratur, quid significat hoc nomen 'causa', potest
dici, quod idem quod haec oratio : 'Aliquid ad cuius
esse sequitur aliud', vel : 'Aliquid potens producere
aliud', vel aliquid huiusmodi.

Huiusmodi autem nomina connotativa sunt omnia
nomina concreta primo modo dicta, de quibus dictum
est in v° capitulo, et hoc quia talia concreta significant
unum in recto et aliud in obliquo, hoc est dictum, in
definitione exprimente quid nominis debet poni unus
rectus significans unam rem, et alius obliquus significans aliam rem, sicut patet de omnibus talibus : 'iustus',
'albus', 'animatus', 'humanus', et sic de aliis.

Huiusmodi etiam nomina sunt omnia nomina relativa,
quia semper in sua definitione ponuntur diversa idem
diversis modis vel distincta significantia. Sicut patet de
hoc nomine 'simile'. Si enim definiatur 'simile', debet
dici sic : 'Simile est aliquid habens qualitatem talem
qualem habet aliud', vel aliquo modo consimili definiri
habet. Unde de exemplis non est magna cura.

expressing the meaning of the name. In such a definition it is often necessary to put one of its terms in the nominative case and something else in an oblique case. This holds, for instance, for the name 'white'. For it has a definition expressing the meaning of the name in which one expression is put in the nominative case, and another in an oblique case. When you ask, therefore, 'What does the name "white" signify?' you will answer: 'It signifies the same as the entire phrase "Something that is qualified by whiteness", or "Something that has whiteness".' It is manifest that one part of this phrase is put in the nominative case and another in the oblique case. Sometimes it may happen that a verb appears in the definition expressing the meaning of the name. If, for instance, it is asked 'What does the name "cause" signify?' it can be answered that it means the same as the phrase 'Something whose existence is followed by the existence of something else', or 'Something that can produce something else', or the like.

Such connotative names include all the concrete names of the first kind, mentioned in Chapter V, because such concrete names signify one thing in the nominative case and something else in the oblique case; that is to say, in the definition expressing the meaning of the name, one term signifying one thing must be put in the nominative case, and another term signifying another thing must be put in the oblique case. That becomes evident as regards all such names as 'just', 'white', 'animated', 'human' and the like.

Also to this type belong all relative names. For their definition has to contain distinct parts which either signify the same thing in different ways, or signify distinct things; this is evident as regards the name 'similar'. For if 'similar' is defined, we have to say 'The similar is something that has such a quality as another thing has', or some such definition. However, it does not matter which examples we take.

Ex quo patet, quod hoc nomen commune 'connotativum' est superius ad hoc nomen 'relativum', et hoc
accipiendo hoc nomen commune 'connotativum' lar-
gissime. Talia enim nomina sunt omnia nomina perti-
nentia ad genus quantitatis secundum illos, qui ponunt
quantitatem non esse aliam rem a substantia et qualitate,
sicut 'corpus' secundum eos debet poni nomen connotativum. Unde secundum eos debet dici, quod corpus
non est aliud nisi aliqua res habens partem distantem
a parte secundum longum, latum et profundum ; et
quantitas continua et permanens non est nisi res habens
partem distantem a parte, ita quod ista est definitio
exprimens quid nominis ipsius. Tales etiam consequenter
habent ponere, quod 'figura', 'rectitudo', 'longitudo',
'altitudo', et huiusmodi, sunt nomina connotativa. Immo
qui ponunt, quod quaelibet res est substantia vel qualitas,
habent ponere, quod omnia contenta in aliis praedicamentis a substantia et qualitate sunt connotativa, et
etiam quaedam de genere qualitatis sunt connotativa,
sicut ostendetur inferius.

Sub istis nominibus etiam comprehenduntur omnia
talia : 'verum', 'bonum', 'unum', 'potentia', 'actus',
'intellectus', 'intelligibile', 'voluntas', 'volibile', et huiusmodi. Unde de intellectu est sciendum, quod habet
quid nominis istud : 'Intellectus est anima potens
intelligere', ita quod anima significatur per rectum et
actus intelligendi per aliam partem. Hoc autem nomen
'intelligibile' est nomen connotativum et significat intellectum tam in recto quam in obliquo, quia definitio sua
est ista : 'Intelligibile est aliquid apprehensibile ab
intellectu' ; ibi intellectus significatur per hoc nomen
'aliquid' et per istum obliquum 'intellectu' significatur

From this it becomes clear that the common name 'connotative' is a higher genus than the name 'relative', at least if we take the common noun 'connotative' in its broadest sense. For such names include all names pertaining to the genus of quantity, according to those who maintain that quantity is not a different thing from substance and quality. Thus, for them, 'body' has to be considered a connotative name. Hence, according to them, it must be said that a body is nothing else but a thing which has part distant from part in length, breadth and height, and a continuous and permanent quantity is a thing which has part distant from part. This, then, would be a definition expressing the meaning of the name. In consequence, these people have also to maintain that 'figure' or 'shape', 'curvature', 'straightness', 'length', 'height', and the like are connotative names. Further, those who maintain that everything is either a substance or a quality, have to suppose also that all terms contained in the categories other than substance and quality are connotative names, and also some of the genus quality are connotative names, as will be shown later on.

To this group of names belong also such terms as 'true', 'good', 'one', 'potency', 'act', 'intellect', 'intelligible', 'will', 'willable' and the like. The word 'intellect', for instance, has the meaning : 'Intellect is soul able to understand'. Thus the soul is signified by the nominative case and the act of understanding by the rest of the phrase. The name 'intelligible' is also a connotative term. It signifies the intellect, both in the nominative and in the oblique case, since its definition is this : 'The intelligible is something that can be apprehended by the intellect'. In this definition the intellect is signified by the name 'something', and also by the oblique case 'by

etiam intellectus. Et eodem modo dicendum est de
'vero' et 'bono', quia 'verum', quod ponitur convertibile
cum 'ente', significat idem quod 'intelligibile'. 'Bonum'
etiam, quod est convertibile cum 'ente', significat idem,
quod haec oratio : 'Aliquid secundum rectam rationem
volibile et diligibile'.

De nominibus primae et secundae impositionis

5. Positis divisionibus, quae possunt competere tam terminis naturaliter significantibus quam etiam terminis ad
placitum institutis, dicendum est de quibusdam divisionibus competentibus terminis ad placitum institutis.

Est autem prima divisio talis : Nominum ad placitum
significantium quaedam sunt nomina primae impositionis et quaedam sunt nomina secundae impositionis.
Nomina secundae impositionis sunt nomina imposita ad
significandum signa ad placitum instituta et illa quae
sequuntur talia signa, sed non nisi dum sunt signa.

Verumtamen hoc commune 'nomen secundae impositionis' potest dupliciter accipi, scilicet large et proprie.
Large, tunc omne illud est nomen secundae impositionis,
quod significat voces ad placitum institutas, sed non nisi
quando sunt ad placitum institutae, sive illud nomen sit
commune etiam intentionibus animae, quae sunt signa
naturalia, sive non. Talia autem nomina sunt huiusmodi : ' nomen', 'pronomen', 'verbum', 'coniunctio',
'casus', 'numerus', 'modus', 'tempus', et huiusmodi,
accipiendo ista vocabula illo modo, quo utitur eis gram-
maticus. Et vocantur ista nomina nomina nominum
quia non imponuntur nisi ad significandum partes
orationis, et hoc non nisi dum istae partes sunt significativae. Illa enim nomina, quae praedicantur de
vocibus ita quando non sunt significativae sicut quando
sunt significativae, non vocantur nomina secundae im-

the intellect'. The same must be said of 'true' and 'good';
for 'true', which is convertible or co-extensive with
'being', signifies the same as 'intelligible'. Likewise
'good', which is co-extensive with 'being', signifies the
same as the phrase 'Something which can be willed and
loved according to right reason'.

On names of first and second imposition

5. We have thus given the divisions that apply both to terms
which signify naturally and to those which are made by
convention ; we have now to say something about
certain divisions which concern only terms made by
convention.

A first division is this : Some of the conventional
names are names of first imposition and some are names
of second imposition. Names of second imposition are
names which are applied to signify conventional signs,
and also what goes with such signs, but only as long as
they are signs.

But the general term 'name of second imposition' can
be taken in two senses ; one broad, the other strict. In
a broad sense a name of second imposition is one that
signifies utterances conventionally used, but only as long
as they have this conventional use, whether or not such
a name be also shared by mental contents, which are
natural signs. Such names are 'noun', 'pronoun', 'verb',
'conjunction', 'case', 'number', 'tense' and the like,
when used as the grammarian understands them. These
names are called names of names, because they are
applied only to signify parts of speech, and only as long
as these are significative. For names which are predicated of words both when they are significant and when
they are not are not called names of second imposition.

positionis. Et ideo talia nomina 'qualitas', 'prolatum',
'vox', et huiusmodi, quamvis significent voces ad placitum institutas et verificentur de eis, quia tamen ita
significarent eas, si non essent significativae sicut nunc,
ideo non sunt nomina secundae impositionis. Sed
'nomen' est nomen secundae impositionis, quia ista vox
'homo' nec aliqua alia, antequam imponebatur ad
significandum, non erat nomen ; et similiter 'hominis',
antequam imponebatur ad significandum, nullius casus
erat, et ita est de aliis.

Stricte autem dicitur nomen secundae impositionis
illud quod non significat nisi signa ad placitum instituta,
ita quod non potest competere intentionibus animae,
quae sunt naturalia signa, cuiusmodi sunt talia : 'figura',
'coniugatio', et huiusmodi. Omnia autem alia nomina
ab istis, quae scilicet non sunt nomina secundae impositionis nec uno modo nec alio, vocantur nomina
primae impositionis.

Verumtamen 'nomen primae impositionis' dupliciter
accipi potest, scilicet large : et sic omnia nomina, quae
non sunt nomina secundae impositionis sunt nomina
primae impositionis. Et sic talia signa syncategorematica 'omnis', 'nullus', 'aliquis', 'quilibet', et huiusmodi,
sunt nomina primae impositionis. Aliter potest accipi
stricte, et tunc sola nomina categorematica, quae non
sunt nomina secundae impositionis, vocantur nomina
primae impositionis, et non nomina syncategorematica.

Nomina autem primae impositionis, stricte accipiendo
'nomen primae impositionis', sunt in duplici differentia :
quia quaedam sunt nomina primae intentionis, et quaedam sunt nomina secundae intentionis. Nomina secundae intentionis vocantur illa nomina, quae praecise
imposita sunt ad significandum intentiones animae, quae
sunt signa naturalia, et alia signa ad placitum instituta

Hence such names as 'quality', 'spoken,' 'utterance' and the like, are not names of second imposition, though they signify conventional utterances, since they would signify them even if they were not significant as they now are. But 'noun' is a name of second imposition, since neither the word 'man' nor any other word was a noun before it was employed to signify. Likewise 'man's' was of no case, before it was used to signify what it does. The same holds good for the other words of this kind.

In the strict sense, however, 'name of the second imposition' is that which signifies only a conventional sign, and therefore does not refer to mental contents, which are natural signs. Such names are 'figure', 'conjugation' and the like. All other names that are not names of second imposition in one or the other way, are called names of first imposition.

'Name of first imposition', however, can be taken in two senses. In a broad sense all names not of second imposition are names of first imposition. Thus all such syncategorematic signs as 'every', 'none', 'some', 'any' and the like, are names of first imposition. In a strict sense, however, only categorematic names not of second imposition are called names of first imposition, and not syncategorematic names.[1]

Names of first imposition, in the strict sense, are of two classes. Some are names of first intention, others of second intention. Names of second intention are those nouns which are used precisely to signify mental con-

---

[1] Or nouns. *Cf.* p. 50 *n.* 1

vel consequentia talia signa. Et talia nomina sunt
omnia talia : 'genus', 'species', 'universale', 'praedicabile', et huiusmodi, quia talia nomina non significant
nisi intentiones animae, quae sunt signa naturalia, vel
signa voluntarie instituta. Unde potest dici, quod hoc
commune 'nomen secundae intentionis' potest accipi
stricte et large. Large illud dicitur nomen secundae
intentionis, quod significat intentiones animae quae sunt
naturalia signa, sive etiam significent signa ad placitum
instituta, tantum dum sunt signa, sive non. Et sic
aliquod nomen secundae intentionis et primae impositionis est etiam nomen secundae impositionis. Stricte
autem illud solum dicitur nomen secundae intentionis,
quod praecise significat intentiones animae, quae sunt
naturalia signa, et sic nullum nomen secundae intentionis
est nomen primae impositionis.

Nomina autem primae intentionis vocantur omnia alia
nomina a praedictis, quae videlicet significant aliquas
res, quae non sunt signa nec consequentia talia signa,
cuiusmodi sunt omnia talia 'homo', 'animal', 'Sortes',
'Plato', 'albedo', 'album', 'verum', 'bonum', et huiusmodi, quorum aliqua significant praecise res, quae non
sunt signa nata supponere pro aliis, aliqua significant
talia signa et simul cum hoc alias res.

Ex quibus omnibus colligi potest, quod quaedam
nomina significant praecise signa ad placitum instituta,
et non nisi dum sunt signa, quaedam autem praecise
significant signa, sed tam ad placitum instituta quam
signa naturalia, quaedam vero significant praecise res,
quae non sunt signa talia, quae sunt partes propositionis,
quaedam indifferenter significant tales res, quae non sunt
partes propositionis nec orationis et etiam signa talia,
cuiusmodi sunt talia nomina 'res', 'ens', 'aliquid', 'unum',
et huiusmodi.

cepts, which are natural signs, and also other conventional signs, or what goes with such signs. All the following are of this kind : 'genus', 'species', 'universal', 'predicable' and the like. For such names signify only mental contents, which are natural signs, or conventional signs.

Hence it can be said that this common term, 'name of second intention', can be taken strictly or broadly. Broadly speaking, that is said to be a name of second intention which signifies mental contents that are natural signs, whether or not it also signifies conventional signs for just such time as they function as signs. In this sense some names of first imposition and second intention are also names of second imposition. Strictly speaking, however, that only is called a name of second intention which precisely signifies mental contents that are natural signs. In this sense no name of second intention is a name of first imposition.

Names of first intention, on the other hand, are all names that differ from the former ; that is, they signify some things which neither are signs nor go with such signs, as for instance, 'man', 'animal', 'Socrates', 'Plato', 'whiteness', 'white', 'true', 'good' and the like. Some signify precisely things that are not signs able to stand for other things ; some signify such signs and other things as well.

From all this it may be gathered that certain names precisely signify conventional signs, but only as long as they are signs ; some signify both natural and conventional signs ; some, however, signify only those things which are not such signs, which are parts of propositions ; some indifferently signify both things which are not parts of propositions or speech, and also such signs ; of this kind are the following names : 'thing', 'being', 'something', 'one' and the like.

De univocis, aequivocis et denominativis

6. Sequitur post praedicta tractare de divisione terminorum ad placitum institutorum, quae est per aequivocum, univocum et denominativum. Quamvis enim Aristoteles in *Praedicamentis** tractet de aequivocis, univocis et denominativis, tamen ad praesens intendo tantum de univocis et aequivocis tractare, quia de denominativis dictum est superius.

Est autem primo sciendum, quod sola vox vel aliquod signum ad placitum institutum est aequivocum vel univocum ; et ideo intentio animae vel conceptus non est aequivocus nec univocus proprie loquendo.

Est autem vox illa aequivoca, quae significans plura non est signum subordinatum uni conceptui, sed est signum unum pluribus conceptibus seu intentionibus animae subordinatum. Et hoc intendit Aristoteles,† quando dicit nomen esse commune et idem sed rationem substantialem esse diversam, hoc est, conceptus vel intentiones animae, cuiusmodi sunt descriptiones et definitiones, et etiam conceptus simplices sunt diversi, tamen vox una est. Hoc expresse patet de dictione diversorum idiomatum ; nam in uno idiomate imponitur ad significandum illud idem, quod significatur per talem conceptum, et in alio imponitur ad significandum illud idem, quod significatur per alium conceptum. Et ita pluribus conceptibus seu passionibus animae subordinatur in significando.

Tale autem aequivocum est duplex : Unum est aequivocum a casu : quando scilicet vox pluribus conceptibus subordinatur, et ita uni ac si non subordinaretur alteri, et ita significat unum ac si non significaret aliud,

---

* cap. i (1ᵃ)   † *loc. cit.*

Univocal, equivocal and denominative terms

6. The next thing to be dealt with is the division of conventional terms into equivocal, univocal and denominative terms. Although Aristotle in the *Categories* deals with equivocal and univocal and denominative terms, nevertheless at present I intend to treat only univocal and equivocal terms, since I have spoken about denominative terms before.

First it must be known that only a spoken word or a conventional sign is an equivocal or univocal term ; therefore a mental content or concept is, strictly speaking, neither equivocal nor univocal.

That word is equivocal which, although it signifies several things, still is not a sign subordinated to one concept, but one sign subordinated to several concepts or mental contents. This is what Aristotle means when he says that the name is common and the essential meaning is diverse. That is, the concepts or mental contents, for example descriptions or definitions and even simple concepts, are diverse, though they are referred to by one word. This is manifestly clear as regards an expression found in different languages ; for in one language it is employed to signify the same thing as is signified by a certain concept, and in another language it is applied to that which is signified by a different concept. Thus the same word is subordinated in its significance to several concepts or mental impressions.

Such equivocal terms are of two sorts. There is the term that is equivocal by chance, namely when a word is subordinated to several concepts and is subordinated to one just as if it were not subordinated to another, and thus it signifies one thing just as if it did not signify

sicut est de hoc nomine 'Sortes', quod imponitur pluribus hominibus. Aliud est aequivocum a consilio : quando vox primo imponitur alicui vel aliquibus et subordinatur uni conceptui, et postea propter aliquam similitudinem primi significati ad aliquid aliud vel propter aliquam aliam rationem imponitur illi alteri, ita quod non imponeretur illi alteri, nisi quia primo imponebatur alii. Sicut est de hoc nomine 'homo'; 'homo' enim primo imponebatur ad significandum omnia animalia rationalia, ita quod imponebatur ad significandum omne illud, quod continetur sub hoc conceptu 'animal rationale' ; postea utentes videntes similitudinem inter talem hominem et imaginem hominis, utebantur quandoque hoc nomine 'homo' pro tali imagine, ita quod nisi hoc nomen 'homo' fuisset primo impositum hominibus, non uterentur nec imponerent hoc nomen 'homo' ad significandum vel standum pro tali imagine ; et propter hoc dicitur aequivocum a consilio.

Univocum autem dicitur omne illud quod est subordinatum uni conceptui, sive significet plura sive non. Tamen proprie loquendo non est univocum nisi significet vel natum sit significare plura aeque primo, ita tamen quod non significet illa plura nisi quia una intentio animae significat illa, ita quod sit signum subordinatum in significando uni signo naturali, quod est intentio seu conceptus animae.

Talis autem divisio non tantum competit nominibus sed etiam verbis et universaliter cuilibet parti orationis, immo etiam sic quod aliquid potest esse aequivocum, eo quod potest esse diversarum partium orationis, puta tam nomen quam verbum vel tam nomen quam participium vel adverbium, et sic de aliis partibus orationis.

Est autem intelligendum, quod ista divisio terminorum per aequivocum et univocum non est per simpliciter

another thing. This is the case with the name 'Socrates', which is applied to several men. There is also the term that is intentionally equivocal ; namely when a word is first applied to some thing or things and subordinated to one concept, and then, later on, because of some resemblance that the thing first signified bears to some other thing, or for some other reason, the same word is applied to this other thing in such a way that it would not have been applied to the second thing, had it not previously been applied to the first. Such is the case with the name 'man'. For 'man' was first applied to signify all rational animals, so that it was applied to signify everything that is contained under the concept 'rational animal'. Later, however, when those who used the word saw the resemblance between such a man and the image of a man, they sometimes called the image a man ; hence if the noun 'man' had not first been applied to men, it would not have been used or applied to signify or stand for such an image. And for this reason it is called intentionally equivocal.

'Univocal', on the other hand, is a term for every name that is subordinated to one concept, whether it signifies several things or not. However, properly speaking, a term is not univocal if it does not or cannot primarily signify several things alike ; in such a manner, however, that it signifies these several things only because one mental content signifies them. Therefore, it is a sign subordinated in its significance to one natural sign, which is a mental content or concept.

This division does not only refer to nouns, but also to verbs, and, in general, to every part of a sentence. Furthermore, something can be equivocal because it can function as different parts of speech ; for instance, as a noun and a verb, or as a noun and a participle or adverb, and the same with other parts of speech.

It must be understood, however, that this division of terms into equivocal and univocal is not one of un-

opposita, ita quod haec sit omnino falsa : 'Aliquod aequivocum est univocum', immo vera est, quia vere et realiter eadem vox est aequivoca et univoca, sed non respectu eorumdem. Sicut idem est pater et filius, non tamen respectu eiusdem, et idem est simile et dissimile, non tamen eidem per idem. Unde si sit aliqua dictio diversorum idiomatum, manifestum est quod potest esse univoca in utroque idiomate. Unde ille qui sciret alterum idioma tantum, nullam propositionem, in qua poneretur, distingueret ; scienti tamen utrumque idioma est aequivoca. Unde scientes utrumque idioma in multis casibus distinguerent propositiones, in quibus talis dictio poneretur. Et ita idem terminus est uni univocus et alteri aequivocus.

Ex praedictis colligi potest, quod non semper univocum habet unam definitionem, quia non semper proprie definitur. Et ideo, quando Aristoteles dicit,* quod univoca sunt illa, quorum nomen commune est et ratio substantialis eadem, accipit 'rationem' pro intentione animae, cui tamquam primario signo vox subordinatur.

Est autem sciendum, quod 'univocum' dupliciter accipitur, scilicet large pro omni voce vel signo ad placitum instituto correspondente uni conceptui. Aliter accipitur stricte pro aliquo tali praedicabili per se primo modo de aliquibus, quibus est univocum, vel de pronomine demonstrante aliquam rem.

Terminus autem denominativus ad praesens potest accipi dupliciter, scilicet stricte, et sic terminus incipiens sicut abstractum incipit, et non habens consimilem finem et significans accidens dicitur terminus denominativus,

qualified opposition, such that the proposition 'Something equivocal is univocal', would be completely false. On the contrary, it is true, since really and truly the same word is equivocal and univocal, though not in reference to the same things (just as the same man may be a father and a son, but not of the same person ; or one and the same thing may be similar and dissimilar, though not to the same thing under the same aspect). Hence, if some expression occurs in different languages, it is manifest that it can be univocal in each language. Hence he who knows but one of these languages would not make distinctions over a proposition in which this expression occurred, whereas to one who knows both languages the term is equivocal, and he would in many cases make distinctions over propositions in which such an expression occurs. Thus the same term would be univocal for the one and equivocal for the other.

From the aforesaid it can be gathered that what is univocal does not always have just one definition, since it does not always admit of a proper definition. Hence when Aristotle says that univocal terms are those which have the same name in common and which have the same essential meaning, he takes 'meaning' (*rationem* [λόγον]) for a mental content to which, as a primary sign, the word is subordinated.

It has to be known that 'univocal' can be understood in two senses. In a broad sense it refers to every spoken word or conventional sign that corresponds to one concept. In another sense it is taken strictly for something which is predicable in the first mode of *per se* predication of things relatively to which it is univocal, or of the pronoun which points to some such thing.

A denominative term can for the present be taken in two senses. If it is taken strictly, a denominative term

sicut a 'fortitudine' 'fortis', a 'iustitia' 'iustus'. Aliter dicitur large terminus habens consimile principium cum abstracto sed non consimilem finem, sive significet accidens sive non, sicut ab 'anima' dicitur 'animatus'.

Et haec de divisionibus terminorum sufficiant. Aliqua autem in praedictis omissa inferius supplebuntur.

is one which begins as the abstract term does but does not have the same ending, and signifies an accident ; e.g. from 'bravery' we have the denominative term 'brave', or from 'justice', 'just'. Taken broadly, a denominative term is one which has the same beginning as the abstract term and does not have the same ending ; but it does not matter, whether it signifies an accident or not. As for instance, from 'life' something is said to be 'living'.

Let this suffice about the division of terms. Some details left out here will be added later on.

IV

THE THEORY OF 'SUPPOSITIO'

Sources :

De suppositione terminorum

1. Dicto de significatione terminorum restat dicere de suppositione, quae est proprietas conveniens termino, sed numquam nisi in propositione.

Est autem primo sciendum, quod 'suppositio' accipitur dupliciter, scilicet large et stricte. Large accepta non distinguitur contra appellationem, sed appellatio est unum contentum sub suppositione. Aliter accipitur stricte 'suppositio', secundum quod distinguitur contra appellationem. Sed sic non intendo loqui de suppositione, sed primo modo tantum. Et sic tam subiectum quam praedicatum supponunt; et universaliter quidquid potest esse subiectum propositionis vel praedicatum supponit.

Dicitur autem 'suppositio' quasi pro alio positio, ita quod, quando terminus stat in propositione pro aliquo, ita quod utimur illo termino pro aliquo, de quo sive de pronomine demonstrante ipsum ille terminus vel rectus illius termini, si sit obliquus, verificatur, supponit pro illo; et hoc saltem verum est, quando terminus supponens significative accipitur. Et sic universaliter terminus supponit pro illo, de quo vel de pronomine demonstrante ipsum per propositionem denotatur praedicatum praedicari, si supponens sit subiectum; si autem terminus sit praedicatum, denotatur, quod subiectum subiicitur respectu illius vel respectu pronominis demonstrantis ipsum, si propositio formetur. Sicut per istam: 'Homo est animal', denotatur, quod Sortes vere est animal, ita quod haec sit vera, si formetur: 'Hoc est animal', demonstrando Sortem. Per istam autem: ' "Homo" est nomen', denotatur, quod

'Suppositio' of terms [in general]

1. Up to now we have been speaking about the signification of terms. It remains now to discuss *suppositio*, which is a property belonging to a term, but only when used in a proposition.

We have to know first that *suppositio* is taken in two meanings. In a broad sense, it is not contrasted with appellation ; appellation is rather a subclass of *suppositio*. In a strict sense, *suppositio* is contrasted with appellation. However, I do not intend to speak about *suppositio* in this sense, but only in the former. Thus, both subject and predicate have *suppositio*. Generally speaking, whatever can be subject or predicate in a proposition has *suppositio*.

'Suppositio' means taking the position, as it were, of something else. Thus, if a term stands in a proposition instead of something, in such a way (*a*) that we use the term for the thing, and (*b*) that the term (or its nominative case, if it occurs in an oblique case) is true of the thing (or of a demonstrative pronoun which points to the thing), then we say that the term has *suppositio* for the thing. This is true, at least, when the term with *suppositio* is taken in its significative function. Hence, in general, when a term with *suppositio* is the subject of a proposition, then the thing for which the term has *suppositio*, or a demonstrative pronoun pointing to this, is that of which the proposition denotes that the predicate is predicated. But where the term with *suppositio* is predicate, the thing or pronoun is the one of which the proposition, if formulated, denotes that the subject is a subject. For instance, the proposition 'Man is an animal' denotes that Socrates is truly an animal, so that the proposition 'This is an animal' would be true, if it were formulated while pointing at Socrates. The proposition ' "Man" is a noun', however, denotes that the

haec vox 'homo' sit nomen, ideo in ista supponit 'homo' pro illa voce. Similiter, per istam : 'Album est animal', denotatur, quod illa res, quae est alba, sit animal, ita quod haec sit vera : 'Hoc est animal', demonstrando illam rem, quae est alba, et propter hoc pro illa re subiectum supponit. Et sic proportionaliter dicendum est de praedicato. Nam per istam : 'Sortes est albus', denotatur, quod Sortes est illa res, quae habet albedinem, et ideo praedicatum supponit pro ista re, quae habet albedinem. Et si nulla res haberet albedinem nisi Sortes, tunc praedicatum praecise supponeret pro Sorte.

Est autem una regula generalis, quod numquam terminus in aliqua propositione, saltem quando significative accipitur, supponit pro aliquo, nisi de quo praedicatur vere.

Ex quo sequitur, quod falsum est, quod aliqui ignorantes dicunt, quod concretum a parte praedicati supponit pro forma, videlicet quod in ista : Sortes est albus, li 'albus' supponit pro albedine ; nam haec est simpliciter falsa : 'Albedo est alba', qualitercumque termini supponant. Ideo numquam concretum tale supponit pro forma tali significata per suum abstractum secundum viam Aristotelis. In aliis autem concretis, de quibus dictum est, hoc est bene possibile. Eodem modo in ista : 'Homo est Deus', 'homo' vere supponit pro Filio Dei, quia Filius Dei vere est homo.

De divisione suppositionis

2. Sciendum autem est, quod suppositio primo dividitur in suppositionem personalem, simplicem et materialem.

Suppositio personalis universaliter est illa, quando terminus supponit pro suo significato, sive illud significatum sit res extra animam, sive sit vox, sive intentio

vocal sound 'man', is a noun. Therefore in this proposition 'man' stands for this vocal sound. Likewise, the proposition 'A white thing is an animal' denotes that this thing which is white is an animal, so that this proposition would be true : 'This'—pointing at that thing which is white—'is an animal'. Hence the subject stands for that thing. Much the same must be said as regards the predicate. For the proposition 'Socrates is white' denotes that Socrates is *that* thing, which has whiteness ; and for that reason the predicate stands for *that* thing, which has whiteness. And if no other thing had whiteness but Socrates, then the predicate would stand for Socrates alone.

There is a general rule, namely that in any proposition a term never stands for something of which it is not truly predicated, at least if the term is taken in its significative function. From this it follows that it is false to say, as some ignorant people do, that the concrete term as a predicate stands for a form—for instance to say that in the proposition 'Socrates is white' the term 'white' stands for whiteness. For whichever *suppositio* the terms may have, the proposition 'Whiteness is white' is simply false. Therefore, according to the teaching of Aristotle, a concrete term of this kind never stands for such a form as is signified by the corresponding abstract term. But in regard to other concrete terms of which we have spoken before, this is quite possible. In the same way in this proposition 'A man is God', 'man' truly stands for the Son of God, because He is truly man.

The division of 'suppositio'

2. We have to know that '*suppositio*' is primarily divided into personal, simple and material *suppositio*.

Generally speaking, we have personal *suppositio* when a term stands for the objects it signifies, whether the latter be things outside the mind, or vocal sounds, or

animae, sive sit scriptum, sive quodcumque imaginabile,
ita quod, quandocumque subiectum vel praedicatum
propositionis supponit pro suo significato, ita quod significative tenetur, semper est suppositio personalis. Exemplum primi sic dicendo : 'Omnis homo est animal', li
'homo' supponit pro suis significatis, quia 'homo' non
imponitur ad significandum nisi istos homines ; non
enim proprie significat aliquod commune eis, sed ipsos-
met homines, secundum Damascenum.* Exemplum
secundi sic dicendo : 'Omne nomen vocale est pars
orationis', li 'nomen' non supponit nisi pro vocibus, quia
tantum imponitur ad significandum illas voces, ideo
supponit personaliter. Exemplum tertii sic dicendo :
'Omnis species est universale', vel : 'Omnis intentio
animae est in anima', utrumque subiectum supponit
personaliter, quia supponit pro illis, quibus imponitur
ad significandum. Exemplum quarti sic dicendo :
'Omnis dictio scripta est dictio', subiectum non supponit
nisi pro significatis suis, puta pro dictionibus scriptis,
ideo supponit personaliter.

Ex quo patet, quod non sufficienter describunt suppositionem personalem dicentes, quod suppositio personalis
est, quando terminus supponit pro re. Sed ista est
definitio : Suppositio personalis est, quando terminus
supponit pro suo significato et significative.

Suppositio simplex est, quando terminus supponit pro
intentione animae, sed non tenetur significative. Verbi
gratia sic dicendo : 'Homo est species' ; iste terminus
'homo' supponit pro intentione animae, quia illa intentio
est species, et tamen iste terminus 'homo' non significat
proprie loquendo illam intentionem ; sed illa vox et
illa intentio animae sunt tantum signa subordinata in

---

* Cf. Dialectica, cap. v (Migne PG, TOM. XCIV, col. 549 B–C)

mental concepts, or writing, or anything else imaginable. Whenever the subject or the predicate of a proposition stands for the object signified, so that it is taken in its significative function, we always have personal *suppositio*.

An example of the first would be 'Every man is an animal', where 'man' stands for the objects it signifies, since 'man' is a conventional sign meant to signify *these* men and nothing else ; for properly speaking it does not signify something common to them, but, as St John Damascene says, these very men themselves. An example of the second would be to say 'Every vocal noun is a part of speech'. In this case 'noun' stands only for vocal signs ; therefore its *suppositio* is personal. An example of the third would be to say 'Every species is universal', or 'Every mental content is in the mind'. In either case the subject has personal *suppositio*, since it stands for what it conventionally signifies. An example of the fourth would be to say 'Every written expression is an expression'. Here the subject stands only for the thing it signifies, namely for written signs. Hence it has personal *suppositio*.

From this it is clear that personal *suppositio* is not adequately described by those who say that personal *suppositio* occurs when a term stands for a thing. But the definition is this : 'Personal *suppositio* obtains when a term stands for what it signifies and is used in its significative function'.

Simple *suppositio* is that in which the term stands for a mental content, but is not used in its significative function. For instance 'Man is a species'. The term 'man' stands for a mental content, because this content is the species ; nevertheless, properly speaking, the term 'man' does not signify that mental content. Instead, this vocal sign and this mental content are only signs, one subordinate to the other, which signify the same thing,

significando idem, secundum modum alibi expositum.
Ex quo̅ patet falsitas opinionis communiter dicentium,
quod suppositio simplex est, quando terminus supponit
pro suo significato, quia suppositio simplex est, quando
terminus supponit pro intentione animae, quae proprie
non est significatum termini, quia terminus talis significat
veras res et non intentiones animae.

Suppositio materialis est, quando terminus non supponit significative, sed supponit pro voce vel pro scripto.
Sicut patet hic : ' "Homo" est nomen' ; hi̅c 'homo'
supponit pro seipso, et tamen non significat seipsum.
Similiter in ista propositione : ' "Homo" scribitur',
potest esse suppositio materialis, quia terminus supponit
pro illo, quod scribitur.

Et est sciendum, quod sicut ista triplex suppositio
competit voci prolatae, ita potest competere voci scriptae. Unde si scribantur istae quatuor propositiones :
'Homo est animal', 'Homo est species', 'Homo est vox
dissyllaba', 'Homo est dictio scripta', quaelibet istarum
poterit verificari, et tamen non nisi pro diversis : Quia
illud, quod est animal, nullo modo est species nec vox
dissyllaba nec dictio scripta. Similiter illud, quod est
species, non est animal nec vox dissyllaba etc., et sic de
aliis. Et tamen in duabus ultimis propositionibus habet
terminus suppositionem materialem.

Sed illa potest subdistingui, eo quod subiectum potest
supponere pro voce vel pro scripto. Et si essent nomina
imposita, ita posset distingui suppositio pro voce et̅
scripto, sicut suppositio pro significato ve̅l pro intentione
animae, quarum unam vocamus 'personalem' et aliam
'simplicem' ; sed talia nomina non habemus.

---

[1] Note, again, that in Ockham's day there were no quotation
marks ; in fact, they partly dispel the ambiguity which he is
discussing.

in the manner explained elsewhere. This shows the falsity of the opinion held by those who say (as is commonly accepted) that simple *suppositio* occurs when a term stands for the object it signifies. For simple *suppositio* obtains when a term stands for a mental content, which is not properly speaking the object signified by the term, because the term signifies real things and not mental contents.

Material *suppositio* occurs when a term does not stand for what it signifies, but stands for a vocal or written sign, as ' "Man" is a noun'. Here, 'man' stands for itself ; and yet it does not signify itself. Likewise in the proposition ' "Man" is written', we can have material *suppositio*, since the term stands for that which is written.

As the three sorts of *suppositio* apply to a spoken sign, so also they can be applied to a written sign. Hence, if the following four propositions are written, 'Man is an animal', 'Man is a species', ' "Man" is a monosyllabic word', ' "Man" is a written word',[1] each one of these could be true, but each one for a different object. For that which is an animal is by no means a species, nor a monosyllabic word, nor a written word. Likewise, that which is a species is not an animal nor a monosyllabic sign. And so with the others. Yet in the two latter propositions the term has material *suppositio*.

Material *suppositio* could be subdivided according as the subject stands for a spoken sign or for a written sign. If we had terms for them, we could distinguish *suppositiones* for a spoken sign and for a written sign, just as we distinguish *suppositio* for the object signified and *suppositio* for a mental content, calling one 'personal' and the other 'simple' *suppositio*. However, we have no such names.

Sicut autem talis diversitas suppositionis potest competere termino vocali et scripto, ita etiam potest competere termino mentali, quia intentio potest supponere pro illo, quod significat, et pro seipsa et pro voce et scripto.

Est autem sciendum, quod non dicitur 'suppositio personalis', quia supponit pro persona, nec 'simplex', quia supponit pro simplici, nec 'materialis', quia supponit pro materia, sed propter causas praedictas. Et ideo isti termini 'materiale', 'personale', 'simplex' aequivoce usitantur in logica et in aliis scientiis. Tamen in logica non usitantur frequenter nisi cum isto termino addito 'suppositio'.

Quod terminus in omni propositione potest supponere personaliter

3. Notandum etiam est, quod semper terminus, in quacumque propositione ponatur, potest habere suppositionem personalem, nisi ex voluntate utentium arctetur ad aliam. Sicut terminus aequivocus in quacumque propositione potest supponere pro quolibet significato suo, nisi ex voluntate utentium arctetur ad certum significatum. Sed terminus non in omni propositione potest habere suppositionem simplicem vel materialem, sed tunc tantum, quando terminus talis comparatur alteri extremo, quod respicit intentionem animae vel vocem vel scriptum. Verbi gratia, in ista propositione : 'Homo currit', li 'homo' non potest habere suppositionem simplicem vel materialem, quia ' currere' non respicit intentionem amimae nec vocem nec scriptum. Sed in ista propositione : 'Homo est species', quia 'species' significat intentionem animae, ideo potest habere suppositionem simplicem, et est propositio distinguenda penes tertium modum aequivocationis, eo quod subiectum potest

As such a difference of *suppositio* can apply to a vocal and written term, so also it can apply to a mental term. For a mental content may stand for that which it signifies, or for itself, or for a spoken or written sign.

It should be noted, however, that personal *suppositio* is not called 'personal' because a term stands for a person, nor is simple *suppositio* so called because a term stands for a simple thing, nor is material *suppositio* so called because a term stands for matter ; but only for the reasons mentioned. Therefore the terms 'material', 'personal' and 'simple' are being used in an equivocal meaning in logic and in other sciences. In logic, however, they are not used frequently except in conjunction with the term '*suppositio*'.

In whatever proposition a term is placed, it may have
personal 'suppositio'

3. In whatever proposition a term is placed, it may have personal *suppositio*, if it is not arbitrarily limited to another *suppositio* by those who use it. In the same manner an equivocal term may stand in any proposition for any one of the objects it signifies, if it is not arbitrarily limited to only one such object by those who use it. However, a term cannot have simple and material *suppositio* in every proposition. It can have these *suppositiones* only when the other term of the proposition, to which it is being compared, relates to a mental content or a spoken or written sign. For instance, in the proposition 'Man is running', 'man' cannot have simple or material *suppositio*, since 'to run' does not refer to a mental content, nor to a spoken or written sign. But it is different in the proposition 'Man is a species', for 'species' signifies a mental content. For that reason the term can have simple *suppositio*. Hence the proposition must have its various senses distinguished according to the third mode of equivocation, because the subject may have either

habere suppositionem simplicem vel personalem. Primo modo est propositio vera, quia tunc denotatur, quod una intentio animae sive conceptus sit species, et hoc est verum. Secundo modo est̄ falsa simpliciter, quia tunc denotatur, quod aliqua res significata per 'hominem' sit species, quod est manifeste falsum.

Eodem modo sunt tales distinguendae : ' "Homo" praedicatur de pluribus', ' "Risibile" est passio hominis', ' "Risibile" praedicatur primo de homine', et sunt istae distinguendae tam a parte subiecti quam a parte prae- dicati. Similiter ista propositio est distinguenda : ' "Animal rationale" est definitio "hominis",' quia si habeat suppositionem simplicem, est vera, si personalem, est falsa. Et sic de multis talibus, sicut de istis : 'Sa- pientia est attributum Dei', ' "Creativum" est passio Dei', 'Bonitas et sapientia sunt attributa divina', 'Bonitas praedicatur de Deo', 'Innascibilitas est proprietas Patris', et huiusmodi.

Similiter, quando terminus comparatur ad aliquod extremum respiciens vocem vel scripturam, est pro- positio distinguenda, eo quod talis terminus potest habere suppositionem personalem vel materialem. Et isto modo sunt istae distinguendae : ' "Sortes" est nomen', ' "Homo" est vox dissyllaba', ' "Paternitas" significat proprietatem Patris'. Nam si 'Paternitas' supponat materialiter, sic est haec vera : ' "Paternitas" significat proprietatem Patris' ; si autem supponeret̄ personaliter, sic est falsa, quia Paternitas est proprietas Patris vel est ipse Pater. Et isto modo sunt distinguendae istae : ' "Animal rationale" significat quidditatem

simple or personal *suppositio*. In the first sense the proposition is true, for then it denotes that a mental content or concept is a species, and that is true. In the second sense, the proposition is simply false, since then it denotes that something signified by 'man' is a species, and that is manifestly false.

In like manner the following propositions have to have their possible senses distinguished : ' "Man" is predicated of many' ; ' "Risible" is a property of man' ; ' "Risible" is predicated primarily of man'. These propositions must have various senses distinguished on the side both of the subject and of the predicate. Likewise in the proposition ' "Rational animal" is the definition of "man",' a distinction must be made, for if the subject has simple *suppositio* it is true, if it has personal *suppositio* it is false. Thus it is with many other propositions, such as 'Wisdom is an attribute of God', ' "Creative" is a property of God', 'Goodness and wisdom are divine attributes', 'Goodness is predicated of God', 'Innascibility is a property of the Father', etc.

In a similar manner, if a term is compared with the other extreme [viz. the predicate], which refers to a vocal or written sign, the proposition must be distinguished. For the term may have personal *suppositio* or material *suppositio*. Thus the following propositions have to have their senses distinguished : ' "Socrates" is a name' ; ' "Man" is a monosyllable' ; ' "Paternity" signifies a property of the Father'. For if 'paternity' has material *suppositio*, this proposition is true ; ' "Paternity" signifies a property of the Father'. If, however, its *suppositio* is personal, then the proposition would be false, because paternity is a property of the Father or is the Father Himself [i.e. when we use 'paternity' with personal *suppositio*, we must say it *is* a property of the Father]. In the same manner the following propositions must have their senses distinguished : ' "Rational animal"

hominis', ' "Rationale" significat partem hominis',
' "Homo albus" significat aggregatum per accidens',
' "Homo albus" est terminus compositus', et sic de multis
aliis talibus.

Potest igitur ista regula dari : Quod quando terminus
potens habere praedictam triplicem suppositionem comparatur extremo communi incomplexis sive complexis,
sive prolatis sive scriptis, semper terminus potest habere
suppositionem materialem, et est talis propositio distinguenda. Quando vero comparatur extremo significanti
intentionem animae, est distinguenda, eo quod potest habere suppositionem simplicem vel personalem. Quando
autem comparatur extremo communi omnibus praedictis,
tunc est distinguenda, eo quod potest habere suppositionem simplicem, materialem et personalem. Et sic
est haec distinguenda : ' "Homo" praedicatur de pluribus' ; quia si 'homo' habeat suppositionem personalem,
sic est falsa, quia tunc denotatur, quod aliqua res significata per hunc terminum 'homo' praedicatur de pluribus ; si habeat suppositionem simplicem vel materialem,
sive pro voce sive pro scripto, est vera, quia tam intentio
communis quam vox quam illud quod scribitur praedicatur de pluribus.

De suppositione personali in speciali

4. Suppositio personalis potest dividi primo in suppositionem discretam et communem. Suppositio autem
discreta est, in qua supponit nomen proprium alicuius
vel pronomen demonstrativum significative sumptum ;
et talis suppositio reddit propositionem singularem, sicut
hic : 'Sortes est homo', 'Iste homo est homo', et sic de
aliis. Et si dicatur, haec est vera : 'Haec herba crescit
in horto meo', et tamen subiectum non habet supposi-

signifies the quiddity of "man" ' ; ' "White man" signifies an accidental aggregate' ; ' "White man" is a composite term', and so on as regards many other propositions.

Therefore the following rule can be given : When a term capable of this threefold *suppositio* is compared with an extreme [of a proposition] which is a common term for complex and non-complex, spoken and written, terms, the first term can always have material *suppositio*, and therefore with such a proposition a distinction must be made. When, on the other hand, a term is compared with an extreme that signifies a content of the mind, the proposition has to have its possible meanings distinguished, since the term may have simple *or* personal *suppositio*. When, however, the term is compared with an extreme which is a common term for all the aforesaid classes, then its meanings must be distinguished, since it may have simple, material *and* personal *suppositio*. A proposition which must have its meanings distinguished in this manner is ' "Man" is predicated of many' ; because if man has personal *suppositio*, then it is false, since then it denotes that something signified by the term 'man' is predicated of many. If it has simple *suppositio*, or material *suppositio* either for the vocal or the written sign, then it is true, because both the common concept and the spoken and written sign *are* predicated of many.

Personal 'suppositio' in particular

4. Personal *suppositio* can be divided in the first place into discrete and common *suppositio*. Discrete *suppositio* is that belonging to a proper name of something or to the demonstrative pronoun taken as significative. Such a *suppositio* makes a proposition singular, like these : 'Socrates is a man' ; 'This man is a man' ; and so with others. It may be objected that the proposition 'This plant grows in my garden' is true, yet the subject has

tionem discretam : dicendum, quod ista propositio est
falsa de virtute sermonis ; sed per istam intelligitur talis
propositio : 'Talis herba crescit in horto meo', ubi subiectum supponit determinate. Unde advertendum est, quod
quando aliqua propositio falsa est de virtute sermonis,
sed tamen aliquem verum sensum habet, ipsa accepta
in illo sensu debent subiectum et praedicatum habere
eandem suppositionem, quam habent in illa, quae de
virtute sermonis est vera.

Suppositio personalis communis est quando terminus
communis supponit sicut hic : 'Homo currit', 'Omnis
homo est animal'. Suppositio personalis communis
dividitur in suppositionem confusam et determinatam.

Suppositio determinata est, quando contingit descendere per aliquam disiunctivam ad singularia, sicut bene
sequitur : 'Homo currit, igitur iste homo currit, vel
ille', et sic de singulis. Et ideo dicitur suppositio determinata, quia per talem suppositionem denotatur, quod
talis propositio sit vera pro aliqua singulari determinata,
quae singularis determinata sola sine veritate alterius
singularis sufficit ad talem propositionem verificandam ;
sicut ad veritatem istius : 'Homo currit', requiritur, quod
aliqua singularis determinata sit vera, et quaelibet
sufficit, etiam posito, quod quaelibet alia esset falsa.
Tamen frequenter multae vel omnes sunt verae. Est
igitur regula certa : Quod quando sub termino communi contingit descendere ad singularia per propositionem disiunctivam et ex qualibet singulari infertur
talis propositio, tunc ille terminus habet suppositionem
personalem determinatam. Et ideo in ista propositione :
'Homo est animal', utrumque extremum habet suppositionem determinatam, quia sequitur : 'Homo est animal,

no discrete *suppositio*. To this we have to say that the proposition taken as it stands is false. However, what is understood by it is the proposition 'A plant of this kind grows in my garden', and in this case the subject has determinate *suppositio*. From this it should be noted that when a proposition which as it stands is false, has nevertheless a true sense, then, taking it in this sense, the subject and predicate must have the same *suppositio* as in the proposition which *is* true as it stands.

Common personal *suppositio* is that of a common term, as in 'A man is running', 'Every man is an animal'.

Common personal *suppositio* is divided into confused *suppositio* and determinate *suppositio*. There is determinate *suppositio* when it is possible to make the logical descent to singulars by a disjunctive proposition, as in the correct inference 'A man is running, therefore this man is running, or that man (and so on for every individual)'. It is called 'determinate' *suppositio* because such *suppositio* denotes that a proposition of this kind is true in the case of a determinate singular proposition, which determinate singular proposition by itself, without the truth of any other singular proposition, is sufficient to make such a proposition true. Thus for the truth of the proposition 'A man is running', it is required only that some determinate singular proposition be true; and any one would suffice, even if every other such singular proposition were false. Frequently, however, others also, or even all, of the singular propositions are true. Therefore it is a sure rule that when (1) the logical descent from a common term to its singular inferior terms can legitimately be made by a disjunctive proposition, and (2) from any singular proposition such a proposition is inferable, then this term has determinate personal *suppositio*. Therefore, in the proposition 'A man is an animal', both extremes have determinate *suppositio* ; for this follows : 'A man is an animal, therefore, this

igitur ille homo est animal, vel ille (et sic de singulis)'.
Similiter sequitur : 'Ille homo est animal', quocumque
demonstrato, 'igitur homo est animal'. Similiter sequitur : 'Homo est animal, igitur homo est hoc animal, vel
homo est illud animal, vel illud (et sic de singulis)'. Et
bene sequitur : 'Homo est hoc animal', quocumque
animali demonstrato, 'igitur homo est animal'. Et ideo
tam 'homo' quam 'animal' habet suppositionem determinatam.

Suppositio personalis confusa est omnis suppositio
personalis termini communis, quae non est determinata.
Et illa dividitur : quia quaedam est suppositio confusa
tantum, quaedam est suppositio confusa et distributiva.

Suppositio confusa tantum est, quando terminus communis supponit personaliter et non contingit descendere
ad singularia per disiunctivam nulla variatione facta a
parte alterius extremi, sed per propositionem de disiuncto praedicato, et contingit eam inferre ex quacumque singulari. Verbi gratia in ista : 'Omnis homo est
animal', li 'animal' supponit confuse tantum, quia non
contingit sub 'animali' ad sua contenta per disiunctivam
descendere, quia non sequitur : 'Omnis homo est animal,
igitur omnis homo est hoc animal, vel omnis homo est
illud animal, et sic de singulis', sed bene contingit
descendere ad propositionem de disiuncto praedicato ex
singularibus. Quia bene sequitur : 'Omnis homo est
animal, igitur omnis homo est hoc animal vel illud vel
illud (et sic de singulis)' ; quia consequens est una cate-
gorica composita ex hoc subiecto 'homo' et hoc praedicato 'hoc animal vel illud (et sic de singulis)' ; et
manifestum est, quod hoc praedicatum vere praedicatur
de omni homine, ideo ista universalis est simpliciter
vera. Et similiter ista infertur ex quolibet contento sub

man is an animal, or this (and so on in regard to each man)'. Likewise this follows : 'This man is an animal' —if we point at any man—'therefore a man is an animal'. Likewise, it follows : 'A man is an animal, therefore a man is this animal, or, a man is that animal, or that animal (and so on with each animal)'. And this correctly follows : 'A man is this animal'—pointing at any animal —'therefore a man is an animal'. Therefore, both 'man' and 'animal' have determinate *suppositio*.

Confused personal *suppositio* is any personal *suppositio* of a common term which is not determinate *suppositio*. This again is subdivided into merely confused *suppositio*, and confused distributive *suppositio*. Merely confused *suppositio* occurs when (1) a common term has personal *suppositio* ; (2) we are unable to make the logical descent to the singulars by means of a disjunctive proposition without any change of the other extreme ; (3) we can, however, make the logical descent by way of a proposition with a disjunctive predicate ; and (4) the original proposition can be inferred from any singular. For instance, in the proposition 'Every man is an animal', 'animal' has merely confused *suppositio*. For (2) it is not open to us to make the logical descent from 'animal' to its inferior terms ; for this does not follow : 'Every man is an animal, therefore every man is this animal, or every man is that animal (and so on for every animal)'. However, (3) the logical descent can validly be made to a proposition whose predicate is a disjunction of singular terms. For this does validly follow : 'Every man is an animal, therefore every man is either this animal or that or that (and so on for every animal)', for the consequent is a single categorical proposition composed of the subject 'man' and the predicate 'this animal or that or that (and so on for every animal)'. And it is manifest that this predicate is truly predicated of every man, and for that reason this universal proposition is simply true. And likewise (4) this proposition

animali ; nam bene sequitur : 'Omnis homo est hoc animal', quocumque animali demonstrato, 'igitur omnis homo est animal'.

Suppositio confusa et distributiva est, quando convenit aliquo modo descendere copulative, si habeat multa contenta, et ex nulla formaliter infertur, sicut est in ista : 'Omnis homo est animal', cuius subiectum supponit confuse et distributive ; sequitur enim : 'Omnis homo est animal, igitur iste homo est animal, et ille, et sic de singulis' ; et non sequitur formaliter : 'Ille homo est animal', quocumque demonstrato, 'igitur omnis homo est animal'.

Quod dixi, aliquo modo* contingit descendere, hoc dixi, quia non semper contingit eodem modo descendere ; nam contingit aliquando descendere nulla variatione facta circa propositiones, nisi quod in prima subiicitur vel praedicatur terminus communis, et postea accipiuntur singularia, sicut patet in exemplo praedicto. Aliquando autem contingit descendere aliqua variatione facta, immo aliquo dempto in una propositione, quod accipitur in alia, quod nec est terminus communis nec contentum sub termino communi. Verbi gratia sic dicendo : 'Omnis homo praeter Sortem currit', bene contingit aliquo modo descendere ad aliqua singularia copulative ; nam bene sequitur : 'Omnis homo praeter Sortem currit, igitur Plato currit et sic de aliis a Sorte'. Sed in istis singularibus aliquid dimittitur, quod accipiebatur in universali, quod non fuit terminus communis nec signum

---

* aliquo modo *coni. Geach* ; *cf. supra, l. 5* : aliquando *textus vulg.*

is inferred from every thing contained under 'animal'. For this follows correctly : 'Every man is this animal' —pointing at any animal—'therefore every man is an animal'.

Confused distributive *suppositio* occurs when it is licit to make a logical descent in some way to a copulative proposition if the term has many inferiors, but a formal inference cannot be made to the original proposition from one of the instances. So it is with this proposition, 'Every man is an animal'. The subject of this proposition has confused distributive *suppositio*. For this follows : 'Every man is an animal, therefore this man is an animal and that one is (and so on for every individual)'. But this does not formally follow : 'This man is an animal' —pointing at any man—'therefore every man is an animal'.

When I said 'It is licit to make a logical descent in some way', I said so because this logical descent cannot always be made in the same manner. For sometimes it is possible to make this descent without making any change on the part of the propositions, except that in the first proposition a common term is subject or predicate, whereas in the consequent the corresponding singulars are taken, as is clear in the aforesaid example. Sometimes, however, it is allowed to make the logical descent with some variation, even omitting something in one proposition which is put in the other and is not the common term nor contained under the common term. For instance, when we say 'Every man except Socrates is running', it is legitimate to make the logical descent to some individuals in a copulative proposition. For this follows : 'Every man except Socrates is running, therefore Plato is running (and so on for every man who is different from Socrates)'. However, in these singular propositions something is omitted, which was put in in the universal proposition ; and that which was omitted is not the common term nor the sign distributing the

ipsum distribuens, scilicet dictio exceptiva cum parte
extra capta, et ita non eodem modo contingit descendere
sub ista : 'Omnis homo praeter Sortem currit', et sub
ista : 'Omnis homo currit', nec etiam ad omnia eadem
contingit descendere.

Prima suppositio confusa et distributiva vocatur
'suppositio confusa distributiva mobilis', secunda vocatur
'confusa et distributiva immobilis'.

common term [viz. the quantifier], for what was omitted was the word expressing exception [i.e. 'except'], together with the term to be excepted. Hence the logical descent is not made in the same manner in the two propositions 'Every man except Socrates is running', and 'Every man is running', nor can the logical descent be made altogether to the same things. The first kind of confused distributive *suppositio* is called 'mobile confused distributive *suppositio*', the second is called 'immobile confused distributive *suppositio*'.

V

TRUTH

Source :

Summa totius logicae, II, c. ii

76

Quid requiritur ad veritatem propositionis singularis?

. . . Primo dicendum est de propositionibus singularibus
de inesse et de praesenti et de recto, tam a parte subiecti
quam a parte praedicati, et non aequivalentibus propositioni hypotheticae. Unde dicendum est, quod ad
veritatem talis propositionis singularis, quae non aequivalet multis propositionibus, non requiritur quod subiectum et praedicatum sint idem realiter, nec quod
praedicatum ex parte rei sit in subiecto, vel insit realiter
ipsi subiecto, nec quod uniatur a parte rei extra animam
ipsi subiecto, sicut ad veritatem istius : 'Iste est angelus',
non requiritur quod hoc commune 'angelus' sit idem
realiter cum hoc, quod ponitur a parte subiecti, nec
quod insit illi realiter, nec aliquod tale, sed sufficit et
requiritur, quod subiectum et praedicatum supponant
pro eodem. Et ideo si in ista : 'Hic est angelus',
subiectum et praedicatum supponant pro eodem, propositio est vera. Et ideo non denotatur, quod hic habeat
angelitatem, vel quod in isto sit angelitas vel aliquid
huiusmodi, sed denotatur, quod hic sit vere angelus, non
quidem quod sit illud praedicatum, sed quod sit illud
pro quo supponit praedicatum.

Similiter etiam per tales propositiones : 'Sortes est
homo', 'Sortes est animal', non denotatur, quod Sortes
habeat humanitatem vel animalitatem, nec denotatur,
quod humanitas vel animalitas sit in Sorte, nec quod
homo vel animal sit in Sorte, nec quod homo vel animal
sit de essentia vel de quidditate Sortis vel de intellectu
quidditativo Sortis, sed denotatur, quod Sortes vere est
homo et vere est animal, non quidem quod Sortes sit
hoc praedicatum 'homo' vel hoc praedicatum 'animal',
sed denotatur, quod est aliqua res, pro qua stat vel

What is requisite to the truth of a singular proposition?

. . . Let us first speak of singular propositions of inherence in the present tense [and not determined by a modality], which have both the predicate and the subject in the nominative case, and are not equivalent to a hypothetical proposition. For the truth of such a singular proposition, which is not equivalent to many propositions, it is not required that the subject and the predicate be really the same, nor that the predicate be really in the subject, or really inhere in the subject, nor that it be really united with the subject outside the mind. For instance, for the truth of the proposition 'This is an angel' it is not required that this common term 'angel' be really the same with that which has the position of subject in this proposition, or that it be really in it, or anything of the sort ; but it is sufficient and necessary that subject and predicate should stand for the same thing. If, therefore, in the proposition 'This is an angel' subject and predicate stand for the same thing, the proposition is true. Hence it is not denoted, by this proposition, that this [individual] has 'angelity', or that 'angelity' is in him, or something of that kind, but it is denoted that this [individual] is truly an angel. Not indeed that he is this predicate ['angel'], but that he is that for which the predicate stands. In like manner also the propositions 'Socrates is a man', 'Socrates is an animal', do not denote that Socrates has humanity or animality, nor that humanity or animality is in Socrates, nor that man or animal is in Socrates, nor that man or animal belongs to the essence or quiddity of Socrates or to the quidditative concept of Socrates. They rather denote that Socrates is truly a man and that he is truly an animal ; not that Socrates is the predicate 'man' or

supponit hoc praedicatum 'homo' et hoc praedicatum
'animal', quia pro Sorte stat utrumque illorum praedicatorum.

Ex hoc patet, quod omnes tales de virtute sermonis
sunt falsae : 'Homo est de quidditate Sortis', 'Homo
est de essentia Sortis', 'Humanitas est in Sorte', 'Sortes
habet humanitatem', 'Sortes est homo humanitate', et
multae tales propositiones, quae quasi ab omnibus con-
ceduntur. Falsitas istarum patet ; nam accipio unam
istarum, scilicet istam : 'Humanitas est in Sorte', et
quaero : Pro quo stat li 'humanitas' ? Aut pro re, aut
pro intentione, hoc est, aut denotatur per istam quod
res vera extra animam sit in Sorte, vel quod intentio
animae sit in Sorte. Si supponat pro re, quaero : Pro
qua re ? Aut pro Sorte, aut pro parte Sortis, aut pro
re quae nec est Sortes nec est pars Sortis. Si pro Sorte,
tunc est f̄alsum, quia nulla res, quae est Sortes, est in
Sorte, quia Sortes non est in Sorte, quamvis Sortes sit
Sortes. Et eodem modo humanitas non est in Sorte, sed
est Sortes, si 'humanitas' supponat pro re quae est
Sortes. Si autem 'humanitas' stet pro re quae est pars
Sortis, hoc est falsum : quia quaelibet res, quae est pars
Sortis, vel est materia vel forma vel compositum ex
materia et forma, et una forma hominis et non alia, vel
est pars integralis Sortis ; sed nulla talium partium est
humanitas, sicut patet inductive : Quia anima intellectiva non est humanitas ; tunc enim vera humanitas
remansisset in Christo in triduo, ēt per consequēns vere

the predicate 'animal', but that he is something that the predicate 'man' and the predicate 'animal' stand for or represent; for each of these predicates stands for Socrates.

From this it becomes clear that all the following propositions are false in their literal meaning : 'Man belongs to the quiddity of Socrates', 'Man is of the essence of Socrates', 'Humanity is in Socrates', 'Socrates has humanity', 'Socrates is a man by his humanity', and many such propositions, which almost everyone concedes. The falsity of such propositions is clear ; I take one of them, viz. 'Humanity is in Socrates', and I ask : For what does 'humanity' stand ? Either for a thing, or for a mental content ; that is, such a proposition denotes either that a real thing outside the mind is in Socrates, or that a mental content is in Socrates. If 'humanity' stands for a thing, then I ask, For which thing ? Either for Socrates, or for a part of Socrates, or for a thing that is neither Socrates nor a part of Socrates. If it stands for Socrates, then the proposition is false. For no thing that is Socrates is in Socrates, because Socrates is not in Socrates, although Socrates is Socrates. And likewise humanity is not in Socrates, but *is* Socrates, if 'humanity' stands for a thing that is Socrates. If, however, 'humanity' stands for a thing that is part of Socrates, then, again, the proposition is false, because every thing which is part of Socrates is either matter, or form, or a composite of matter and form (only one human substantial form, not any other such form, is in question), or else an integral part of Socrates. But none of these parts is humanity, as can be shown case by case. For the intellective soul is not humanity ; because then true humanity would have remained in Christ during the three days after his death, and consequently humanity

fuisset humanitas unita Verbo in triduo, et per consequens
vere fuisset homo, quod falsum est. Similiter nec materia
est humanitas, nec corpus Sortis est humanitas, nec pes
nec caput et sic de aliis partibus Sortis, quia nulla pars
Sortis est humanitas, sed tantum pars humanitatis, et
per consequens 'humanitas' non potest supponere pro
parte Sortis. Si supponat pro re quae nec est Sortes nec
est pars Sortis, cum talis res non sit nisi accidens vel
aliqua alia res, quae non est in Sorte, 'humanitas' supponeret pro accidente Sortis vel pro aliqua alia re, quae
nec est Sortes nec pars Sortis, quod manifestum est esse
falsum.

Si autem 'humanitas' supponat pro intentione animae,
tunc est manifeste falsa, quia intentio animae non est
in Sorte. Et ita patet, quod ista est omnino falsa :
'Humanitas est in Sorte'.

would have been truly united with the divine Word during this time, and therefore the Word would then have been truly a man, which is false. Likewise, matter is not humanity, nor is the body of Socrates humanity, nor the foot nor the head, nor any of the other parts of Socrates, because no part of Socrates is humanity, but only a part of humanity. Consequently, 'humanity' cannot stand for a part of Socrates. If, however, it stands for a thing which is neither Socrates nor a part of Socrates, such a thing is only an accident or some other thing which is not Socrates ; and therefore 'humanity' in this case would stand for an accident or for some other thing which is neither Socrates nor a part of Socrates. This is manifestly false. If, however, 'humanity' stands for a content of the mind, then also our proposition is manifestly false, since a content of the mind is not Socrates. It is clear then that the proposition 'Humanity is in Socrates' is utterly false.

VI

INFERENTIAL OPERATIONS

Sources :

De propositione copulativa

1. Copulativa est illa, quae componitur ex pluribus categoricis coniunctis mediante hac coniunctione 'et' vel
mediante aliqua parte aequivalente tali coniunctioni.
Sicut ista est copulativa : 'Sortes currit et Plato disputat'.
Similiter ista est copulativa : 'Sortes nec est albus nec
niger'. Similiter ista : 'Sortes est tam albus quam
calidus'. Quia prima aequivalet isti : 'Sortes non est
albus et Sortes non est niger' ; et secunda isti : 'Sortes
est albus et Sortes est calidus'.

Ad veritatem copulativae requiritur, quod utraque
pars sit vera. Et ideo si quaecumque pars copulativae
sit falsa, ipsa copulativa est falsa. Similiter, ad necessitatem copulativae requiritur, quod quaelibet pars sit
necessaria. Et ad hoc quod sit possibilis, requiritur,
quod quaelibet pars sit possibilis. Sed ad hoc quod sit
impossibilis, non requiritur, quod utraque pars sit impossibilis. Nam haec est impossibilis : 'Sortes sedet et
non sedet', et tamen utraque pars est possibilis. Sed ad
hoc quod copulativa sit impossibilis, requiritur quod
altera pars sit impossibilis, vel quod una est incom-
possibilis alteri. Sicut haec est impossibilis : 'Sortes
est albus et Sortes est asinus', quia haec est impossibilis :
'Sortes est asinus'. Et haec est impossibilis : 'Sortes
sedet et non sedet', quia duae partes sunt incompossibiles.

Sciendum est etiam, quod opposita contradictorie
copulativae est una disiunctiva composita ex contradictoriis partium copulativae. Et ideo idem requiritur

Copulative propositions

1. A copulative proposition is that which is composed of several categorical propositions connected by the conjunction 'and' or some part of speech equivalent to such a conjunction. For instance, 'Socrates is running and Plato is debating' is a copulative proposition ; and so are 'Socrates is neither white nor black', and 'Socrates is no less white than hot', for the former is equivalent to the proposition 'Socrates is not white and Socrates is not black', the second to 'Socrates is white and Socrates is hot'.

For the truth of a copulative proposition, it is required that each part be true. For this reason, if any part of the copulative proposition is false, then the copulative proposition itself is false. Likewise, for the necessity of a copulative proposition it is required that each part be necessary, and for its possibility each part must be possible. But in order that it be impossible it is not required that each part be impossible. For the proposition 'Socrates is sitting and not sitting' is impossible, nevertheless each part is possible. But what is necessary in order that a copulative proposition be impossible, is that one part be impossible or that one part be not possible along with the other. For instance, the proposition 'Socrates is white and Socrates is a donkey' is impossible, since the proposition 'Socrates is a donkey' is impossible. The proposition 'Socrates is sitting and he is not sitting' is also impossible, since the two parts are not possible together.

We should also know that the contradictory opposite of a copulative proposition is a disjunctive proposition composed of the contradictory opposites of its parts. Therefore what is necessary and sufficient for the truth of the disjunctive proposition is what is necessary and

et sufficit ad veritatem oppositae copulativae, quod sufficit et requiritur ad veritatem disiunctivae. Unde istae non contradicunt : 'Sortes est albus et Plato est niger', 'Sortes non est albus et Plato non est niger'. Sed illi copulativae contradicit ista : 'Sortes non est albus vel Plato non est niger'.

Oportet autem scire, quod semper a copulativa ad utramque partem est consequentia bona. Sicut sequitur : 'Sortes non currit et Plato disputat, ergo Plato disputat'. Sed econverso est fallacia consequentis. Tamen sciendum est, quod quandoque ab altera parte copulativae ad copulativam potest esse consequentia bona gratia materiae, puta si una pars copulativae inferat aliam, tunc ab illa parte ad totam copulativam est consequentia bona.

De disiunctiva propositione

2. Disiunctiva est illa, quae componitur ex pluribus categoricis mediante hac coniunctione 'vel' vel mediante aliquo aequivalente sibi. Sicut ista est disiunctiva : 'Tu es homo vel tu es asinus'. Similiter ista est disiunctiva : 'Tu es homo vel Sortes disputat'.

Ad veritatem autem disiunctivae requiritur, quod altera pars sit vera. Et hoc est intelligendum, quando propositiones sunt de praesenti et non de futuro nec aequivalentes propositionibus de futuro ; et hoc diceret Philosophus.* Tamen secundum veritatem ad veritatem disiunctivae requiritur, quod altera pars sit vera, quia secundum veritatem propositio de futuro est vera vel falsa, quamvis evitabiliter.

Sed ad necessitatem disiunctivae non requiritur

* Cf. *Perihermenias,* cap. ix–x (18^a–19^b)

sufficient for the truth of the opposite of the copulative proposition. Hence the propositions 'Socrates is white and Plato is black' and 'Socrates is not white and Plato is not black' are not contradictories ; but 'Socrates is not white or Plato is not black' is the contradictory opposite of the original copulative proposition.

It must also be known that there is a valid inference from a copulative proposition to each part of it. Thus it follows : 'Socrates is not running and Plato is debating; therefore Plato is debating'. To argue from the latter to the former proposition, however, is a fallacy of the consequent. Nevertheless one must know that sometimes from one or other part of a copulative proposition to the copulative proposition itself a valid inference is possible, but only because of the subject-matter. For instance, if one part of the copulative proposition entails the other, then it is legitimate to argue from that part to the whole copulative proposition.

Disjunctive propositions

2. A disjunctive proposition is one composed of several categorical propositions by means of the conjunction 'or' or by means of a conjunction equivalent to it. For instance, the proposition 'You are a man or you are a donkey' is a disjunctive proposition ; and so is the proposition 'You are a man or Socrates is debating'.

For the truth of a disjunctive proposition it is necessary that one or other part be true. However, this must be understood of the case where the propositions are in the present tense, not when they are, or are equivalent to, propositions in the future tense. This is what the Philosopher would say. In fact, however, it is necessary for the truth of a disjunctive proposition that one or other part be true, because in fact a proposition about the future is true or false, though not inevitably so.

For the necessity of a disjunctive proposition the

necessitas alterius partis, sicut ad hoc quod haec sit necessaria : 'Sortes sedet vel non sedet', non requiritur, quod altera pars sit necessaria. Tamen ad necessitatem disiunctivae requiritur necessitas alicuius partis, vel quod partes sibi invicem contradicant, vel aequivalent contradictoriis vel sint convertibilia contradictoriis. Unde haec est necessaria : 'Sortes currit vel Deus est', quia altera pars est necessaria. Haec autem est necessaria : 'Deus creat vel non creat', quia partes contradicunt.

Ad possibilitatem autem disiunctivae sufficit quod altera pars sit possibilis.

Sed ad hoc quod disiunctiva sit impossibilis, requiritur quod utraque pars sit impossibilis.

Sciendum est etiam, quod opposita contradictorie disiunctivae est una copulativa composita ex contradictoriis partium illius disiunctivae. Et ideo idem sufficit et requiritur ad veritatem oppositae disiunctivae, quod sufficit et requiritur ad veritatem copulativae.

Sciendum est etiam, quod ab altera parte disiunctivae ad totam disiunctivam est bonum argumentum, et econverso est fallacia consequentis, nisi sit aliqua causa specialis impediens. Similiter a disiunctiva cum negatione alterius partis ad alteram partem est bonum argumentum. Sicut bene sequitur : 'Sortes est homo vel asinus, et Sortes non est asinus, igitur Sortes est homo'.

necessity of one or other part is not required. For instance, in order that the proposition 'Socrates is sitting or not sitting' be necessary, it is not required that either part be necessary. Rather, for the necessity of a disjunctive proposition it is required that one proposition be necessary or that the parts be contradictories, or equivalent to contradictories, or convertible into contradictories. Hence the proposition 'Socrates is running or God exists' is necessary because the second part is necessary. The following, however, 'God creates or does not create', is necessary because the parts are contradictories.

For the possibility of a disjunctive proposition it is sufficient that either part be possible.

But in order that a disjunctive proposition be impossible it is required that both parts be impossible.

It must be understood that the contradictory opposite of a disjunctive proposition is a copulative proposition composed of the contradictories of the parts of the disjunctive proposition. Therefore the same is necessary and sufficient for the truth of the opposite of a disjunctive proposition as is necessary and sufficient for the truth of the copulative proposition.

Furthermore, it must be understood that from either part of a disjunctive proposition to the entire disjunctive proposition there is a valid argument. To argue the other way round, however, is a fallacy of the consequent, unless there is a special reason which excludes the fallacy. Likewise from the negation of one part of a disjunctive proposition the other part can be validly inferred. Thus from 'Socrates is a man or a donkey' and 'Socrates is not a donkey', it correctly follows 'Therefore Socrates is a man'.

De divisione syllogismi

3. Syllogismorum quidam sunt demonstrativi, quidam topici, quidam nec topici nec demonstrativi.

Syllogismus demonstrativus est ille, in quo ex propositionibus necessariis evidenter notis potest acquiri prima notitia conclusionis. Syllogismus topicus est syllogismus ex probabilibus ; et sunt probabilia, quae videntur vel omnibus vel pluribus vel sapientibus, et de his vel omnibus vel pluribus vel maxime sapientibus.* Et est ista descriptio sic intelligenda, quod probabilia sunt illa, quae cum sint vera et necessaria, non tamen per se nota nec ex per se notis syllogizabilia nec etiam per experientiam evidenter nota nec ex talibus sequentia ; tamen propter sui veritatem videntur esse vera omnibus vel pluribus etc. Ut sic brevis descriptio sit ista : Probabilia sunt necessaria nec principia nec conclusiones demonstrationis, quae propter sui veritatem videntur omnibus vel pluribus etc. Per primam particulam excluduntur omnia contingentia et omnia falsa. Per secundam omnia principia et conclusiones demonstrationis. Per tertiam excluduntur quaedam necessaria, quae tamen omnibus apparent falsa vel pluribus etc. Et sic articuli fidei nec sunt principia demonstrationis nec conclusiones, nec sunt probabiles, quia omnibus vel pluribus vel maxime sapientibus apparent falsi, et hoc accipiendo 'sapientes' pro sapientibus mundi et praecise innitentibus rationi naturali, quia illo modo accipitur

---

* *Cf.* Aristot., *Topica*, I (100^b, 21 sq.)

Syllogism and its main division

3. Some syllogisms are demonstrative, some are topical, some are neither topical nor demonstrative. A demonstrative syllogism is that in which primary knowledge of a conclusion can be obtained from propositions that are necessary and evidently known. A topical syllogism proceeds from probable propositions. Probable propositions are those which appear true to all or to the majority or to wise men, and among the last either to all or to most or to the wisest. This description has to be understood as follows : Probable propositions are of such a nature that, though they are true and necessary, nevertheless they are not known by themselves, nor can they be obtained by a syllogistic process from propositions known by themselves, nor are they evidently known from experience ; nor do they follow from propositions known from experience. Nevertheless, because of their truth, they appear to be true to all or to the majority, etc. A brief description of them could be as follows : Probable propositions are necessary, and they are neither principles nor conclusions of a demonstration, but because of their truth they appear to be true to all or to the majority, etc.

The first part of the description excludes all contingent and false propositions ; the second, all first principles and conclusions of demonstrations. The third excludes certain necessary truths which appear, however, to be false to all or to the majority, etc. And to this class belong the articles of faith ; they are neither principles of demonstration nor conclusions, nor are they probable propositions, since they appear to be false to all or to the majority or to the most wise men. It is understood that we are taking 'wise' here in the sense of 'the wise men of this world', that is of those who are supported by natural reason alone, for in the description of a prob-

'sapiens' in descriptione probabilis.

Ex istis sequitur, quod syllogismus topicus nec peccat in materia nec in forma. Sequitur etiam aliud, quod nullus secundum communem cursum potest evidenter et demonstrative cognoscere de aliquo syllogismo topico ipsum esse topicum, quamvis possit habere fidem quod est syllogismus topicus. Sequitur etiam aliud, quod non omnis syllogismus topicus facit semper praecise dubitationem et formidinem, sed etiam frequenter facit firmam fidem sine omni dubitatione, quia ita aliquando adhaeremus probabilibus sicut evidenter notis.

De regulis generalibus consequentiarum

4. Regulae generales sunt multae.

Una est : *Quod ex vero numquam sequitur falsum.*

Et ideo quando antecedens est verum et consequens falsum, consequentia non valet. Et haec ratio est sufficiens ad probandum consequentiam non valere. Sciendum est, quod antecedens est totum quod praecedit consequens. Et ideo aliquando antecedens est tantum una propositio et aliquando continet plures propositiones, sicut patet in syllogismo, et tunc, quamvis una illarum propositionum sit vera, conclusio poterit esse falsa ; sed si quaelibet illarum fuerit vera, non poterit conclusio esse falsa, si sequatur ex eis.

Alia regula est : *Quod ex falsis potest sequi verum.*

Et ideo ista consequentia non valet : 'Antecedens est falsum, igitur consequens est falsum'. Sed ista consequentia est bona : 'Consequens est falsum, igitur et antecedens'. Ita quod si consequens sit falsum, oportet quod totum antecedens sit falsum, vel quod aliqua propositio sit falsa quae est pars antecedentis. Sed non oportet quod quaelibet propositio quae est pars ante-

able proposition 'wise' is taken in this sense.

From this it follows that a topical syllogism is not deficient in matter or form. It also follows that no-one, according to the common course of nature, can know, evidently and demonstratively, that a topical syllogism is topical, though he can have the belief that it is a topical syllogism. Also something else follows, viz. that not every topical syllogism makes us doubt or fear that we are wrong, but it often makes us have primary belief without any doubt, because sometimes we adhere to probable propositions as we do to evidently known propositions.

General rules of inference

4. There are many general rules of inference :

(1) *From truth falsity never follows.*

Therefore when the antecedent is true and the consequent is false, the inference is not valid. This reason is sufficient to prove that an inference is not valid. However, it is to be understood that 'antecedent' means everything that precedes the consequent. Therefore sometimes the antecedent is only one proposition, and sometimes it contains several propositions, as is obvious in a syllogism. In this case, though one of the propositions of the antecedent may be true, the conclusion may be false ; but if every one of the propositions is true, the conclusion cannot be false, if it follows from them.

(2) *From false propositions a true proposition may follow.*

Hence this inference does not hold : 'The antecedent is false, therefore the consequent is false'. But the following inference holds : 'The consequent is false, therefore so is the antecedent'. Therefore, if the consequent is false, it is necessary that the antecedent as a whole is false or that some proposition which is part of the antecedent is false. But it is not required that every proposition which

cedentis sit falsa, quia aliquando ex una propositione
vera et alia falsa sequitur conclusio falsa, sicut patet
hic : 'Omnis homo est animal, lapis est homo, igitur
lapis est animal'.

Alia regula est : *Si aliqua consequentia sit bona, ex
opposito consequentis sequitur oppositum totius antecedentis.*

Notandum est quod quando antecedens est una propositio, semper, si sit consequentia bona, ex opposito
consequentis sequitur oppositum totius antecedentis ;
sed quando antecedens continet plures propositiones,
tunc non oportet quod ex opposito consequentis sequitur
oppositum cuiuslibet propositionis, quae est pars antecedentis, sed oportet quod ex opposito consequentis cum
una propositione sequatur oppositum alterius propositionis. Sicut bene sequitur : 'Omnis homo est albus,
Sortes est homo, igitur Sortes est albus' ; et tamen non
sequitur : 'Sortes non est albus, igitur Sortes non est
homo' ; sed bene sequitur : 'Omnis homo est albus,
Sortes non est albus, ergo Sortes non est homo' ; et ita
ex opposito conclusionis et maiore sequitur oppositum
minoris, et non ex solo opposito conclusionis. Similiter
bene sequitur : 'Omnis homo est animal, asinus est
homo, igitur asinus est animal', et tamen ex solo
opposito conclusionis non sequitur oppositum maioris.
Nam non sequitur : 'Nullus asinus est animal, igitur
non omnis homo est animal' ; sed ex opposito conclusionis et minore sequitur oppositum maioris sic : 'Nullus
asinus est animal, asinus est homo, igitur non omnis
homo est animal'.

is part of the antecedent should be false. For sometimes from one true and one false proposition a false conclusion follows, as is obvious in the following instance : 'Every man is an animal, a stone is a man, therefore a stone is an animal'.

(3) *If an inference is valid, then from the opposite of the consequent the opposite of the antecedent follows.*

It has to be noted that when the antecedent is one proposition and the inference is valid, then from the opposite of the consequent the opposite of the entire antecedent always follows. However, when the antecedent contains several propositions, then it is not required that from the opposite of the consequent the opposite of every proposition which is part of the antecedent should follow ; but it is required that from the opposite of the consequent combined with one of the propositions of the antecedent the opposite of the other proposition should follow. Thus this inference follows : 'Every man is white, Socrates is a man, therefore Socrates is white' ; but this one does not follow : 'Socrates is not white, therefore Socrates is not a man'. On the other hand, this is correct : 'Every man is white, Socrates is not white, therefore Socrates is not a man'. Thus from the opposite of the conclusion and the major premise the opposite of the minor premise follows, but it does not follow from the opposite of the conclusion alone. Likewise this is correct : 'Every man is an animal, a donkey is a man, therefore a donkey is an animal' ; nevertheless from the opposite of the conclusion alone the opposite of the major premise does not follow. For this does not follow : 'No donkey is an animal, therefore not every man is an animal'. But from the opposite of the conclusion and the minor premise, the opposite of the major premise follows in this way : 'No donkey is an animal, a donkey is a man, therefore not every man is an animal'.

Alia regula est : *Quidquid sequitur ad consequens, sequitur ad antecedens.* Sicut si sequitur : 'Omne animal currit, igitur omnis homo currit', quidquid sequitur ad istam : 'Omnis homo currit', sequitur ad istam : 'Omne animal currit'.

Et ex ista regula sequitur alia, scilicet : *Quidquid antecedit ad antecedens, antecedit ad consequens.* Quia aliter aliquid sequeretur ad consequens, quod non sequeretur ad antecedens.

Sed istae regulae falsae sunt : *Quidquid sequitur ad antecedens, sequitur ad consequens.* Nam sequitur : 'Omne animal currit, igitur omnis homo currit', et tamen non sequitur : 'Omnis asinus currit, igitur omnis homo currit'. Similiter ista regula est falsa : *Quidquid antecedit ad consequens, antecedit ad antecedens,* propter idem.

Ex istis sequuntur aliae regulae. Una est : *Quidquid stat cum antecedente, stat cum consequente.* Sicut quidquid stat cum ista : 'Omne animal currit', stat cum ista : 'Omnis homo currit' ; sed non quidquid stat cum consequente, stat cum antecedente. Nam cum ista consequente : 'Omnis homo currit', stat ista : 'Aliquis asinus non currit', et tamen non stat cum ista antecedente : 'Omne animal currit', et hoc quando antecedens non sequitur ad consequens nec consequentia simplici nec consequentia ut nunc.

(4) *Whatever follows from the consequent follows from the antecedent.*

For instance, if this follows, 'Every animal is running therefore every man is running', then, whatever follows from the proposition 'Every man is running' follows also from 'Every animal is running'.

From this rule follows another :

(5) *Whatever is antecedent to the antecedent is antecedent also to the consequent.*

For, it it were not so, then something would follow from the consequent which does not follow from the antecedent.

The following rules, however, are false : *Whatever follows from the antecedent, follows from the consequent.* For this follows : 'Every animal is running, therefore every man is running' ; and nevertheless this does not follow : 'Every donkey runs, therefore every man is running'. Likewise this rule is false, for the same reason : *Whatever is antecedent to the consequent, is antecedent to the antecedent.*

From these other rules follow :

(6) *Whatever is consistent with the antecedent is consistent with the consequent.*

For instance, whatever is consistent with the proposition. 'Every animal is running' is consistent with 'Every man is running'. But not everything that is consistent with the consequent is consistent with the antecedent. For with the consequent 'Every man is running', the following is consistent, ' Some donkey is not running' ; but this is not consistent with the antecedent 'Every animal is running'. This is the case, when the antecedent does not follow from the consequent either in simple or in factual inference.

Alia regula est : *Quidquid repugnat consequenti, repugnat antecedenti.* Sicut quidquid repugnat isti : 'Omnis homo currit', $\overline{\text{repugnat}}$ isti : 'Omne animal currit', sed non econverso. Quia aliquid repugnat antecedenti, quod non repugnat consequenti. Quia $\overline{\text{istae}}$ repugnant : 'Tantum homo currit', et : 'Aliud ab homine currit' ; sed $\overline{\text{istae}}$ non repugnant : 'Homo currit, et aliud ab homine currit'. Et ideo tales consequentiae sunt bonae : 'Oppositum consequentis stat cum antecedente, igitur consequentia non valet ; oppositum consequentis non stat cum antecedente, igitur consequentia est bona'.

Sed sciendum, quod consequentia poterit esse bona ut nunc, quia ut nunc oppositum consequentis potest stare cum antecedente ; sed si oppositum consequentis stet vel possit stare cum antecedente, non poterit esse consequentia simplex.

Alia regula est : *Quod ex necessario non sequitur contingens.* $\overline{\text{Alia}}$: *Ex possibili non sequitur impossibile.* Istae duae regulae sunt intelligendae de consequentia simplici. $\overline{\text{Nam}}$ ex necessario non sequitur contingens consequentia simplici, nec ex possibili impossibile. Tamen consequentia ut nunc bene poterit sequi. $\overline{\text{Sicut}}$ sequitur : 'Omne ens est, igitur omnis homo est' ; et tamen antecedens est necessarium et consequens contingens. Similiter bene sequitur : 'Omne coloratum est homo, igitur omnis asinus est homo', et tamen antecedens est possibile

(7) *Whatever is inconsistent with the consequent is inconsistent with the antecedent.*

For instance, whatever is inconsistent with the proposition 'Every man is running' is inconsistent with 'Every animal is running', but not vice versa. For something is inconsistent with an antecedent which is not inconsistent with its consequent. The following propositions are inconsistent : 'Only a man is running' and 'Something different from a man is running'. Yet the following propositions are not inconsistent : 'A man is running' and 'Something different from a man is running'. Therefore, such inferences as these are valid : 'The opposite of the consequent is consistent with the antecedent, therefore the inference is not valid' ; and 'The opposite of the consequent is not consistent with the antecedent, therefore the inference is valid'.

However, it is to be understood that such an inference may be valid only at a certain time (*ut nunc*), because at a certain time the opposite of the consequent may be consistent with the antecedent. But if the opposite of the consequent is or could be consistent with the antecedent, it cannot be a simple inference [which holds at any time].

(8) *From something necessary something contingent does not follow.*

(9) *Something impossible does not follow from something possible.*

These two rules have to be understood of simple inference. For in simple inference, from something necessary something contingent does not follow. Nevertheless, it may indeed follow in a factual inference. For instance, this follows : 'Every being exists, therefore every man exists' ; but nevertheless the antecedent is necessary and the consequent contingent. Likewise it follows : 'Every coloured thing is a man, therefore every donkey is a man', but nevertheless the antecedent is possible and the

et consequens impossibile. S̄ed consequentia solum est
bona ut nunc.

N̄otandum est etiam, quod quamvis ex possibili non
sequatur consequentia simplici impossibile, tamen aliquando propter positum possibile, concedendum est
impossibile et negandum est necessarium. Sed hoc
numquam est faciendum nisi in arte obligatoria et
durante tempore obligationis.

Aliae regulae dantur : *Quod ex impossibili sequitur quodlibet.* Et : *Quod necessarium sequitur ad quodlibet.* Et ideo
sequitur : 'Tu es asinus, igitur tu es Deus'. Et sequitur :
'Tu es albus, igitur Deus est trinus et unus'. Sed tales
consequentiae non sunt formales n̄ec sunt multum
usitandae nec usitatae.

consequent impossible.   The consequence is valid only as a factual one.

It is to be noted that though, in a simple consequence, from something possible something impossible does not follow, nevertheless it sometimes happens that if something possible is affirmed, something impossible has to be conceded and something necessary has to be denied ; but this can be done only in the art of *Obligatio* [that is, in the art of purely logical disputation] and only for the course of a given disputation.

Other rules are given :

(10) *From an impossibility anything follows.*
(11) *What is necessary follows from everything.*

Therefore this follows : 'You are a donkey, therefore you are God'.   This also follows : 'You are white, therefore God is triune'.   But these consequences are not formal ones and they should not be used much, nor, indeed, are they used much.

VII

BEING, ESSENCE AND EXISTENCE

Sources :

De ente

1. Circa ens autem est primo sciendum, quod 'ens' dupliciter accipi potest : Uno modo accipitur hoc nomen 'ens' secundum quod sibi correspondet unus conceptus communis omnibus rebus praedicabilis de omnibus in quid illo modo quo transcendens potest in quid praedicari. Quod enim omnibus rebus sit unus conceptus communis praedicabilis de omnibus rebus, ex hoc persuaderi potest : quia si non sit aliquis talis conceptus communis, ergo diversis rebus sunt diversi conceptus communes, qui sunt *A* et *B* ; sed ostendo quod aliquis conceptus est communior tam *A* quam *B* praedicabilis de quocumque, pu̅t̅a *C*. Gratia exempli : Quia sicut possunt formari tales tres propositiones vocales : '*C* est *B*', '*C* est *A*', '*C* est aliquid', ita possunt in mente tales tres propositiones formari, quarum duae sunt dubiae et tertia est scita ; nam possibile est, quod aliquis dubitet utramque istarum : '*C* est *B*', '*C* est *A*', et tamen quod sciat istam : '*C* est aliquid'. Quo dato arguo sic : Duae istarum propositionum sunt dubiae, et una est scita, et istae tres habent idem subiectum ; igitur habent distincta praedicata. Quia si non, eadem propositio esset scita et dubia, ex quo duae sunt hic dubiae. Si habent distincta praedicata, igitur aliud praedicatum est in ista : '*C* est aliquid', quod non est praedicatum in aliqua istarum : '*C* est *B*', '*C* est *A*' ; igitur illud praedicatum est distinctum ab illis. Sed manifestum est, quod illud praedicatum non est minus commune nec convertibile cum

---

[1] i.e., so that it answers the question 'What is it ?'

The notion of being

1. The first thing to know about 'being' (*ens*) is that 'being' can assume two meanings. In the first sense, the noun 'being' is associated with a concept which is common to all things and can be predicated of all things in the manner of a quiddity,[1] in the way that a transcendental term can be predicated in the manner of a quiddity. In favour of the statement that there is a concept common to and predicable of all things, the following persuasive argument can be adduced. If there is no such common concept, then diverse concepts—let us call them *A* and *B*—are common to diverse things. However, I can show that there is a concept, more common than *A* and *B*, and predicable of any given subject, let us say *C*. For example : just as the three spoken propositions '*C* is *B*', '*C* is *A*', '*C* is something', can be formulated, so likewise three such mental propositions can be formed. Of these mental propositions two are doubtful and the third is known to be true. For it is possible that someone should doubt both propositions '*C* is *B*' and '*C* is *A*', and nevertheless know that *C* is something. If this is granted, then I argue in the following manner : Two of the aforesaid propositions are doubtful and one is known ; but all three propositions have the same subject, consequently they must have distinct predicates. For if they did not, then the same proposition would be known and would be dubious, since we assumed that the two are doubtful. If, however, they have distinct predicates, then there is another predicate in this proposition, '*C* is something', which is not the predicate in one of the other two propositions, viz. '*C* is *B*', '*C* is *A*'. Therefore this predicate 'something' is distinct from the other predicates. Yet it is manifest that this predicate is not less common than

aliquo illorum, igitur est communius quam aliquid
illorum.   Quod est propositum, scilicet quod aliquis
conceptus mentis alius ab istis inferioribus est communis
cuilibet enti.   Quod est concedendum ; nam de omni
ente vel de pronomine demonstrante quodcumque ens
potest idem conceptus mentis vere praedicari : sicut
eadem vox potest de quolibet vere praedicari.

Non tamen obstante quod sic sit unus conceptus communis omni enti, tamen hoc nomen 'ens' est aequivocum
quia non praedicatur de omnibus subiicibilibus, quando
significative sumuntur, secundum unum conceptum, sed
sibi diversi conceptus correspondent, sicut super Por-
phyrium declaravi.*

Ulterius sciendum est, quod secundum Philosophum
IV° *Metaphysicae* † 'ens' dicitur hoc quidem secundum
accidens, illud vero secundum se.   Quae distinctio non
est intelligenda, quasi aliquod ens sit per se et aliud per
accidens ; sed ostendit ibi diversum modum praedicandi
unius de reliquo mediante hoc verbo 'est'.   Quod satis
clarum est per exempla Philosophi, quia dicit quod
dicimus musicum secundum accidens esse iustum, et
similiter :   Musicus secundum accidens est homo, et :
Musicum dicimus aedificare secundum accidens.   Ex
quo patet, quod non loquitur nisi de diverso modo praedicandi alicuius de aliquo.   Quia aliquid dicitur de
aliquo per se, et aliquid dicitur de aliquo per accidens.

Quod enim aliqua res non sit ens per se et alia per
accidens, patet : quia nulla res est, quin sit substantia
vel accidens ; sed tam substantia quam accidens est ens
per se ; igitur etc.

---

* *Expositio aurea,* super Porphyrii cap. De specie, ad ' Sed in
familiis'

† cap. vii (1017*a*, 7)

either, and with at least one of them it is not coextensive ; consequently, it is more common than at least one of them. This is what was to be proved, namely that some concept of the mind other than these less extensive concepts is common to every being. And this must be conceded. For of every being, or of the pronoun pointing to any being, the same mental concept can be truly predicated, just as the same word can be predicated of every thing.

Notwithstanding there is a concept thus common to every being, the name 'being' is equivocal. For it is not in accordance with one concept that it is predicated of all its possible subjects taken in their significative function. Rather, to the name 'being' there correspond diverse concepts, as I have explained in my exposition of Porphyry.

Furthermore, it is known that according to the Philosopher in the fourth book of the *Metaphysics*, 'is' is applied both to what *is* incidentally and to what *is* intrinsically. This distinction does not mean that some being exists intrinsically and another exists incidentally. Aristotle is rather pointing out the different ways of predicating one term of another by means of the verb 'is'. This is sufficiently clear from the examples used by the Philosopher. He says : 'We say that the musician is incidentally just, and also that the musician is incidentally a man, and we say that the musician is incidentally building'. From this it is clear that he is speaking only about the diverse modes of predicating one term of another. For something is asserted of something intrinsically, and something is asserted of something incidentally. For it is manifest that there is not one thing which is intrinsically existent and another that is incidentally existent, for this reason : there is nothing besides substance or accident ; but both substance and accident exist intrinsically ; therefore, etc. However, notwithstanding this, something is predicated of another

Hoc tamen non obstante aliquid praedicatur de aliquo per se et aliquid per accidens.

Similiter distinguitur ens in ens in potentia et in ens in actu. Quod non est intelligendum, quod aliquid quod non est in rerum natura, sed potest esse, sit vere ens, vel aliquid aliud quod est in rerum natura sit etiam ens. Sed Aristoteles dividendo ens in potentiam et in actum, v⁰ *Metaphysicae*, intendit quod hoc nomen 'ens' de aliquo praedicatur mediante hoc verbo 'est' in propositione mere de inesse non aequivalenti propositioni de possibili sic dicendo : 'Sortes est ens', 'Albedo est ens' ; de aliquo autem non praedicatur nisi in propositione de possibili vel aequivalenti propositioni de possibili sic dicendo : 'Antichristus potest esse ens', sive : 'Antichristus est ens in potentia' ; et sic de aliis. Unde vult ibidem, quod ens est divisibile potestate et actu sicut sciens et quiescens ; et tamen nihil est sciens vel quiescens, nisi actualiter sit sciens vel quiescens.

Utrum esse rei et essentia sint duo distincta in re ?

2. Et quia tactum est de esse existere, aliquantulum disgrediendo considerandum est, qualiter esse existere se habet ad rem : Utrum esse rei et essentia rei sint duo extra animam distincta inter se. Et mihi videtur, quod non sunt talia duo, nec 'esse existere' significat aliquid distinctum a re. Quia si sic, aut esset substantia aut accidens. Non accidens, quia tunc esse existere hominis esset qualitas vel quantitas, quod est manifeste falsum,

thing intrinsically, and something else of something else incidentally.

The distinction between potential existence and actual existence is similar. It does not mean that something which is not in the universe, but can exist in the universe, is truly a being, or that something else which is in the universe is also a being. Rather, when Aristotle divides 'being' into potentiality and actuality in the fifth book of the *Metaphysics*, he has in mind that the name 'being' is predicated of some thing by means of the verb 'is', in a proposition which merely states a fact concerning a thing and is not equivalent to a proposition containing the mode of possibility. For instance, 'Socrates is a being', 'Whiteness is a being'. About something, however, 'being' is predicated only in a proposition containing the mode of possibility or equivalent to one containing this mode. For instance, 'The Antichrist can be a being', or 'The Antichrist is potentially a being', and so also with other propositions. Hence, Aristotle declares in the same place that 'being is divisible into potential and actual, as knowledge and rest are' ; but nothing is knowing or resting unless it is actually knowing or resting.

The distinction between existence and essence

2. Since we have touched upon 'existence' (*esse existere*), we shall make a digression for a while and consider how the existence of a thing is related to the thing, i.e. whether the existence of a thing and its essence are two entities extra-mentally distinct from each other. It appears to me that they are not two such entities, nor does 'existence' signify anything different from the thing itself. For if there were something distinct, then it would be either a substance or an accident. But it is not an accident, because in that case the existence of a man would be a quality or a quantity, which is manifestly false, as can

sicut inductive patet. Nec potest dici, quod sīt substantia : quia omnis substantia vel est materia vel forma vel compositum, vel substantia absolūta ; sed manifestum est, quod nullum istorum potest dici esse, si esse sit alia res ab entitate rei.

Item : Si essent duae res, aut facerent per se unum, aut non. Si sic, oporteret quod unum esset actus et reliquum potentia, et per consequens unum esset materia et aliud forma, quod est absurdum. Si non facerent per se unum, igitur essent unum aggregatione tantum vel facerent unum tantum per accidens, ex quo sequitur, quod unum est accidens alterius.

Item : Si essent duae res, non esset contradictio, quin Deus conservaret entitatem rei in rerum natura sine existentia, vel econverso existentiam sine entitate, quorum utrumque est impossibile.

Ideo dicendum est, quod entitas et existentia non sunt duae res. Sed ista duo vocabula 'res' et 'esse' idem et eadem significant, sed unum nominaliter et aliud verbaliter, propter quod unum non potest convenienter poni loco alterius, quia non habent eadem officia. Unde 'esse' potest poni inter duos terminos sic dicendo : Homo est animal. Non est sic de hoc nomine 'res' vel 'entitas'.

Unde 'esse' significat ipsam rem. Sed significat causam primam simplicem, quando dicitur de ea non significando ipsam ab alio dependere. Quando autem praedicatur de aliis, significat ipsas res dependentes et ordinatas ad causam primam. Et hoc, quia istae res non sunt res,

be shown by considering cases. Nor can it be a substance, because every substance is either matter or form, or a composition of matter and form, or a separated substance. But it is manifest that none of these can be called the existence of a thing, if existence is a thing distinct from the essence (*entitas*) of the thing itself.

Furthermore, if essence and existence were two things, then either they would constitute something that is intrinsically one, or they would not. If they did, then the one must be actuality and the other potentiality ; hence the one would be matter and the other form ; but that is absurd. If, however, they did not constitute something that is intrinsically one, then they would be one as an aggregate is one, i.e. they could constitute some one thing only incidentally. From this, however, it would follow that the one is an accident of the other.

Furthermore, if they were two things, then no contradiction would be involved if God preserved the essence of a thing in the world without its existence, or vice versa, its existence without its essence ; both of which are impossible.

We have to say, therefore, that essence (*entitas*) and existence (*existentia*) are not two things. On the contrary, the words 'thing' and 'to be' (*esse*) signify one and the same thing, but the one in the manner of a noun and the other in the manner of a verb. For that reason, the one cannot be suitably substituted for the other, because they do not have the same function. Hence the verb 'to be' can be put between two terms by saying 'Man is (*est*) an animal', but the same cannot be done with the noun 'thing' or 'essence' (*entitas*). Hence 'existence' (*esse*) signifies the thing itself. Now, it signifies the first simple cause, when it is predicated of this cause without signifying that it depends on something else. However, when it is predicated of other things, it signifies them in their dependence on, and subordination to, the first cause. And this is so, because these things are things

nisi sint sic dependentes et ordinatae ad causam primam, sicut non sunt aliter. Unde, quando homo non dependet ad Deum, sicut tunc non est, ita tunc non est homo.

Et ideo non est plus imaginandum, quod essentia est indifferens ad esse et non esse, quam quod est indifferens ad essentiam et non essentiam : quia sicut essentia potest esse et non esse, ita essentia potest esse essentia et potest non esse essentia. Et igitur talia argumenta : 'Essentia potest esse et non esse, igitur esse distinguitur ab essentia' ; 'Essentia potest esse sub opposito esse, igitur essentia differt ab esse', non valent. Sicut nec talia valent : 'Essentia potest non esse essentia, et potest esse essentia, igitur essentia differt ab essentia' ; 'Essentia potest esse sub opposito essentiae, igitur essentia differt ab essentia'. Et ideo non plus sunt essentia et esse duae res, quam essentia et essentia sunt duae res. Et ita esse non est alia res ab entitate rei.

Et haec est sententia Lincolniensis, quando dicit ii° *Posteriorum* * : ' "Esse" dictum de causa prima non praedicat nisi ipsam essentiam causae primae omnino simplicem ; "esse" dictum vero de aliis non praedicat nisi ordinem et dependentiam eorum ab ente primo, quod est per se. Et haec ordinatio vel dependentia nihil multiplicat in essentia dependente. Propter hoc, sive quaeratur de ente primo sive de re dependente ab ente primo, an sit, haec quaestio non ponit in numerum'.

Causa autem, quare sancti et alii dicunt Deum esse ipsum esse, est quia Deus sic est esse, quod non potest

---

* ed. Venet. 1494, fol. 21r

only in as much as they are dependent on and ordered towards the first cause, just as it is only thus that they exist. Hence, just as a man does not exist when he is not depending on God, so likewise he is not, in that case, a man.

Therefore there is no more reason to imagine that essence (*essentia*) is indifferent in regard to being (*esse*) and non-being, than that it is indifferent in regard to being an essence and not being an essence. For as an essence may exist and may not exist, so an essence may be an essence and may not be an essence. For this reason the following arguments are invalid : 'Essence may exist and may not exist, therefore existence is distinct from essence' ; 'Essence can come under the opposite of existence, therefore essence differs from existence'. Just as the following ones are not valid : 'Essence may be or may not be an essence, therefore essence differs from essence' ; 'Essence can come under the opposite of essence, therefore essence differs from essence'. Hence, there is no more reason for essence and existence to be two things, than for essence and essence to be two things. Therefore existence is not a thing different from the essence of a thing.

This is the teaching of the Lincolnian [Robert Grosseteste], when he says on the second book of the *Posterior Analytics* : 'When "it exists" is said of the first cause, what is predicated is just the absolutely simple essence of the first cause ; but when "it exists" is said of other things, what is predicated only is just their order and dependence on the first being, which exists of itself. And this ordering or dependence does not add anything to the dependent essence. For that reason, the question whether or not a thing exists does not figure among the demonstrative questions, whether it be raised about the first being or about a being dependent on the first being'.

The reason why the saints and others say that God is His very existence is this. God exists in such a manner

non esse, immo necesse est esse, nec ab aliquo alio est. Creatura autem sic est esse, quod non est necessario esse, sicut nec necessario est res ; et ab alio est, sicut ab alio est res effective. Et ideo non differunt in Deo 'quod est' et 'quo est', quia non est aliquid aliud a Deo quo Deus est. Sed in creatura differunt, quia illud quod est creatura et quo est creatura sunt distincta simpliciter, sicut Deus et creatura differunt.

that He cannot not exist ; in fact, He exists necessarily ;
and He is not from something else. A creature, on the
other hand, exists in such a manner that it does not
necessarily exist, just as it is not necessarily a thing ;
and it is from something else, just as it is a thing on
account of something else as its efficient cause. For that
reason, there is no distinction in God between 'that
which is' and 'that in virtue of which it is', because there
is not anything different from God in virtue of which
God is. But in a creature there is a distinction, because
that which a creature is and that in virtue of which
a creature is are simply distinct, just as God and a
creature are distinct.

VIII

THE POSSIBILITY OF A
NATURAL THEOLOGY

Sources :

1. *Utrum eadem veritas theologica specie vel numero possit probari in theologia et in scientia naturali ?*

Quod non : Quia eadem conclusio specie non potest sciri duplici scientia alterius rationis ; sed media alterius rationis in theologia et scientia naturali causant scientiam alterius rationis ; ergo necessario conclusiones erunt alterius rationis.

Contra : Nisi eadem veritas posset probari in scientia naturali et in theologia, philosophia non iuvaret theologiam.

Hic primo distinguo de 'scientia', secundo dico ad quaestionem.

Circa primum dico, quod 'naturalis scientia' accipitur dupliciter : Uno modo pro habitu, naturali sive theologico, unius conclusionis tantum, alio modo pro aggregato ex omnibus habitibus habentibus determinatum ordinem respectu unius conclusionis, sive illi habitus sint incomplexorum sive complexorum.

Circa secundum supponendo quod quaelibet veritas sit theologica, quae est necessaria ad salutem, dico tunc, quod eadem conclusio specie theologica non potest probari in theologia et scientia naturali primo modo acceptis, et hoc, quia quot sunt scientiae sic distinctae, tot sunt conclusiones scitae. Ideo sicut unius conclusionis non possunt esse diversae scientiae, quia pluralitas non est ponenda sine necessitate, ita eadem conclusio non potest probari in diversis scientiis. Sed accipiendo theologiam et scientiam naturalem secundo modo, sic potest non solum eadem conclusio specie sed etiam

[*On the knowability of God*]

1. *Whether a truth specifically and numerically the same can be proved in theology and in natural knowledge?*

No : For the same specific truth cannot be known by two different kinds of knowledge : but the specifically different middle terms in theology and natural knowledge cause specifically different knowledge ; hence the conclusion must necesarily have a different meaning.

On the contrary : Unless the same truth could be proved in natural knowledge and in theology, philosophy would be of no help to theology.

Answer : First, I distinguish the senses of the term 'knowledge' ; secondly, I answer the question.
Concerning the first point I say : 'Natural knowledge' is taken in two senses. In one sense, it means the possession of just one conclusion, whether this is a natural or a theological *habitus*. In the second sense, it means an aggregate formed of all those *habitūs* which have a definite order as regards one conclusion, whether they relate to non-complex or complex contents.
Concerning the second point, assuming that every truth necessary for salvation is theological, I maintain that the same specific theological conclusion cannot be proved in theology and in natural knowledge, if we understand 'knowledge' in the first sense. The reason is, because there are as many distinct cognitions as there are distinct conclusions known. Hence, just as there cannot be different acts of knowledge of one conclusion, since plurality must not be asserted without necessity, so also the same conclusion cannot be proved in different sciences. If, however, we understand 'theology' and 'knowledge' in the second sense, then a conclusion that is not only specifically the same but also numerically

numero probari in theologia et scientia naturali, si
existant in eodem intellectu, puta talis : 'Deus est
sapiens', 'Deus est bonus'.

Hoc probo : Quia hoc non est magis inconveniens
quam quod eadem conclusio specie et numero probetur
propter quid et *quia*. Hoc est possibile : Tum quia idem
effectus specie et numero potest causari a causis diversae
speciei ; et per consequens, licet media sint alterius
rationis hinc inde, tamen conclusio potest esse eiusdem
rationis. Tum quia ista propositio in mente : 'Nullum
ens infinitum est', contradicit primo huic propositioni in
mente : 'Aliquod infinitum est', quae probatur tam in
theologia quam in scientia naturali, et per consequens
est eiusdem rationis in utraque scientia.

Sed contra : Theologus intelligit per nomen 'Deus'
ens infinitum nobilius quibuscumque infinitis alterius
rationis ; si essent simul, non solum divisim sed coniunctim est nobilius omnibus. Tunc sic accipiendo
'Deum' hoc modo Deum esse non est naturaliter evidens ;
ergo sic accepto 'Deo' nihil probatur naturaliter et
evidenter de Deo. Consequentia patet. Antecedens
probatur : Quia non est naturaliter evidens, quod
aliquid sit infinitum nisi ex motu vel causalitate solum
probatur infinitum esse quod est melius quolibet infinitorum divisim et non coniunctim, ergo etc.

Praeterea : Aut probant istam conclusionem per
medium eiusdem rationis vel alterius. Si primo modo,

the same can be proved in theology and in natural knowledge, provided that both [sciences] exist in the same intellect. For instance, the conclusions 'God is wise', 'God is good'.

I prove this because there is no more reason against it than against holding that a specifically and numerically identical conclusion can be proved both in a demonstration *quia* [a proof of the fact] and in a demonstration *propter quid* [a proof giving the reason for the fact]. Yet the latter is possible : first, because a specifically and numerically identical effect can be caused by specifically different causes ; consequently, though in either case the middle terms are different in kind, nevertheless the conclusion may have the same meaning. Secondly, because the mental proposition 'No infinite being exists' contradicts immediately the mental proposition 'An infinite being exists', which is proved both in theology and in natural knowledge, and, therefore, has the same meaning in both.

It is objected : A theologian understands by the term 'God' an infinite being which is nobler than an infinity of beings of a different type ; if these were coexistent, it would be nobler than all of them, not only taken separately, but even taken together. Then the argument runs as follows : If we understand 'God' in this sense, then the existence of God is not naturally known. The inference is clearly valid. The antecedent is proved thus : It is not naturally evident that something infinite exists, except from motion or from causality ; but in this way it can only be proved that something infinite exists which is better than each one of an infinity of beings taken separately, not better than all taken together ; therefore, etc.

Furthermore, the middle terms by which they [theologian and philosopher] prove the conclusion either have the same meaning, or they have different meanings. If the first alternative is admitted, then the conclusion

tunc praecise conclusio et termini essent eiusdem rationis,
et sic non probaretur in diversis scientiis. Si secundo
modo, tunc medium proprium conclusionis specialis est
quaedam definitio vel descriptio data per praedicabilia
in quid ; illa descriptio est alterius rationis ibi in una
scientia et in alia, et per consequens cognitio simplex
causata per illam descriptionem erit alterius rationis, et
ita conclusio, cuius illa cognitio simplex est subiectum,
erit alterius rationis.

Ad primum istorum dico, quod nisi conclusio eiusdem
rationis posset probari in diversis scientiis, aliter theologus fidelis et philosophus paganus non possent sibi
contradicere de ista propositione : 'Deus est trinus et
unus', quia propositiones in voce non contradicunt, nisi
quia propositiones in mente contradicunt, eo quod sunt
signa subordinata. Sed propositio affirmativa et
negativa in mente non contradicunt primo nisi com-
ponantur ex conceptibus eiusdem rationis, licet possit
inferri contradictio ex propositionibus compositis ex
conceptibus alterius rationis aliquando. Aliter enim,
nisi istud esset verum, in terminis aequivocis posset fieri
contradictio ; sicut hic : Omnis canis currit, Aliquis
canis non currit, ubi sunt conceptus alterius rationis,
puta animalis latrabilis et caelestis sideris, quod patet
esse falsum, quia contradictio est oppositio rei et nominis,
non solum vocalis sed mentalis. Dico ergo, quod aliqua
conclusio eiusdem rationis probatur in diversis scientiis,
et aliqua non. Et istam propositionem particularem
teneo veram, licet non universalem.

Ad argumentum ergo dico, quod sicut illa conclusio,

and its terms would have precisely the same meaning [for both theologian and philosopher], and thus the conclusion would not be proved by different kinds of knowledge. On the second alternative, a proper middle term of a specific conclusion is a definition or description given in terms that are predicable as answers to the question 'What is it?' Such a description is different for different kinds of knowledge, and consequently the simple cognition caused by such a description will be different in kind ; therefore the conclusion of which the simple cognition is the subject will be different in meaning.

To the first objection I reply : If a conclusion of the same meaning could not be proved in different sciences, then a theologian who is a believer and a pagan philosopher could not contradict each other in regard to the proposition 'God is three and one', since propositions in words (being subordinate signs) are not contradictory unless the propositions in the mind are contradictory. But affirmative and negative propositions in the mind are not primarily contradictory unless they are composed of concepts of the same kind, though a contradiction can sometimes be inferred from propositions composed of concepts different in kind. Otherwise, if this were not true, a contradiction could happen with equivocal terms as in the case of 'Every dog is running, some dog is not running', where the concepts are different in kind, viz. one of a barking dog and one of a star in the sky. This is obviously false, since a contradiction is an opposition of thing and name (meaning by 'name' not only a vocal but a mental name). I maintain, therefore, that some conclusions of the same meaning are proved in different sciences and some conclusions are not. This particular proposition I hold as true ; not, however, the universal one [viz. that all conclusions can be proved by different kinds of knowledge].

To the argument I reply : Just as the conclusion in

in qua praedicatur 'esse trinum et unum' de quocumque
conceptu Dei non potest probari in diversis scientiis, sed
solum probatur in theologia praesupposita fide, ita illa
conclusio, in qua subiicitur conceptus Dei vel 'Deus'
secundum istam descriptionem, quod est aliquid melius
omnibus aliis a se, quodcumque praedicatum de eo praedicetur, non probatur in diversis scientiis, sed solum in
theologia.   Unde tales conclusiones : 'Deus est bonus',
'Deus est sapiens', etc., sic accepto Deo non possunt
probari in diversis scientiis.   Et ratio est, quia sic accipiendo Deum non est naturaliter evidens Deum esse,
sicut deducit ratio, ut patet in primo *Quodlibet*.*   Et per
consequens non est naturaliter evidens Deum sic acceptum esse bonum.   Sed ex hoc non sequitur, quin alia
conclusio, in qua 'bonum' vel 'sapiens' praedicatur de
conceptu Dei, ut per illum intelligimus, quod est aliquid
quo nihil est perfectius nec prius, quia sic potest demonstrari Deum esse, quia aliter esset processus in infinitum,
nisi esset aliquid in entibus, quo nihil est perfectius.   Vel
etiam potest demonstrari conclusio, in qua praedicatur
'bonum' de prima causa ; vel de quocumque alio conceptu, ad quem philosophus potuerit naturaliter devenire,
possit probari in theologia et in aliqua scientia naturali.

Unde ad formam argumenti concedo antecedens et
consequens, quia non est contra me.

Ad aliud dico, quod theologus et philosophus naturalis
probant eandem conclusionem specie per medium alterius rationis.

Et quando dicitur, quod medium proprium est definitio
vel quaedam descriptio subiecti, dico quod non semper
medium est quaedam definitio vel descriptio subiecti, sed
aliquando medium est definitio exprimens [partes]
integrales definiti, puta quando demonstratur habere

* *Quodlibeta*, i, Q.i

which 'being three and one' is predicated of any concept of God cannot be proved in different kinds of knowledge, but is proved only in theology under the supposition of faith, so also a conclusion in which the subject is God described as 'Something better than anything besides Him' (no matter what is predicated of God) cannot be proved in different sciences, but only in theology. Hence the conclusions 'God is good', 'God is wise', etc., cannot be proved in different kinds of knowledge, if 'God' is understood in the sense of the aforesaid description. The reason for this is that the existence of God, understood in this sense, is not naturally evident, as the argument infers ; this is shown in the first *Quodlibet*. And, therefore, it is not naturally evident that God, understood in this sense, is good. But from this it does not follow that we cannot prove another conclusion in which 'good' or 'wise' is predicated of a concept of God, if by 'God' we understand 'something to which nothing is superior in perfection or prior'. For the existence of God in this sense can be demonstrated ; because otherwise we should have to go on *in infinitum*, unless among existents there were one than which nothing is more perfect. Or again, the conclusion in which 'good' is predicated of 'the first cause', or of some other concept at which a philosopher could arrive by natural means, could be proved both in theology and by natural knowledge.

Hence, concerning the form of the argument I concede the antecedent and the consequent, since it is not against me.

To the other argument I reply that a theologian and a natural philosopher prove the same specific conclusion by middle terms different in meaning.

And when it is said that the proper middle term is a definition or a sort of description of the subject, I reply that this is not always the case. Sometimes the middle term is a definition that expresses the integral parts of

tres de triangulo ; aliquando medium est subiectum
primum passionis, sicut demonstratur esse susceptibile
disciplinae de homine per animam intellectivam ;
aliquando medium est conceptus communis ; et variis
modis potest esse aliquid medium. Et ultra, dato quod
medium semper sit descriptio subiecti, dico quod ista
descriptio erit alterius rationis in diversis scientiis.

Et quando ultra dicitur, quod descriptio alterius
rationis causat cognitionem simplicem alterius rationis,
illud multipliciter peccat : Tum quia definitio subiecti
numquam causat notitiam incomplexam subiecti, quia
illa praesupponitur omni definitioni et acquiritur mediante notitia intuitiva, licet definitio possit partialiter
causare cognitionem aliquam complexam per discursum,
qui discursus praesupponit notitiam incomplexam subiecti. Tum quia dato quod descriptio subiecti causaret
effective talem cognitionem simplicem subiecti, non
sequitur propter hoc, quod descriptiones alterius rationis
causent cognitiones incomplexas alterius rationis, quia
causae diversae rationis possunt habere aliquem effectum
eiusdem rationis ; patet de sole et igne respectu caloris,
similiter de cognitione et voluntate respectu amoris.
Tum quia talis cognitio simplex, si esset, non esset
subiectum in conclusione probanda per descriptionem,
sed esset medium, sicut ipsa descriptio est medium ;
nam secundum Philosophum iᵒ *Posteriorum* † de subiecto
dicitur praecognosci quid est et quia est, et per consequens
subiectum debet praehaberi ante demonstrationem. Et

---

* *Cf.* i. x (76ᵃ, 31 sqq.)

the thing defined, for instance when the property of having three angles is proved about a triangle. Sometimes the middle term is the first subject of a property, as for instance when the property of being receptive of education is demonstrated of man by means of the intellective soul. Sometimes the middle term is a common concept. And there are many ways in which something can be a middle term. In addition, even granted that the middle term is always the description of the subject, I nevertheless maintain that such a description will be of a different kind in different kinds of knowledge.

When it is said, furthermore, that a description different in meaning causes simple cognition of a different kind, the statement is in many ways faulty. First, because the definition of the subject never causes a non-complex cognition of the subject, since that knowledge is presupposed by every definition and is acquired by intuitive cognition ; though the definition might partially cause a complex cognition by means of reasoning—reasoning that presupposes non-complex cognition of the subject. Furthermore, even granted that the description of the subject were an efficient cause of such simple cognition of the subject, nevertheless because of this it does not follow that descriptions of different meanings cause non-complex cognitions of different kinds, since causes of different kinds can have an effect of the same kind. This is evident from the fact that heat can be caused by the sun and by fire, and likewise from the fact that both cognition and will cause love. Furthermore, if such a simple cognition existed it would not be the subject of the conclusion to be proved by a description, but it would be the middle term, just as the description itself is a middle term. For according to the Philosopher in the first book of the *Posterior Analytics* : 'Of the subject it is said that we have to know previously what it is and that it is' ; consequently, the subject must already be had before the demonstration. Hence,

ideo licet illa cognitio simplex, si esset possibilis, posset
esse subiectum in aliqua conclusione, tamen illa conclusio
numquam probaretur per illam descriptionem.

Ad argumentum principale concedo, quod eadem
conclusio non potest sciri duplici scientia alterius rationis,
sed nego minorem, scilicet quod media alterius rationis
in theologia et scientia naturali causant scientias alterius
rationis, et hoc accipiendo scientiam pro habitu conclusionis.

2. . . . . Deo et creaturae est aliquis conceptus unus communis praedicabilis de eis in quid et per se primo modo.

Circa quod ostendendum primo ostendam, quod Deus
non potest cognosci in se, ita quod ipsamet divina essentia
terminet immediate actum intelligendi nullo alio concurrente in ratione obiecti.

Secundo, quod non potest concipi a nobis pro statu
isto in aliquo conceptu simplici proprio sibi.

Tertio, quod potest concipi a nobis in aliquo conceptu
communi praedicabili de eo et aliis.

Quarto, quod aliquis talis, in quo potest concipi a
nobis, sit sibi quidditativus.

Et quinto ex his sequitur, quod aliquis conceptus unus
est praedicabilis de Deo et aliis in quid per se primo
modo.

Primum ostendo sic : Omnis intellectus cognoscens
aliquam naturam in se nullo alio concurrente in ratione
obiecti potest vere cognoscere illam rem esse in re vel
non includere contradictionem, immo non potest dubitare illud obiectum includere contradictionem ; sed
viator intelligens Deum notitia incomplexa, quantum est

though this simple cognition, if it were possible, could be the subject in some conclusion, nevertheless such a conclusion would never be proved by such a description.

Concerning the main argument, I concede that the same conclusion cannot be known in knowledge of two different kinds ; however, I deny the minor premise, viz. that the different meanings of the middle terms in theology and a natural science cause knowledge of different kinds, if we take 'knowledge' as possession of one conclusion.

[On the knowableness of God in a common concept]

2. There is a concept, common to God and creatures, which can be predicated of them in the manner of an essence and in the first mode of intrinsic (per se) predication.

In order to show this, I shall show :

first that God cannot be so known in Himself: that the divine essence itself is the immediate term of an act of understanding without the help of an accompanying thought-object.

secondly, that we cannot know God in this life in a concept that is simple and proper to Him ;

thirdly, that we can know God in a common concept that is predicable of Him and others ;

fourthly, that some such concept, in which we can conceive of God, is quidditative [answers the question 'What thing is this ?'] ; and,

fifthly, from this it follows that some one concept is predicable of God and others in the manner of an essence and in the first mode of intrinsic predication.

I prove the first thesis in the following manner : Every intellect that knows some nature in itself without the help of an accompanying thought-object can truly know that this thing exists in reality, or that it does not include a contradiction. Indeed, it cannot even suspect that this object includes a contradiction. But a man in this life

possibile viatori, potest dubitare, an includat contradictionem, quia potest dubitare, an includat contradictionem Deum esse, etiam posito quod firmiter credat,
quod nihil est impossibile esse, nisi includens contradictionem ; ergo talis non cognoscit Deum in se modo
exposito.   Maior videtur manifesta : quia hoc est
evidenter notum, quod numquam concipitur aliquid
includens contradictionem sine pluribus obiectis
conceptis ; ergo concipiens tantum unam rem sine
pluralitate obiectorum non potest dubitare illam rem
includere contradictionem.   Minor etiam est manifesta :
quia multi dubitant Deum esse, et utrum sit possibile
Deum esse.

Praeterea, omnis res cognita in se aut cognoscitur
intuitive aut abstractive ; ergo si essentia divina in se
cognoscitur, aut cognoscitur a nobis intuitive aut
abstractive.   Non intuitive, manifestum est, quia illa
est beatifica, quae ex puris naturalibus non est possibilis
nobis.   Nec abstractive, quia sicut declaratum est in
prologo,* nulla res potest cognosci abstractive in se a
nobis ex puris naturalibus, nisi ipsa praecognoscatur
intuitive.   Quia si cognoscatur abstractive, aut hoc erit
per notitiam intuitivam eiusdem, et habetur propositum,
aut per speciem rei, et hoc est inconveniens : Tum quia
talis species, ut post probabitur, non est ponenda.   Tum
quia in aliis patet, quod species non sufficit ad notitiam
abstractivam sine notitia intuitiva praevia.   Aut cognoscitur abstractive per notitiam intuitivam alicuius
alterius rei, et hoc est impossibile, quia sicut probatum
est in prologo,† nulla notitia incomplexa unius rei potest
esse causa sufficiens notitiae alterius rei.

* *Ordinatio*, prol., Q. ix E   † *loc. cit.*

who knows God by a non-complex cognition (in as far as this is possible for such a man) can still doubt whether the statement 'God exists' contains a contradiction. He can have such a doubt, even if we admit that he firmly believes that it is not impossible for anything to exist except what includes a contradiction. Therefore such a man does not know God in Himself in the manner before explained. The major premise seems to be manifest. For it is evident that nothing is ever conceived as including a contradiction unless several objects are conceived ; therefore he who conceives only one thing, and not several, cannot suspect that this thing includes a contradiction. The minor premise is also manifest, since many do doubt whether God exists, and whether it is possible that God exists.

Furthermore, everything known in itself is known either intuitively or abstractively. Therefore if the divine essence is known in itself, we know it either intuitively or abstractively. It is clear that it is not intuitively known ; for such cognition is beatific, which it is not possible for us to have by purely natural means. Nor is such a cognition abstractive ; because, as has been declared in the prologue [of the *Commentary on the Sentences*], we can know nothing abstractively in itself by purely natural means without first knowing it intuitively. For if it is abstractively known, it is known either by intuitive cognition of the same thing, and we have our intended thesis, or by the *species* of a thing. But the latter will not do. First, because such a *species*, as will be proved later, is not to be admitted ; secondly because, as is clear in other cases, a *species* is not sufficient to produce abstractive cognition without a previous intuitive cognition. Or, finally, it is known abstractively through intuitive cognition of another thing ; but this is impossible, for, as we have proved in the prologue, no non-complex cognition of one thing can be sufficient cause for the cognition of another thing.

Secundum ostendo : Quia nihil potest cognosci a
nobis ex puris naturalibus in conceptu simplici sibi proprio, nisi ipsum in se praecognoscatur.   Ista patet
inductive. Aliter enim posset dici, quod color posset
cognosci a caeco a nativitate in conceptu proprio coloribus, quia non est maior ratio, quod Deus cognoscatur
in conceptu sibi proprio sine praecognitione ipsius in se
quam color, sicut declarabitur distinctione sequenti. Sed
manifestum est, quod a tali non potest concipi color in
conceptu sibi proprio.   Ergo nec Deus.   Et ista ratio
aequaliter probat conclusionem priorem, ex qua sequitur
ista.

Tertium ostendo : Quia omne cognoscibile a nobis
aut cognoscitur in se aut in conceptu simplici sibi proprio
aut conceptu composito proprio aut in conceptu communi sibi et aliis ; sed Deus aliquo modo cognoscitur
a nobis, et non primis duobus modis, sicut declaratum
est, ergo tertio modo vel quarto modo.   Et si tertio,
oportet quod cognoscatur quarto modo, quia conceptus
compositus proprius, ex quo non potest componi ex
conceptibus simplicibus propriis, oportet quod com-
ponatur ex simplicibus et communibus.

Quartum ostendo per unam rationem, quam facit iste
Doctor Subtilis,* quae mihi concludit. Et arguo sic :
Si Deus concipitur in aliquo conceptu communi sibi et
aliis, quaero : aut ille conceptus est quidditativus aut
denominativus? Si quidditativus, habetur propositum.
Si denominativus, tunc quaero de illo : cui attribuis
istum conceptum denominativum ?   Aut est denominativus, et erit processus in infinitum, aut quidditativus,
et habetur propositum.   Verbi gratia, habeo istum conceptum, puta 'esse creativum', quem scio esse denomi-

_____

* *Opus Oxoniense*, I, DIST. III, Q.i, *n.* v

[1] For 'quidditative', 'denominative', see above, pp. xli and 59 sq.

I prove the second thesis : We can know nothing by purely natural means in a simple concept proper to it without first knowing it in itself. This is clear by considering cases. For otherwise it could be said that a man born blind can know colour in a concept proper to colour, since it is no more reasonable that God, than that colour, should be known in a proper concept without being first known in Himself or itself ; as will be explained in the following distinction. But it is manifest that colour cannot be known by such a man in a proper concept. Consequently neither can God. This reasoning establishes equally well the preceding conclusion, from which the present conclusion follows.

The third thesis is proved in this way : Everything knowable by us is known either in itself, or in a simple concept proper to it, or in a composite concept proper to it, or in a concept common to it and others. Now, God is known in some manner by us, but not in the two first modes, as has been explained. Therefore, God is known in the third or the fourth mode. But if God is known in the third mode, then He must be known in the fourth mode. For a proper composite concept must be composed of simple and common concepts, since it cannot be composed of simple and proper concepts.

The fourth point I show by a proof advanced by the Subtle Doctor [Duns Scotus], which is conclusive for me. I reason in the following way. If God is conceived in a concept common to Him and others, then I ask 'Is this concept quidditative or denominative ?'[1] If it is quidditative, I have the intended thesis. If it is denominative, then I ask about this concept 'Of what kind of concept do you make the denominative concept a predicate ?' Either this concept is in turn denominative, and then we shall have to go on *in infinitum* ; or it is quidditative, and then I have the intended thesis. For instance, I have, let us say, the concept 'creative', and I know that it is denominative ; hence I must have

nativum, et ideo oportet praehabere unum conceptum,
cui istum attribuo, puta dicendo, quod aliquod ens est
creativum ; et certum est, quod iste conceptus, cui iste
attribuitur, non est denominativus, vel, si sit, erit processus in infinitum, vel stabitur ad aliquem conceptum
quidditativum. Et tunc quaero de illo conceptu ultimo
quidditativo : aut est communis Deo et creaturae, et
habetur propositum, aut est proprius Deo, et hoc est
improbatum, aut est proprius creaturae, et hoc est
impossibile, quia tunc non posset supponere nisi pro
creatura ; et tunc haec esset falsa : 'Aliquod ens est
creativum'.

Ista ratio confirmatur : Quia omnis conceptus denominativus habet definitionem exprimentem quid
nominis, in qua ponitur aliquid in recto et aliquid in
obliquo. Tunc quaero de una parte illius definitionis :
aut habet definitionem consimilem exprimentem quid
nominis, aut non? Si non, habetur propositum, quod
talis necessario est quidditativus. Aut habet talem
definitionem quid nominis, et quaero tunc de partibus,
sicut prius : et ita vel erit procesus in infinitum, vel
stabitur ad aliquem conceptum quiddidativum praedi-
cabilem de illo, de quo primus conceptus denominativus
praedicabitur.

Ex isto sequitur, quod est aliquis conceptus unus praedicabilis in quid et per se primo modo de Deo et de
creatura. Ex quo sequitur ultra, quod vox correspondens
illi conceptui est simpliciter univoca.

Et ideo dico, quod sine omni compositione a parte rei
aliquid est univocum sibi et creaturae : quia sicut
univocum quibuscumque individuis cuiuscumque speciei
specialissimae non facit compositionem cum ipsis indi-

a previous concept of which I make this an attribute, saying, for instance, 'Some being is creative'. Now, it is certain that this concept of which the other is made an attribute is not denominative ; or, if it is denominative, either this will go on *in infinitum*, or we shall finally stop at some quidditative concept. Then I ask about this ultimate quidditative concept 'Is it common to God and creature ?' If so, then I have the intended thesis. Or is it proper to God ? But that is already disproved. Or is it proper to a creature ? That, however, is impossible, because in that case it could stand only for a creature, and therefore the proposition 'Some being is creative' would be false.

This proof is confirmed as follows : Every denominative concept has a definition expressing the meaning of the term, and in this definition something is put in the nominative case and something in another case. Now, I ask about one part of this definition [sc. the part in the nominative case] 'Does it have a definition like the former, expressing the meaning of the term, or not?' If not, then I have the intended thesis, viz. that such a concept is necessarily quidditative. If so, then it has a definition expressing the meaning of the term ; and then again I ask about its parts as before. Thus, either this will go in *in infinitum*, or we shall finally stop at some quidditative concept predicable of that of which the first denominative concept is predicated.

From this it follows that there is a concept which is one and is predicable of God and of creatures in answer to the question 'What thing is this ?' and in the first mode of intrinsic predication. And from this it follows, further, that the spoken word corresponding to this concept is simply univocal.

I maintain, therefore, that something is univocal to God and creatures without there being any composition in God Himself. For just as that which is univocal to any individuals of the same lowest species does not enter

viduis nec cum quibuscumque existentibus in individuis,
ita nec univocum Deo et creaturae facit aliquam compositionem in Deo. Et causa est, quia universaliter nihil
quod est a parte rei est univocum Deo et creaturae,
accipiendo 'univocum' stricte, quia nihil est in creatura
nec essentiale nec accidentale, quod habeat perfectam
similitudinem cum aliquo, quod realiter est in Deo. Et
istam univocationem sancti et auctores negant respectu
Dei et creaturae et nullam aliam.

3. . . . De analogia dico primo, quot modis accipitur
'univocum'. Ubi sciendum, quod uno modo accipitur
pro conceptu communi aliquibus habentibus perfectam
similitudinem in omnibus essentialibus sine omni dis-
similitudine, ita quod hoc sit verum tam in substantiali-
bus quam in accidentalibus, sic quod in forma accidentali
non est reperire quod est dissimile cuilibet formae in alia
forma accidentali eiusdem rationis. Exemplum : si
albedo in quarto gradu et in tribus gradibus non sunt
omnino similes, non tamen est reperire aliquid in una
albedine, quod est dissimile cuilibet in alia albedine. Et
sic accipiendo 'univocum' conceptus solus speciei specialissimae est univocus, quia in individuis eiusdem speciei
non est reperire aliquid alterius rationis in uno et alio.

Alio modo accipitur 'univocum' pro conceptu communi aliquibus, quae nec sunt omnino similia nec
omnino dissimilia, sed in aliquibus similia et in aliquibus
dissimilia, vel quantum ad intrinseca vel ad extrinseca.
Hoc modo homo et asinus conveniunt in conceptu
animalis sicut in conceptu univoco, et licet formae
specificae eorum sunt alterius rationis, tamen materia

into composition with the individuals themselves nor
with anything existing in the individuals, so that which
is univocal to God and creatures does not make for any
composition in God. The reason for this is that, generally speaking, nothing real is univocal to God and
creatures, if we take 'univocal' in its strict meaning;
for nothing that exists in a creature, whether it be
essential or accidental, has perfect similitude with something which really exists in God. It is this strict univocation and no other that the saints and [recognised]
authors deny is found between God and creatures.

[Univocity and analogy]

3. Concerning 'analogy' I first maintain that it is taken in
as many distinct ways as is 'univocity'. We have to
know here that 'univocal' denotes a concept common
to things which are perfectly alike in all essentials without any dissimilarity. This is true not only for concepts
of substances but also for concepts of accidents; for in
one accidental form nothing can be found dissimilar to
any form in another accidental form of the same kind.
For instance, though whiteness in the fourth degree and
in the first three degrees are not absolutely similar; still
nothing is to be found in one whiteness which is dissimilar to anything in the other whiteness. If 'univocal'
is understood in this sense, then only the concept of the
lowest species is univocal, since in individuals of the
same species there is nothing to be found which differs
in kind in the one and the other.

   In another sense, 'univocal' denotes a concept common
to things which are not absolutely similar and not
absolutely dissimilar, but in certain respects similar and
in certain others dissimilar, either intrinsically or extrin-
sically. In this manner, man and donkey agree in the
concept 'animal' as a univocal concept; though their
specific forms are different, yet the matter in both is

in eis est eiusdem rationis, et sic conveniunt in aliquo
essentiali et in aliquo differunt. Hoc modo etiam homo
et angelus conveniunt in conceptu substantiae sicut in
conceptu univoco, quia licet non conveniant in aliquo
intrinseco, tamen in aliquibus extrinsecis conveniunt,
quia habent aliqua accidentia eiusdem rationis, puta
intellectionem et volitionem. Hoc modo etiam nigredo
et albedo in conceptu coloris conveniunt, quia licet non
conveniant in aliquo intrinseco, quia quodlibet unius est
alterius rationis a quolibet alterius, tamen extrinsece
conveniunt, quia habent aliquod subiectum eiusdem
rationis. Et de isto univoco dicit Philosophus vii°
Physicorum,* quod in genere latent multae aequivo-
cationes, quia accipiendo 'aequivocationem', ut distinguitur contra similitudinem perfectam vel contra
univocationem aliquorum habentium similitudinem
perfectam, sic conceptus generis tam subalterni quam
generalissimi non est univocus sed potius in genere sic
est aequivocatio.

Tertio modo accipitur 'univocum' pro conceptu communi multis non habentibus aliquam similitudinem, nec
quantum ad substantialia nec quantum ad accidentalia.
Isto modo quilibet conceptus conveniens Deo et creaturae
est eis univocus, quia in Deo et creatura nihil penitus
nec intrinsecum nec extrinsecum est eiusdem rationis.

Primam univocationem et secundam negant Sancti
a Deo. Primam, quia nihil essentiale in Deo et creatura
est eiusdem rationis ; secundam, quia nihil accidentale
est eiusdem rationis in Deo et creatura. Sicut enim
essentia Dei est dissimilis essentiae creaturae, ita sapientia
Dei et bonitas sua. Ideo dicit Damascenus,† quod Deus

---

* cap. iv (249ᵃ, 18 sq.)
† *De fide orthodoxa*, i. iv (Migne *PG*, ᴛᴏᴍ. xciv, col. 799) ; *cf.*
cap. xii (col. 847)

of the same kind. Thus they agree in something essential, and in something else they differ. In this manner also man and angel agree in the concept of 'substance' as a univocal concept ; though they do not agree in something intrinsic, nevertheless they do agree in something extrinsic, because they have accidents of the same kind, viz. intellection and volition. In this manner also blackness and whiteness agree in the concept 'colour' ; though they do not agree in something intrinsic, because everything in the one is different from anything found in the other, nevertheless they agree in something extrinsic, because they have a subject of the same kind. It is of 'univocal' in this sense that the Philosopher says in the seventh book of the *Physics* : 'Many equivocations are implicit in a genus'. For if we understand 'equivocation' in contradistinction to perfect similitude or to univocation as between things which are perfectly similar, then neither the concept of the subordinate nor that of the highest genus is univocal ; but rather there is equivocation in the genus.

In a third sense 'univocal' denotes a concept common to many things which have no likeness, either substantial or accidental. In this manner, every concept which applies to God and to creatures is univocal to them ; for in God and in creatures there is nothing at all, intrinsic or extrinsic, which is of the same kind.

The first and the second univocation the saints deny of God, the first because nothing essential in God and in creatures comes under the same concept, the second because nothing accidental comes under the same concept in God and in creatures. Just as the essence of God is dissimilar to that of creatures, so likewise are the wisdom of God and the goodness of God. For this reason, Damascene says : 'God is not wise, but more-

non est sapiens sed supersapiens, nec bonus sed super-
bonus. Tertiam univocationem ponunt etiam Sancti et
tenentes univocationem et negantes eam, et etiam philosophi posuerunt talem in Deo. Accipiendo 'univocum'
secundo modo, sic in genere latent multae aequivoca-
tiones, quia illa quae solum conveniunt in conceptu
generis sunt multum dissimilia ; quia quantumcumque
aliqua habeant aliqua similia, sicut prius patet, tamen
omnia illa sunt multum dissimilia. . . .

Ad propositum dico, quod 'analogia' accipitur dupliciter. Uno modo pro conceptu univoco tertio modo
dicto, qui nec est pure aequivccus nec pure univocus,
quia est unus conceptus et non plures, nec pure univocus
univocatione perfectissima, puta primo modo dicta, nec
secundo modo. Ideo dicitur esse inter puram univocationem et aequivocationem.

Secundo modo accipitur 'analogia', quando sunt
quatuor, et duo praedicantur de duobus, et sunt imper-
tinentia nisi per conformitatem et proportionem. Et
talis analogia non excludit perfectam univocationem.
Exemplum, hic est analogia tali modo : 'Sicut se habet
homo ad animal, ita albedo ad colorem' ; modo illud
quod praedicatur in utraque propositione est univocum
secundo modo dictum. Similiter hic est talis analogia :
'Sicut se habet Sortes ad hominem, ita haec albedo ad
albedinem', ubi est perfecta univocatio.

Ad aliud de 'sano' dico, quod alio modo significat 'ens'
et dicitur de subiecto et accidente sub istis nominibus
vel conceptibus et alio modo de substantia, qualitate,
quantitate etc. Nam sicut 'sanum' significat principaliter
sanitatem in animali et significat dietam et urinam, ita

than-wise ; God is not good, but more-than-good'.
However, the third univocation is admitted even by the
saints, and both by those who hold univocation and
those who deny it. Even the philosophers admitted such
univocation in God. If we take 'univocal', however, in
the second sense, there is much dissimilarity between
things which agree only in a generic concept ; for, no
matter how much they may have something similar, as
was made clear before, still all of them are very dissimilar. . . .

Concerning our present problem, I say that 'analogy'
is taken in two senses. In one sense it is taken for a
univocal concept of the third kind, which is neither
purely equivocal nor purely univocal. For it is one
concept and not many ; but neither is it purely univocal
by having the most perfect univocation, viz. the first
type, nor by having the second type. For that reason,
it is said that it is midway between pure univocation
and equivocation.

In the second sense, we speak of 'analogy' when we
have four terms and two of them are predicated of the
other two, but they are related to each other only by
conformity and proportion. Such analogy does not
exclude perfect univocation. For instance, in the
following case we have such an analogy : 'As man is
related to animal, so is whiteness to colour'. Here that
which is predicated in each proposition is univocal in
the second way. Likewise in this case we have such
an analogy : 'As Socrates is related to man, so is this
whiteness to whiteness'. Here perfect univocation
obtains.

To an objection concerning the analogous use of the
term 'healthy', I say that when 'being' (*ens*) is applied
to 'subject' and 'accident' and we use these names or
concepts, it signifies and is predicated otherwise than
when it is applied to 'substance', 'quality', 'quantity',
etc. 'Healthy' primarily signifies the health of an

tamen quod semper connotat sanitatem animalis, ita
quod cibus dicitur sanus denominative, quia hoc nomen
vel conceptus, ut praedicatur de dieta, connotat aliquid
extrinsecum dietae, puta sanitatem animalis, similiter
dicitur de urina denominative propter eandem causam.
Unde dicitur de cibo, quia efficit sanitatem, de urina,
quia est signum sanitatis in animali. Tamen 'sanitas'
dicta de sanitate cuiuslibet animalis dicitur de eis in
quid et univoce non denominative, ita quod formaliter
'sanum' primo modo dictum est tantum vox una, sed
secundo modo est unus conceptus.

Eodem modo est de 'ente' : Quia haec vox uno modo
accepta significat substantiam principaliter mediante
aliquo conceptu proprio omnibus substantiis, et secundario significat omnia accidentia mediantibus pluribus
conceptibus. Et 'ens' sic dictum dicitur in quid de
omnibus substantiis, quia mediante uno conceptu, et
denominative de quolibet accidente, quia sic non dicitur
de accidente nisi connotando substantiam, cui attribuitur
tamquam dispositio eius et tamquam principale significatum illius. Sicut 'sanum' dicitur de sanitate in omni
animali univoce, quia significat omnem talem sanitatem
mediante uno conceptu ; et significat cibum et urinam
mediantibus pluribus conceptibus et secundario, tamen
semper connotando sanitatem in animali, ideo dicitur
denominative de cibo et urina. Et sic intelligit Philosophus iv⁰ *Metaphysicae* * ; et ita forte in lingua Graeca,

* cap. vii (1017ᵃ)

animal, and it also signifies a diet and urine, but in such
a way that it always connotes the health of an animal.
Thus food is called 'healthy' by denomination, because
this name or concept, as it is predicated of 'diet', connotes
something extrinsic to the diet, namely the health of an
animal. Likewise it is predicated of 'urine' denominatively for the same reason.

Hence food is said to be healthy, because it effects
health, and urine is said to be healthy, because it is an
indicator of health in an animal. Yet when 'health' is
affirmed of the health of any animal, it is affirmed of it
as an answer to the question 'What thing is this?' and
affirmed univocally, not by denomination. Therefore,
formally speaking, 'health' taken in the first manner [as
applied to 'animal', 'food' and 'urine'] is only one and
the same *word* ; taken in the second manner it is one and
the same *concept.*

It is the same with 'being' (*ens*). This word, taken
in one sense, primarily signifies a substance by means
of one concept proper to all substances, and secondarily
it signifies all accidents by means of several concepts.
'Being' thus predicated is affirmed of all substances as
an answer to the question 'What thing is this?' because
only one concept is involved ; but it is affirmed of every
accident denominatively, because when taken in this
manner 'being' is affirmed of an accident only because
it connotes the substance to which the accident is
attributed as its disposition and as that which is principally signified by 'accident'. In the same way,
'healthy' is affirmed univocally of the health of every
animal, since it signifies every such instance of health
by means of one concept ; and secondarily it signifies
food and urine by means of several concepts, but always
connotes at the same time the health of an animal ;
therefore, it is affirmed denominatively of food and urine.
This is what the Philosopher has in mind in the fourth
book of the *Metaphysics* [where he says that 'being' is

in qua loquebatur Philosophus ; sed sic non loquimur
de ente in proposito, sed de ente, quod omnem naturam
positivam substantialem et accidentalem significat aeque
primo et non prius substantiam quam accidens.

Pro univocatione nescio nisi tantum unam rationem,
in cuius virtute omnes aliae rationes tenent, et est ista :
Omnes concedunt quod aliquam notitiam incomplexam
habemus de Deo pro statu isto, et etiam de substantia
creata materiali et immateriali. Tunc quaero : Quando
intelligo Deum intellectione complexa, aut cognosco eum
in se aut in alio ? Non in se secundum omnes, quia nec
intuitive nec abstractive. Non intuitive, patet. Nec
abstractive, quia illa semper praesupponit intuitivam,
saltem in illa forma, in qua est abstractiva respectu
eiusdem rei, sicut alibi patet, igitur etc. Unde Deus in
se non plus cognoscitur a me abstractive pro statu isto
quam Papa quem numquam vidi, sed tantum eum
cognosco in conceptu hominis. Deus igitur in se non
intelligitur a me pro statu isto nec aliqua substantia.
Si in alio, tunc aut in aliquo conceptu communi sibi et
aliis, aut in alio reali. Si in aliquo reali, aut illud distinguitur a Deo secundum rationem tantum, aut realiter.
Non primo modo, quia probatum est in primo, quod res
non potest distingui a re ratione, nec distinguitur realiter,
quia tunc cum intelligo Deum, aliqua res singularis creata
terminat intellectionem meam, et tunc non plus cognosco Deum quam quamcumque aliam rem, de qua

not predicated univocally or equivocally or denominatively, but in a manner between them, viz. analogously],
and so it was perhaps in the Greek language, which the
Philosopher used. However, in the present investigation
we are not speaking about 'being' in this way. We only
speak of that 'being' which primarily signifies every
positive nature equally, be it substantial or accidental,
and which does not signify substance as prior to accident.

In favour of univocation I know of only one argument
on which all the others depend ; and it is this : All
agree that we have some non-complex knowledge about
God in this life, and also about created material and
immaterial substance. Then I ask 'When I think of
God by understanding a proposition (*complexum*), do I
know Him in Himself or in something different ?' I do
not know him in Himself, as all concede, since I know
Him in Himself neither intuitively nor abstractively.
Not intuitively, as it is manifest. Nor abstractively, since
abstractive cognition always presupposes intuitive cognition, at least where it is an abstractive cognition of the
same thing, as it is shown elsewhere ; therefore, etc.
Hence I no more know God in Himself abstractively in
this life than I know in himself the Pope, whom I have
never seen, and whom I know only in the concept of
'man'. Hence I do not know God in Himself in this life,
nor any substance [in itself]. If He is known in something different from Him, then He is known either in
a concept common to Him and others, or in something
real which is different from Him. If in something real
different from Him, this is distinct from God either only
in thought or in reality. It is not distinct only in
thought, since we proved in the first book that a thing
cannot be distinct from a thing by a distinction of
thought ; nor is it really distinct, for, on that supposition,
when I think of God, some singular created thing is the
term of my act of intellect, and then I do not know God
more than any other thing about which I do not think,

nihil cogito, quia cognosco tantum illam rem singularem,
quae terminat cognitionem meam. Igitur oportet necessario ponere, quod intelligendo Deum pro statu isto
cognoscam eum in conceptu communi sibi et aliis, ita
quod illud quod terminat actum intelligendi est aliquid
unum sine multitudine, et illud est commune ad multa.

Item, ex notitia incomplexa unius rei in se non potest
causari notitia incomplexa alterius rei in se, sicut in
prologo primi * dictum est. Unde quantumcumque
videas essentiam divinam clare, numquam per hoc
videbis asinum in se, ita quod una notitia causetur ex
alia. Igitur, si notitia incomplexa creaturae ducit in
notitiam incomplexam Dei, hoc erit in conceptu communi creaturae et Deo. Et hoc modo concedo, quod
notitia incomplexa alicuius creaturae in se ducit in
notitiam alterius incomplexam in conceptu communi.
Sicut per notitiam incomplexam albedinis, quam vidi,
ducor in notitiam alterius albedinis, quam numquam
vidi, per hoc quod a prima albedine abstraho conceptum
albedinis, qui indifferenter respicit unam albedinem et
aliam. Eodem modo ex aliquo accidente, quod vidi,
abstraho conceptum entis, qui non plus respicit illud
accidens quam substantiam, nec plus creaturam quam
Deum. Et ideo in illo conceptu non est aliqua prioritas,
quamvis una res in se sit prior altera ; sicut nec in conceptu hominis est Plato prior Sorte, licet Sortes in re
sit prior.

In virtute rationis praedictae tenet ratio prima
Ioannis † de conceptu dubio et certo, aliter non. . . .

Eodem modo tenet aliud argumentum Ioannis:‡
Nullum obiectum ducit in notitiam alterius obiecti, nisi

---

* *Ordinatio,* prol., Q. ix E
† *Opus Oxoniense,* I, DIST. III, Q. i et ii, *n.* vi
‡ *loc. cit., n.* viii et ix

since I know only that singular thing which is the term
of my cognition. Hence it must necessarily be stated
that when I know God in this life, I know Him in a concept which is common to Him and to other things, so
that the term of the act of knowing is some one thing
and not a plurality, and is common to many things.

Furthermore, the non-complex cognition of one thing
in itself cannot cause non-complex cognition of another
thing in itself, as has been said in the prologue of the
first book. Hence no matter how clearly you may see
the divine essence, you will never on this account see
a donkey in itself, in such a way that one cognition is
caused by the other. Therefore if non-complex cognition
of a creature leads to the non-complex cognition of God,
it can only be in a concept common to creatures and
God. In this manner I concede that non-complex
cognition of some creature in itself leads to the non-
complex cognition of another in a common concept.
For instance, through non-complex cognition of a whiteness that I have seen I am led to the cognition of another
whiteness which I have never seen, since I abstract from
the former whiteness a concept of whiteness which indifferently refers to the one or the other whiteness. In
like manner, from an accident that I have seen I abstract
the concept of a being (ens), which does not refer more
to this accident than to substance, nor more to a creature
than to God. Therefore in this concept there is no
priority, though one thing in itself is prior to the other ;
just as in the concept of 'man', Plato is not prior to
Socrates, though Socrates in reality may be prior.

The first proof of John [i.e. Duns Scotus, for uni-
vocation] concerning a dubious and a certain concept
holds in virtue of this argument, otherwise not. . . .

In the same manner the other argument of John holds :
'No object leads to the cognition of another object, unless
it be virtually or essentially contained in it' ; for the

contineat illud virtualiter vel essentialiter, quia notitia
illius accidentis in se continet virtualiter notitiam incomplexam Dei in conceptu communi sibi et aliis.

Eodem modo tenet alia ratio * de remotione imper-
fectionis a sapientia creaturae et attribuendo sibi quod
est perfectionis. Hoc non est nisi abstrahere a sapientia
creata conceptum sapientiae, quae nullam rem creatam
vel increatam dicit, quia quaelibet res creata dicit
imperfectionem. Et ideo abstrahere imperfectionem a
sapientia creaturae non est nisi abstrahere conceptum
sapientiae a creatura imperfecta, qui non plus respicit
creaturam quam non creaturam, et tunc illud quod
resultat attribuendum est Deo per praedicationem. Et
illud dicitur perfectionis, quatenus potest praedicari de
Deo et supponere pro eo. Nisi enim posset talis abstrahi
a creatura, modo non plus per sapientiam creaturae
deveniretur in cognitionem sapientiae divinae, puta quod
Deus sit sapientia, quam per cognitionem lapidis deve-
nitur ad cognitionem quod Deus sit lapis, quia sicut
sapientia creaturae continetur virtualiter in Deo, ita et
lapis. Unde non obstante quod tanta sit distinctio inter
sapientiam creaturae et sapientiam Dei sicut inter Deum
et lapidem nec sunt plus eiusdem rationis ex parte una
quam alia, tamen a sapientia creaturae potest abstrahi
conceptus communis, a lapide non.

Isto modo intelligitur quod dicitur, quod 'ens' est
subiectum metaphysicae, non tantum in voce sed in
conceptu : Quia quaero, pro quo supponit 'ens' quando
dicitur quod 'ens' est subiectum metaphysicae. Non
pro substantia nec pro accidente, quia utraque istarum

* *loc. cit., n.* x

cognition of this accident virtually contains in it the
non-complex cognition of God in a concept common
to Him and others.

In the same manner the other argument holds, about
removing imperfection from the wisdom of a creature
and attributing to it what belongs to perfection. This
just means abstracting from created wisdom a concept
of wisdom which does not mention either a created or
an uncreated thing, since mention of a created thing
brings in imperfection. For that reason, to abstract from
the imperfection in the wisdom of a creature is nothing
else than to abstract from an imperfect creature a concept of wisdom which does not refer more to creatures
than to what is not a creature, and then the result is
attributable to God by way of predication. And what
is thus abstracted is said to belong to perfection in so far
as it can be predicated of God and can stand for Him.
For if such a concept could not be abstracted from a
creature, then in this life we could not arrive at a cognition of God's wisdom—e.g. that God is wisdom—
through the wisdom of a creature any more than, through
the cognition of a stone, we obtain a cognition that God
is a stone. For just as the wisdom of a creature is contained virtually in God, so also a stone is contained
virtually. Therefore, notwithstanding the fact that the
distinction between the wisdom of a creature and the
wisdom of God is as great as the distinction between God
and a stone, and though in neither case do we have things
of the same kind, nevertheless from created wisdom we
can get by abstraction a concept common [to God and
creature], but not from a stone.

When 'being' (*ens*) is said to be the subject of metaphysics, it is to be understood in this way. And this
holds not only in regard to the word 'being', but also
in regard to the concept 'being'. For, I ask, what does
'being' stand for when it is said that 'being' is the subject
of metaphysics ? Not for a substance nor for an accident,

est falsa : 'Substantia est subiectum metaphysicae', 'Accidens est subiectum metaphysicae', etc. Igitur tantum supponit pro se, puta pro conceptu entis, et ille conceptus est subiectum metaphysicae. Similiter intelligitur, quando dicitur quod 'ens' dividitur in creatum et in increatum; 'ens' supponit tantum pro conceptu in mente non pro substantia nec accidente.

because each one of these propositions is false : 'A substance is the subject of metaphysics', 'An accident is the
subject of metaphysics', etc.   Therefore it stands only
for itself, namely for the concept 'being' ; and this
concept is the subject of metaphysics.   Likewise, this is
the meaning when 'being' is said to be divided into
created and uncreated being.   ' Being' stands only for
the concept in the mind, not for substance or accident.

IX

THE PROOF OF GOD'S EXISTENCE

Sources :

1. *Utrum in causis essentialiter ordinatis secunda dependeat a prima?*

Quod sic : Quia in talibus causis secunda causa non potest aliquem effectum suae speciei causare sine causa prima, sed econverso potest. Patet enim, quod Sortes non potest generare hominem sine sole, et sol producere potest hominem sine Sorte, quia mediante Platone, igitur etc.

Contra : Si homo crearetur a Deo solo, tunc non dependeret a sole, et tamen esset causa secunda respectu solis in generatione hominis.

Ad istam quaestionem dico, quod differentia est inter causas essentialiter ordinatas et accidentaliter ordinatas, et causas particulares concurrentes ad producendum eundem effectum numero ; nam in causis essentialiter ordinatis secunda causa dependet a prima quantum ad primum esse et non quantum ad conservationem ; sicut Sortes dependet a Platone quia non potest naturaliter causari sine Platone, cum sit pater eius, sed non conservatur per Platonem, eo quod Sortes vivit mortuo Platone. In causis autem partialibus respectu eiusdem effectus non est aliquis ordo, nec una plus dependet ab alia quam econverso. Verbi gratia, obiectum et intellectus sunt causae partiales respectu actus intelligendi et neuter dependet ex alio nec quantum ad esse nec quantum ad conservationem. . . .

2. *Utrum in causis essentialiter ordinatis causa superior sit perfectior?*

Quod sic : Quia illae causae differunt specie, igitur una est perfectior alia ; sed non inferior, igitur superior.

[The proof of the existence of God]

1. *Whether in essentially ordered causes the second cause depends on the first?*

   Yes : For in causes of this kind the second cause cannot cause an effect of the same kind as itself without the first cause, though the reverse is possible. For it is clear that Socrates cannot generate a man without the sun, but the sun can produce a man without Socrates, because it can do so by means of Plato ; therefore, etc.

   On the contrary : If a man were created by God alone, then this man would not depend on the sun, and nevertheless in reference to the sun he would be a second cause in the generation of a man.

   To this question I answer : There is a difference between essentially ordered causes and accidentally ordered causes, and partial causes concurring in the production of numerically the same effect. For in essentially ordered causes the second cause depends on the first for its first existence ; not, however, for its conservation. For instance, Socrates depends on Plato, since he cannot be naturally caused without Plato, his father ; but he is not conserved by Plato, because Socrates lives on when Plato is dead. However, in partial causes related to the same effect there is no order ; nor is one cause more dependent on the other than conversely. For instance, the object and the intellect are partial causes for the act of knowing, but neither one depends on the other, either for its existence or for its conservation. . . .

2. *Whether in essentially ordered causes the higher cause is more perfect?*

   Yes : For these causes differ in kind, therefore one is more perfect than the other ; but of these the lower is not more perfect, therefore the higher one must be.

Contra : Sol est causa superior respectu hominis, et tamen est imperfectior ; igitur etc.

. . . *Primo ponam* duas distinctiones, secundo dicam ad quaestionem.

Circa primum est prima distinctio ista : Quod quaedam est causa totalis et quaedam partialis. Secunda distinctio est, quod aliquid dicitur perfectius alio uno modo, quia est natura in se perfecta absolute, alio modo, quia sibi competit aliqua conditio vel praedicatio perfectior.

Circa secundum pono tres conclusiones. Prima est, quod causa totalis superior est perfectior causa inferiore. Hoc patet : Quia causa talis includit Deum, solem et omnes causas partiales illius effectus praeter causam posteriorem.

Secunda conclusio est, quod causa partialis superior non est universaliter perfectior causa secunda, et hoc loquendo de perfectione primo modo. Hoc patet : quia sol est causa superior partialis respectu generationis hominis, et tamen non est perfectior homine ; et tamen prima causa superior est perfectior. . . .

Tertia conclusio est quod causa superior est causa perfectior secundo modo loquendo de perfectione. Hoc patet : Nam causa secunda non potest in aliquem effectum suae speciei nisi concausante causa superiore illum effectum. Sed econverso bene potest, quia quamvis Sortes non potest producere naturaliter hominem sine sole, tamen sol potest naturaliter producere hominem sine Sorte, quia mediante Platone ; et per consequens causa superior independentius causat quam inferior. Sed independenter causare est perfectionis ; et per consequens perfectius causat causa superior quantum ad independentiam quam inferior. . . .

On the contrary : The sun is a higher cause [than man] as regards [the generation of] man, and nevertheless it is less perfect ; therefore, etc.

[*Answer* :] . . . First, I shall lay down two distinctions ; secondly I shall answer the question.

The first distinction is this : Some causes are total, others are partial. Second distinction : Something is said to be more perfect than another, in one sense because it is an absolutely perfect nature in itself, in another sense because a more perfect condition or predicate belongs to it.

To fulfil my second task I lay down three conclusions. The first is that the total higher cause is more perfect than an inferior cause. This is clear, for such a cause includes God, the sun and all partial causes of such and such an effect, except the posterior cause.

Second conclusion : A partial superior cause is not universally more perfect than a second cause if we take 'perfection' in the first sense. This is clear, for the sun is a superior partial cause in regard to the generation of a man ; nevertheless the sun is not more perfect than man. Yet the *first* superior cause is more perfect. . . .

Third conclusion : A superior cause is more perfect if we take 'perfection' in the second sense. This is clear, for the second cause is not capable of an effect of its own kind, if the superior cause does not cause the effect together with it. The reverse, however, is quite possible. For though Socrates cannot naturally produce a man without the sun, the sun, however, can produce a man without Socrates, because it can do it by means of Plato. Consequently the superior cause is more independent in its causality than the inferior cause. But independent causality is an aspect of perfection. Consequently, the causality of the superior cause is more perfect than that of the inferior, as regards independence.

3. *Utrum causae essentialiter ordinatae necessario simul requirantur*
   ad producendum effectum cuius sunt causae essentialiter ordinatae?

Quod sic : Quia repugnantia est, quod omnes illae sint
causae essentiales istius effectus, et tamen quod ille idem
effectus possit naturaliter produci aliā illarum circum-
scripta. Quia sequitur : Effectus potest naturaliter produci sine *A,* igitur non requiritur essentialiter ad eius
productionem, et per consequens non est sua causa
essentialis.

Contra : Sol producit vermem cum verme et sine verme.

In ista quaestione dicit Scotus, distinctione ii[a] primi
libri *, necessarium [est] quod una non potest agere
sine alia.

Sed hic sunt tres conclusiones contrariae.   Prima est,
quod effectus eiusdem speciei qui producitur simul ab
omnibus, potest aliquando produci ab una causa per se.
Hoc patet : Quia vermis generatus per propagationem
et putrefactionem sunt eiusdem speciei, manifestum est ;
et tamen vermis productus per propagationem producitur
ab omnibus causis essentialiter ordinatis simul ; vermis
autem productus per putrefactionem producitur a sole
sine actione vermis. . . .

Secunda conclusio est, quod aliquando perfectum
effectum potest causa universalis producere per se sicut
simul.   Hoc patet : quia licet effectus divisibilis sit
perfectior ab omnibus illis causis simul quam ab una
per se, sicut patet de calore causato ab igne et sole
simul, tamen quando effectus est indivisibilis, sicut est
forma substantialis, maxime in eadem parte materiae,
tunc potest esse ita perfectus ab una per se sicut ab
omnibus simul.

Tertia conclusio est, quod idem effectus numero, qui
causatur ab omnibus simul, non potest causari ab uno

* *Opus Oxoniense,* I, DIST. II, Q. i et ii, *n.* xii

3. *Whether the causality of essentially ordered causes must necessarily be simultaneous in order to produce the effect to which they are essentially ordered?*

Yes : For it is a contradiction that all should be essential causes of the same effect, and nevertheless the same effect could be naturally produced where some of them are excluded. For it follows that if an effect can be naturally produced without *A*, then *A* is not essentially required for its production, and consequently *A* is not its essential cause.

On the contrary : The sun can produce a worm both with and apart from a worm.

In reference to this problem, Duns Scotus maintains in the second distinction of the first book [of the *Sentences*] that it is necessary that one cannot act without the other.

But here are three contrary conclusions : The first is that an effect of the same kind which is produced by all causes together can sometimes be produced by one cause alone. This is clear. Worms generated by propagation and by putrefaction are of the same kind, as is manifest. Nevertheless, the worm produced by propagation is produced by all the essentially ordered causes together, whereas a worm produced by putrefaction is produced by the sun without the action of a worm.

Second conclusion : Sometimes a general cause can produce a perfect effect just as well alone as together with others. This is clear. Though a divisible effect produced by all causes together is more perfect than if it is produced by one cause alone—as is clearly true of heat caused by the sun and a fire together—nevertheless, when the effect is indivisible (like a substantial form, especially if the same bit of matter is concerned), then it can be just as perfect, when produced by one cause alone, as when caused by all together.

Third conclusion : Numerically the same effect as is caused by all agents together cannot be caused by one

solo. Hoc patet : quia sicut postea dicetur in materia
de motu, unus effectus numero determinat sibi certum
agens et certam materiam, ita quod ab alio agente non
potest ille effectus produci, et per consequens ille effectus
numero, qui producitur ab omnibus, non potest ab uno
solo produci ab illo ; modo necessario concurrunt ad
producendum effectum ; sed tamen effectus eiusdem
speciei potest produci aliquando ab uno solo, sicut patet
de verme. Et si sic intellexerit Scotus, verum dixit.
Tamen ipse dixit * contrarium ; nam secundum eum,
si Adam stetisset in statu innocentiae, illi qui nunc sunt
electi, tunc fuissent electi, sed habuissent alios patres.
Ita, secundum eum, variatio agentis non variat effectum,
et per consequens secundum eum idem effectus numero
potest habere diversas causas aequivocas, ita quod sine
una illarum potest ille effectus idem numero produci. . . .

Ad argumentum principale concedo conclusionem
loquendo de eodem effectu numero, non autem de eodem
effectu specie.

Ad argumentum in oppositum dico, quod idem
effectus numero non producitur nec potest naturaliter
produci per putrefactionem et propagationem, nec potest
ille idem effectus numero, qui producitur per propagationem, produci naturaliter sine concursione causarum
suarum essentialiter ordinatarum, licet per potentiam
Dei posset aliter fieri.

4. *Utrum possit sufficienter probari primum efficiens per productionem distinctam a conservatione ?*

Quod sic : Quia aliquod ens est effectibile, non a se,
igitur ab alio ; de illo quaero sicut de primo, utrum sit
primum efficiens vel effectibile ; et non est processus
in infinitum, igitur etc.

---

      * *Opus Oxoniense,* II, DIST. XX, Q. ii, *n.* ii et iii

alone. This is clear ; for, as will be explained later when
we deal with motion, an effect numerically one demands
a definite agent and a definite matter, so that the effect
cannot be produced by another agent ; consequently
numerically that effect, which is produced by all agents
cannot be produced by one alone. Rather, they necessarily concur to the production of the effect. Nevertheless, an effect of the same kind can be sometimes produced
by one cause alone, as is clear in the case of the worm.
If Scotus did mean this, then he is right. However, he
said the contrary. For according to him the very same
persons would have been elect [for eternal life] who are
now elect, even if Adam had not sinned ; but they
would have had other fathers. According to him, therefore, the variation of an agent does not vary the effect,
and consequently, according to him, numerically the
same effect can have different equivocal causes, so that
apart from one of them numerically the same effect can
be produced. . . .

To the main argument, I concede the conclusion, if
it is taken to refer to numerically the same effect, but
not if it is taken to refer to specifically the same effect.

To the argument to the contrary I reply : Numerically
the same effect is not produced, and cannot be produced
naturally, by putrefaction and by propagation ; nor can
numerically the same effect which is produced by propagation be naturally produced without the concurrence
of its essentially ordered causes, though it can happen
otherwise by the power of God.

4. *Whether a first efficient cause can be sufficiently proved from
   production as opposed to conservation ?*

It can : For something is such as to be made, but not
made by itself ; therefore, by something different ;
concerning this other I ask as I did about the first : Is
it a first efficient cause or is it such as to be made ?
Now, we cannot go on *in infinitum*, therefore, etc.

Contra : In causis eiusdem rationis est processus, quod sic universitas causatorum primum.

Hic dicit Scotus, quod sic, distinctione ii ª, quaestione iª.* Quod probatur : Essentialiter ordinatorum est causa, igitur aliqua causa, quae non est aliquid illius universitatis, aliter enim idem esset causa sui.

Secundo sic : Universitas causatorum dependet, et a nullo illius universitatis ; aliter enim idem dependeret a se.

Tertio sic : Aliter infinitae causae essentialiter ordinatae essent simul in actu, quia causae essentialiter ordinatae omnes simul concurrunt ad causandum ; si igitur essent infinitae, sequitur etc.

Quarto sic : Prius est principio propinquius ; igitur, ubi nullum est principium, nihil est essentialiter prius.

Quinto : Quia causa superior est perfectior in causando ; igitur causa in infinitum superior est in infinitum perfectior ; tale autem non causat virtute alterius, igitur etc.

Sexto : Quia effectivum non dicit imperfectionem : igitur potest esse in aliquo sine imperfectione ; sed si in nullo est sine dependentia ad aliquid prius, in nullo est sine imperfectione ; igitur primum effectivum est possibile.

Septimo : † Quia aliter infinitas in accidentaliter ordinatis esset impossibilis, quia talis infinitas non potest esse simul sed successive tantum unum post alterum, ita quod causa secunda causatur a prima, non tamen

---

* _Opus Oxoniense,_ I, DIST. II, Q. i et ii, _n._ xiv
† _loc. cit., n._ xv

On the contrary : We can go on with causes of the same kind [*ad infinitum*] for in this case the totality of the things that are caused is what comes first.

Scotus answers this question in the affirmative in the first question of the second distinction. He proves it as follows.

Essentially ordered effects have a cause ; therefore there is some cause which does not belong to this totality, otherwise one and the same thing would be the cause of itself.

Secondly : The totality of the things that are caused is dependent, but not upon something which is part of this totality ; otherwise a thing would be dependent on itself.

Thirdly : Otherwise, an infinity of essentially ordered causes would be in existence at the same time, since all the essentially ordered causes concur for causation ; if, therefore, there were an infinity of causes, an absurdity follows, etc.

Fourthly : What is prior is what is nearer to the first principle ; therefore where there is no first principle, nothing is essentially prior.

Fifthly : A superior cause is more perfect in its way of causing ; therefore a cause infinitely superior is infinitely more perfect ; such a cause, however, does not cause in virtue of another ; therefore, etc.

In the sixth place : [Causal] efficiency does not imply imperfection ; hence it can occur in some being without imperfection ; but if it does not occur in any being without dependence on something prior, then it does not exist in any being without imperfection ; hence a first efficient [cause] is possible.

In the seventh place : Otherwise, an infinity of accidentally ordered causes would be impossible ; for such an infinity cannot exist simultaneously, but only successively, one thing after another, so that the second

dependet ab ea in causando ; quia filius generat patre
mortuo sicut vivo. Talis infinitas non potest esse nisi
ab aliqua natura infinite durante, a qua tota successio
dependet et quidlibet illius.

Octavo : Quia nulla deformitas perpetuatur nisi in
virtute alicuius permanentis, quod nihil est illius successionis, quia omnia successiva sunt eiusdem rationis ;
igitur est aliquid prius essentialiter, a quo quodlibet
illius successionis dependet (et hoc in alio ordine), quam
a causa proxima, quae est aliquid illius successionis. . . .

Sed istae rationes non concludunt sufficienter de productione distincta a conservatione specialiter. . . .

Ad primam rationem in contrarium concedo quod
universitas causatorum est causata ; sed innitens rationi
naturali negaret illam consequentiam, quia diceret, quod
unum causatum causatur ab alio, quod est pars multitudinis, et illud ab [alio] illius multitudinis, et sic in
infinitum, sicut est in accidentaliter ordinatis, secundum
Philosophum, quorum unum potest esse et causare cum
alio, puta unus homo causatur ab alio, et ille ab alio,
et sic in infinitum. Non potest probari contrarium per
productionem. Et tunc non sequitur ultra, quod idem
est causa sui, quia tota illa multitudo non causatur ab
aliqua una causa, sed unum causatur ab uno et aliud
ab alio illius multitudinis.

Ad secundum dico, quod per productionem non potest
sufficienter probari, quod tota universitas simul dependeat, sed solum per conservationem : quia qui non
poneret conservationem, diceret quod unum illius
universitatis solum dependet ab alio illius multitudinis,
et illud ab alio, et sic in infinitum quantum ad primam

cause is caused by the first cause, without, however, depending on the first cause in causing ; for a son generates in the same way whether his father be still living or dead. Such an infinity can have being only from some nature that endures to infinity, on which the whole succession and each part of it depends.

In the eighth place : No deformity is perpetuated except in virtue of something permanent which is not a part of this succession, because all successive things are of the same kind ; therefore, there is something essentially prior on which everything in this succession depends, and that in an order different from that of the proximate cause which is a part of this succession. . . .

However, these reasons are not sufficiently conclusive in regard to production as specifically distinct from conservation.

Concerning the first reason to the contrary, I concede that the totality of things that are caused is itself caused ; but someone basing himself only on natural reason would deny this reasoning, because he would say that one of the things that are caused is caused by another member of this multitude, and this again by another member of this multitude, and so on *ad infinitum*, just as is the case, according to the Philosopher, with accidentally ordered causes of which one can exist and be a cause along with another. For instance, one man is caused by another, and so *ad infinitum*. The opposite cannot be proved from production. In this case it does not follow further that one and the same thing is cause of itself, because this entire multitude is not caused by any one cause, but one member of this multitude is caused by one cause and another by another.

Concerning the second reason I say that as regards production it cannot be sufficiently proved that the entire group is dependent at the same time ; this can be proved only from conservation. For someone not assuming conservation would say that so far as original

productionem ; quo facto a nullo posset dependere nisi
a conservante, quod negatur in proposito. Et tunc non
sequitur ultra, sed intelligendo illud dependet a se, quia
tota multitudo non dependet ab aliquo uno, sed unum
ab alio et aliud ab alio.

Ad tertium dico, quod quamvis omne conservans
aliquid mediate vel immediate est cum conservato,
tamen non omne producens mediate vel immediate
est simul cum producto ; et ideo in producentibus
potest poni processus in infinitum, sunt in finitate actuali.
Unde prius patet, quod non omnes causae essentialiter
ordinatae simul concurrunt ad causandum, licet aliquando simul concurrant ad conservandum.

Ad quartum dico, quod per solam productionem non
potest probari, quod aliquid sit essentialiter prius, sed
tantum accidentaliter.

Ad quintum patet prius, quod non semper causa
superior est perfectior in se, sed frequenter est imperfectior.

Ad sextum dico, quod per productionem non potest
sufficienter probari, quod effectivum non dicit imperfectionem, quia per solam productionem non potest
probari, quin unum effectivum producitur ab alio, et
sic in infinitum.

Ad septimum dico, quod infinitas in accidentaliter
ordinatis potest salvari sine aliqua natura infinite durante
a qua tota successio dependet, quia non potest probari
sufficienter per productionem, quod unus homo non
possit produci ab alio sicut a causa totali, et tunc diceretur, quod unus homo totaliter dependeret ab alio, et ille

production is concerned one member of this totality is merely dependent on another member of this multitude, and this again on another, and so *ad infinitum* ; once produced it may not depend on anything else, except on a conserving cause, which is denied, however, in our case. In this case, then, the further conclusion does not follow, but the multitude depends on itself, in this sense that the multitude as a whole does not depend on some one thing, but it is only that one member depends on another and a second on a third, and so on.

To the third : Though everything which conserves either mediately or immediately coexists with the thing conserved, nevertheless not every thing which mediately or immediately produces a thing coexists with the thing produced. Therefore, in the order of productive beings we could go on *ad infinitum*, and in actuality they are finite [in number]. Hence, as before, it is clear that not all essentially ordered causes concur together in causing, though sometimes they do concur for conservation.

To the fourth : From production alone it can be proved only that something is accidentally prior, but not that something is essentially prior.

To the fifth : It is evident from what was said before that not every superior cause is more perfect, but frequently it is less perfect.

To the sixth : From production it cannot be sufficiently proved that [causal] efficiency does not imply imperfection ; for as regards mere production it cannot be proved that one efficient cause is not produced by another, and so *ad infinitum*.

To the seventh I reply : An infinity of accidentally ordered things can be kept in being without any nature enduring to infinity, on which the entire succession is dependent ; for it cannot be sufficiently proved as regards production, that one man cannot be produced by another as his total cause. In this case it would be said that one man is totally dependent on another man,

ab alio, et sic in infinitum, et non aliqua re in infinitum
durante ; nec potest probari oppositum per productionem, licet per conservationem potest.

Ad octavum potest dici eodem modo, quod ista
successio perpetuatur, quia unum totaliter dependeat ab
alio eiusdem rationis ; nec potest probari per productionem, vel totam, quod ille processus in infinitum non
esset possibilis, nisi esset aliquid unum permanens, a quo
tota illa infinitas dependet, quia quantum ad productionem sufficit, quod unus homo totaliter dependet ab
alio in genere causae efficientis, et ille ab alio, et sic
in infinitum. . . .

Ad argumentum principale dico, quod per primam
productionem non potest sufficienter probari, quin sit
processus in infinitum in causis efficientibus, quarum
una causatur successive ab alia ; sed ex hoc non sequitur
aliqua infinitas actualis, sicut patet ex dictis.

5. *Utrum possit sufficienter probari primum efficiens esse per
conservationem ?*

Quod non : Quia conservare est efficere ; sed per
efficientiam non potest probari primum efficiens ; igitur
nec per conservationem.

Contra : Omnes causae conservantes effectum concurrunt simul ad conservationem ; si igitur in causis
conservantibus sit processus in infinitum, infinita essent
simul actu ; hoc est impossibile, igitur etc.

In ista quaestione dico breviter quod sic. Quod probatur :
Quia quidquid realiter producitur ab aliquo, realiter vel
ab aliquo conservatur, quamdiu manet in esse reali—

and he again on another, and so on, *ad infinitum* ; but he would not be dependent on something with an infinite duration. The opposite cannot be proved from production, though it can be proved from conservation.

To the eighth we can reply in the same manner. This succession is perpetuated, because one member is totally dependent on another member of the same kind ; and it cannot be proved by production, not even by total production, that this process could not go on *ad infinitum* unless there were some one permanent thing on which the whole infinity depends. For in so far as production is concerned, it is sufficient that one man is totally dependent on another in the line of efficient causes, and this man again on another and so on, *ad infinitum*.

To the main argument I reply : From the first production it cannot be sufficiently proved that we do not go on *ad infinitum* in efficient causes of which one is successively caused by the other ; but from this it does not follow that any actual infinity exists, as is clear from the aforesaid.

5. *Whether from conservation it can be sufficiently proved that there is a first efficient cause ?*

No : For to conserve is to effect ; but a first efficient cause cannot be proved from efficiency, consequently neither can it be proved from conservation.

On the contrary : All the conserving causes simultaneously concur for the conservation of an effect ; if, therefore, in the order of conserving causes we go on *ad infinitum*, then an infinite number of things would be actually existing at the same time. This, however, is impossible, therefore, etc.

This question I answer briefly in the affirmative. Proof : Whatever is really produced by something, is also really conserved by something as long as it remains in actual

manifestum est ; sed ille effectus producitur—certum
est ; igitur ab aliquo conservatur, quamdiu manet. De
illo conservante quaero : aut potest produci ab aliquo,
aut non ? Si non, est efficiens primum, sicut est conservans
primum, quia omne conservans est efficiens. Si autem
istud conservans producitur ab aliquo, de illo alio quaero
sicut prius : Et ita vel oportet procedere in infinitum,
vel oportet stare ad aliquid quod est conservans et nullo
modo conservatum, et tale efficiens est primum efficiens.
Sed non est processus in infinitum in conservantibus,
quia tunc aliqua infinita essent in actu, quod est impossibile ; nam omne conservans aliud, sive mediate
sive immediate, est simul cum conservato, et ideo omne
conservatum requirit actualiter omne conservans. Non
autem omne productum requirit omne producens
actualiter mediate vel immediate ; et ideo, quamvis
posset poni processus in infinitum in productionibus sine
infinitate actuali, non potest tamen poni processus in
infinitum in conservantibus sine infinitate actuali.

Sed contra : Videtur quod ratio ista sit evidens de
prima productione sicut de conservatione. Arguitur sic :
Aliquid est productum. Quaero : De quo producente ?
Aut est producens non productum, et habetur propositum ; aut est productum ab alio, et non tamen in infinitum ; igitur est status ad aliquod producens nec productum. Assumptum probatur in essentialiter ordinatis :
Tum quia in essentialiter ordinatis omnes causae simul
requiruntur ad productionem effectus ; si igitur essent

being—this is manifest. But this particular effect is produced—this is certain. Therefore it is being conserved by something as long as it remains in existence. About this conserving being I ask : Can it be produced by something else, or not ? If not, then it is the first productive cause, because every preservative cause is a productive cause. If, however, this preservative cause is produced by something else, then about that I ask as before. And so either this must go on *ad infinitum*, or we must stop at some being which conserves without being conserved by another in any way. And such an efficient cause is the first efficient cause. But we cannot go on *ad infinitum* in the order of preservative causes ; for everything that conserves something else, be it mediately or immediately, exists at the same time with that which is conserved. For that reason, every conserved being requires the actuality of everything that conserves it. But not every thing that is produced requires in actuality every thing that mediately or immediately produces it. Hence, though it is possible to admit that we go on *ad infinitum* in the order of productive causes without an actual infinity, nevertheless going on *ad infinitum* cannot be admitted in the order of conservation without an actual infinity.

But the following objection is raised. It seems that this proof is as evident about the first production as it is about conservation. The argument can be formulated as follows. Something is produced. I now ask : 'From what productive cause ?' Either it is something that produces and is not produced, and then we have the intended thesis, or it is produced by something else ; but this cannot go on *ad infinitum* ; therefore we must stop at something that produces and is not produced. Proof of the minor premise concerning things essentially ordered : In essentially ordered causes all causes are required at the same time for the production of the effect ; if, therefore, they were infinite in number, an

infinitae, infinita essent actu. Tum quia tota multitudo
causatorum essentialiter est causata, et non ab aliquo
illius multitudinis, quia tunc idem causaret se ; igitur
causatur ab aliquo non causato, quod est extra multitudinem causatorum.

Similiter, in accidentaliter ordinatis patet quod tota
multitudo causatorum actualiter est causata, et non
ab aliquo illius multitudinis, quia sic causaret seipsum
causando totam multitudinem ; igitur causatur ab
aliquo extra illam multitudinem ; et tunc, aut est idem
non causatum, et sic habetur propositum ; aut causatur
a causis essentialiter ordinatis, et tunc stat prima pars
istius argumenti.

Respondeo, quod per solam primam productionem
non potest sufficienter probari, quod non sit processus
in infinitum, saltem in causis accidentaliter ordinatis nec
formaliter in essentialiter ordinatis. Et ad primam pro-
bationem pro essentialiter ordinatis dico, sicut prius
patet, quod non omnes causae essentialiter ordinatae
concurrunt ad primam productionem effectus.

Ad utrumque sequens dico, quod tota multitudo tam
essentialiter ordinata quam accidentaliter est causata,
sed non ab aliquo uno, quod est pars illius multitudinis,
vel quod est extra illam multitudinem, sed unum causatur
ab uno, quod est pars multitudinis et aliud ab alio, et
sic in infinitum. Nec per primam productionem potest
sufficienter oppositum probari. Et tunc nec sequitur,
quod idem causat totam multitudinem, nec quod idem
causat se, quia nihil unum est causa omnium.

Ad argumentum principale dico, quod per efficientiam
secundum quod dicit rem immediate accipere esse post
non esse, non potest probari primum efficiens esse, sed
per efficientiam secundum quod dicit rem continuari in

infinity of things would be actually existing. First, because the whole multitude of essentially caused things is caused, but not by some member of this multitude, since in that case, something would be cause of itself. Therefore it is caused by something which is not caused and which is outside the multitude of things that are caused. Likewise, in accidentally ordered things the entire multitude of caused things is caused, as is clear ; but not by something in this multitude, because then this would cause itself in causing the whole multitude. If this is the case, then either it is not caused, and, there-fore, we have our intended thesis, or it is caused by essentially ordered causes, and then our first proof con-cerning essentially ordered causes applies.

I answer : From original production alone it cannot be sufficiently proved that we do not go on *ad infinitum*, at least in accidentally ordered causes, or, formally speaking, in essentially ordered causes.

To the first proof for essentially ordered causes I say, as was made clear before, that not all essentially ordered causes concur for the first production of the effect.

To both arguments that follow I reply that the whole multitude of both essentially and accidentally ordered causes is caused, but not by some one thing which is part of this multitude, or which is outside this multitude, but one part is caused by one thing which is part of this multitude, and another by another thing, and so on *ad infinitum.* Nor can the opposite be sufficiently proved from original production. And in this case it does not follow that one and the same thing causes the whole multitude, nor that one and the same thing causes itself, because no one member is the cause of all.

To the main argument I reply that from efficiency, in so far as it means that a thing receives existence immediately after non-existence, it cannot be proved that a first efficient being exists. Nevertheless, from efficiency, in so far as it means that a thing continues

esse bene potest probari, hoc est per conservationem. Sic patet ad illam quaestionem.

6. *Utrum possit probari per rationem naturalem quod tantum unus sit Deus?*

Quod sic : Quia unius mundi est tantum unus princeps, xii⁰ *Metaphysicae* * ; sed potest probari naturali ratione, quod tantum est unus mundus, secundum Aristotelem i⁰ *De caelo* † ; ergo naturali ratione potest probari, quod tantum unus est princeps ; sed ille est Deus ; ergo etc.

In oppositum : Articulus fidei non potest evidenter probari ; sed quod tantum est unus Deus est articulus fidei ; ergo etc.

In ista quaestione primo exponam, quid intelligendum est per hoc nomen 'Deus', secundo respondebo ad quaestionem.

Circa primum dico, quod hoc nomen 'Deus' potest habere diversas descriptiones. Una est, quod Deus est aliquid nobilius et melius omni alio a se. Alia descriptio est, quod Deus est illud quo nihil est melius et perfectius.

Circa secundum dico, quod accipiendo 'Deum' secundum primam descriptionem non potest demonstrative probari, quod tantum est unus Deus. Cuius ratio est, quia non potest evidenter sciri, quod Deus est, sic accipiendo Deum ; ergo non potest evidenter sciri, quod est tantum unus Deus. Consequentia plana est. Antecedens probatur : Quia haec propositio : 'Deus est', non est per se nota, quia multi dubitant de ea ; nec potest probari ex per se notis, quia in omni ratione accipietur aliquod dubium vel creditum ; nec etiam nota per experientiam, [ut] manifestum est.

Secundo dico, quod si posset evidenter probari, quod

* cap. viii (1074ᵃ, 32 sqq.)   † cap. viii (276ᵃ, 19 sqq.)

in existence, it can well be proved.   That is to say, it
can be proved from conservation.   Thus the answer
to this question is clear.

6. *Can it be proved by natural reason that there is only one God?*

It can be proved : For one world has only one ruler, as
is stated in the 12th book of the *Metaphysics* ; but it can
be proved by natural reason that there is only one
world, according to Aristotle in the first book of the
De Caelo ; therefore by natural reason it can be proved
that there is only one ruler ; but this ruler of the world
is God, therefore, etc.

To the contrary : An article of faith cannot be evidently
proved ; but that there is only one God is an article of
faith ; therefore, etc.

As regards this question, I shall first explain what is meant
by the name 'God' ; secondly I shall answer the question.

Concerning the first point I say that the name 'God'
can have various descriptions.   One of them is : 'God
is some thing more noble and more perfect than anything else besides Him'.   Another is : 'God is that than
which nothing is more noble and more perfect'.

Concerning the second point, I maintain that if we
understand 'God' according to the first description, then
it cannot be demonstratively proved that there is only
one God.   The reason for this is that it cannot be evidently known that God, understood in this sense, exists.
Therefore it cannot be evidently known that there is
only one God.   The inference is plain.   The antecedent
is proved in this way.   The proposition 'God exists' is not
known by itself, since many doubt it ; nor can it be
proved from propositions known by themselves, since
in every argument something doubtful or derived from
faith will be assumed ; nor is it known by experience,
as is manifest.

Secondly I maintain : If it could be evidently proved

Deus est, sic accipiendo D̄eum esse, quod unitas Dei tunc
posset evidenter probari. Cuius ratio est, quia si essent
duo Dii, *A* et *B*, per illam descriptionem *A* esset perfectior omni alio a se, et ita esset perfectior *B* et *B̄* imperfectior *A*. Etiam *B* perfectior esset *A*, quia est Deus
per positum. Et per consequens *B* esset perfectior et
imperfectior *A*, et *A* quam *B*, quod est manifesta contradictio. Ergo si posset evidenter probari, quod Deus
est, sic accipiendo 'Deum', posset evidenter probari
unitas Dei.

Tertio dico, quod unitas Dei non potest evidenter
probari, accipiendo 'Deum' secundo modo. Et tamen
negativa : 'Unitas D̄ei non potest evidenter probari',
non potest demonstrative probari, quia non potest
demonstrari, quod unitas Dei non potest evidenter
probari, nisi solvendo rationes in contrarium. Sicut non
potest probari demonstrative, quod astra sint paria, nec
potest demonstrari Trinitas Personarum. Et tamen illae
negativae non possunt evidenter probari : 'Non potest
demonstrari quod astra sint paria', 'Non potest demonstrari Trinitas Personarum'.

Sciendum tamen, quod potest demonstrari Deum esse,
accipiendo 'Deum' secundo modo prius dicto ; quia
aliter esset processus in infinitum nisi esset aliquid in
entibus quo non est aliquid prius nec perfectius. Sed
ex hoc non sequitur, quod potest demonstrari, quod
tantum est unum tale. Sed hoc fide tantum tenemus. . . .

Ad principale patet ex dictis.

that God exists—'God' being understood in the present sense—then the unicity of God could be evidently proved. The reason for this is the following : If there were two Gods, let us call them *A* and *B*, then in virtue of our description God *A* would be more perfect than anything else, therefore God *A* would be more perfect than God *B*, and God *B* would be more imperfect than God *A*. But God *B* would also be more perfect than God *A*, because according to our assumption God *B* would be God. Consequently God *B* would be more perfect and more imperfect than God *A*, and God *A* than God *B*, which is a manifest contradiction. If, therefore, it could be evidently proved that God exists —'God' being understood in the present sense—then the unicity of God could be evidently proved.

Thirdly I maintain that the unicity of God cannot be evidently proved if we understand 'God' according to the second description. Yet this negative proposition, 'The unicity of God cannot be evidently proved', cannot be proved demonstratively either. For it cannot be demonstrated that the unicity of God cannot be evidently proved, except by rebutting the arguments to the contrary. For instance, it cannot be demonstratively proved that the stars make up an even number, nor can the Trinity of Persons be demonstrated. Nevertheless, these negative propositions, 'It cannot be demonstrated that the stars make up an even number', 'The Trinity of Persons cannot be demonstrated', cannot be evidently proved.

We must understand, however, that it can be proved that God exists, if we understand 'God' according to the second description. For otherwise we could go on *ad infinitum*, if there were not some one among beings to which nothing is prior or superior in perfection. But from this it does not follow that it can be demonstrated that there is only one such being. This we hold only by faith.

The answer to the main objection is clear from the aforesaid.

GOD'S CAUSALITY AND
FOREKNOWLEDGE

Sources :

1. *Utrum Deus sit causa efficiens omnium aliorum a se?*

Quod non : Quia non est causa efficiens entium rationis, quia tunc talia entia essent actualiter in rerum natura, quod est falsum.

Contra : Omne quod non est a Deo effective est incausatum, et omne tale est Deus ; ergo omne aliud a Deo est a Deo effective.

Circa istam quaestionem primo distinguam de causa, secundo dicam ad quaestionem.

Circa primum dico, quod quaedam causa est immediata, sive totalis sive partialis, et quaedam mediata, quae ideo dicitur causa, quia est causa causae, sicut Abraham dicitur pater et causa Iacob, quia est pater patris eius. Sed non intelligo quaestionem praecise de causa immediata, sed tam de mediata quam immediata.

Circa secundum dico primo, quod Deus est causa omnium mediata vel immediata. Licet hoc non possit demonstrari, tamen hoc persuadeo auctoritate et ratione. Auctoritate, quia Ioannis i⁰ dicitur : 'Omnia per ipsum facta sunt' etc. Quod non potest intelligi de Deo, quia ibi non fit distributio pro Deo ; ergo intelligitur, quod omnia alia a Deo per ipsum facta sunt. Et in Symbolo : 'Credo in Deum Patrem omnipotentem', et sequitur : 'creatorem caeli et terrae, visibilium omnium et invisi-

[God's causality and foreknowledge]

1. *Whether God is the efficient cause of all things outside of Him?*

No : For God is not the efficient cause of logical entities ; otherwise such entities would actually exist in the universe.

On the contrary : Everything that is not from God as its efficient cause, is uncaused ; and everything of this nature is God ; therefore everything different from God is from God as its efficient cause.

Concerning this question, I first shall distinguish senses of the term 'cause', and secondly I shall answer the question.

Concerning the first point I say that one sort of cause is immediate, whether it be a total or a partial cause ; whereas another is mediate. The latter is called 'cause' in that it is cause of a cause, just as Abraham is said to be father and cause of Jacob, since he is the father of his father. However, I take the question as regarding not the immediate cause only, but both mediate and immediate causes.

Concerning the second point I first state that God is the mediate or immediate cause of all things. Though this cannot be demonstrated, yet I argue persuasively for it on the basis of authority and reason.

By authority : In the first chapter of the St. John's Gospel it is said : 'All things were made through Him', etc. This term 'all things' cannot be understood of God, since the distribution of this term is not here extended to God. Hence the meaning is that all things *besides* God are made through Him. Again in the Creed : 'I believe in God the Father almighty' ; and then follows 'creator

bilium', etc. Item, *Extra de summa Trinitate et fide catholica, firmiter* * : 'Ipse est creator omnium visibilium et invisibilium, spiritualium et corporalium'.

Praeterea : Hoc probo per rationem primo sic : Omnia dependent essentialiter a Deo, quod non esset verum nisi Deus esset causa illorum. Praeterea, si sic, tunc aliquid aliud a Deo esset increatum, vel esset processus in infinitum in causis : quia accipio aliquid, quod non ponis causari a Deo, et quaero, utrum sit causatum vel incausatum. Si detur primum, quaero de causa illius, et de causa illius eodem modo et sic in infinitum. Si detur secundum, habetur propositum.

Secundo dico, quod Deus est causa immediata omnium. Quod probo : Quia omne aliud a Deo plus dependet a Deo quam una creatura ab alia creatura ; sed una creatura sic dependet ab alia, quod est causa eius immediata ; ergo etc.

Praeterea : Si non, hoc maxime esset verum de culpa actuali ; sed hoc non obstat, quia idem actus numero potest causari ab una causa culpabiliter, et ab alia inculpabiliter ; sicut eadem volitio est a causa naturali, puta a cognitione, et a causa libera, puta a voluntate. Ergo potest idem actus causari a Deo immediate partialiter, sed inculpabiliter, et a voluntate culpabiliter.

Contra tamen hoc sunt aliqua dubia. Primum : quia impossibilia non sunt a Deo, et tamen non sunt Deus.

Secundo : quia figmenta et entia rationis, quae distinguuntur contra entia realia, non sunt Deus nec sunt a Deo.

---

* *Corpus iuris canonici*, cap. i, ii ; x, i, i

of heaven and earth, of all things visible and invisible',
etc. Again, in the Decretal *Extra de summa Trinitate et
fide catholica, firmiter* : 'He is the creator of all things
visible and invisible, corporeal and incorporeal'.

Furthermore, I prove this by reason in the following
manner : All things essentially depend on God. This
would not be true if God were not the cause of them.
Again, if God were not the efficient cause of all things,
then something different from God would be uncreated,
or one could go on *ad infinitum* in the series of causes.
For let me select something which you do not admit to
be caused by God and let me ask : Is it caused or uncaused ? If the first is conceded, I ask again about its
cause, and about the cause of that in the same manner,
and so *ad infinitum*. If the second alternative is conceded,
then I have the intended thesis.

Secondly, I state that God is the immediate cause of
all things. I prove this as follows. Everything different
from God depends more on God than one creature on
any other creature ; but one creature is so dependent
on another that this other is its immediate cause ;
therefore, etc.

Furthermore, if God were not the immediate cause of
all things, this should be true above all for a wrongful
action. But this case raises no difficulty, since numerically the same act may be caused by one cause with
guilt and by another cause without guilt. For instance,
the same act of will comes from a natural cause, viz.
cognition, and from a free cause, viz. the will. Therefore the same act may have God as its immediate part-
cause without His incurring guilt, and also be caused
by a will that does incur guilt.

Nevertheless, some doubts arise against this solution.
First : Impossibilities are not from God and nevertheless
they are not God.

Second : Fictions and logical entities as opposed to
real entities are not God and are not from God.

Tertio : quia esse obiectiva rerum et similiter peccata non sunt a Deo.

Quarto : quia veritates propositionum et privationes non sunt Deus n̅e̅c̅ a Deo effective.

Ad primum istorum dico : Quod omnia impossibilia sunt a Deo, quia omnia impossibilia, vel sunt complexa vel incomplexa, et omnia illa sunt a Deo.

Si dicis, quod chimaera est unum impossibile, et tamen non est a Deo, quia tunc esset aliquid : Respondeo, haec est distinguenda : 'Chimaera est possibilis vel impossibilis', quia 'possibile' accipitur uno modo pro omni illo, quod potest esse, sive sit complexum sive incomplexum ; et sic haec propositio : 'Homo est asinus', est possibilis, quia haec potest esse, et sic 'chimaera', supponens simpliciter, potest esse et est possibilis, quia talis conceptus vel vox potest esse. Alio modo dicitur de propositione, quae non est impossibilis, et sic non praedicatur de ' chimaera'. Similiter 'impossibile' uno modo accipitur prout dicitur de termino aequivalente orationi in significando, de qua nihil vere affirmative praedicatur. Et sic 'chimaera' supponens personaliter est impossibilis. Et sic non est inconveniens, quod idem sit possibile et impossibile secundum diversam suppositionem. Similiter ista : 'Chimaera est aliquid', 'Chimaera est ens', est falsa de virtute sermonis, quia in istis supponit personaliter. Si tamen supponat simpliciter, omnes verae sunt.

Ad secundum dico, quod figmenta sunt a Deo, quia talium quaedam sunt mentalia, quaedam vocalia, quaedam scripta, et omnia sunt entia realia et sunt a Deo, sicut etiam mendacia sunt a Deo, quia realia. Similiter

Third : The existence of things as thought-objects, and likewise sins, are not from God.

Fourth : Propositional truths, and also privations, are not God, nor are they from God as their efficient cause.

To the first of these doubts I answer that all impossibilities are from God, because all impossibilities are either complex or non-complex terms, and all such terms are from God.

You may object that the chimera is an impossibility, and nevertheless is not from God, because if it were from God, it would be something. I answer : The proposition 'A chimera is possible or impossible' has to have its senses distinguished. For 'possible' in one sense can mean all that which can be, whether it be complex or non-complex. In this sense the proposition 'Man is a donkey' is possible since the proposition can exist. In this way 'chimera' (taken in simple *suppositio*) can be and is possible, because such a concept or word can exist. In another sense, 'possible' is predicated of a proposition that is not impossible, and in this sense it is not predicated of 'chimera'. Likewise 'impossible', in one sense, is predicated of a term which in its signification is equivalent to a phrase about which no true affirmative predication is affirmed. In this sense a 'chimera' (in personal *suppositio*) can be made. In this manner it is not improper [to say] that the same term is possible and impossible according to a different *suppositio*. Similarly the propositions 'A chimera is something', 'A chimera is a being', are false in their literal meaning, since 'chimera' has personal *suppositio*. However, if it has simple *suppositio*, both these propositions are true.

To the second I reply that fictions are from God, because some of them are mental entities, some vocal, some written signs, and all of these are real beings and thus are from God, just as lies are from God, since they are real entities. Likewise logical entities are from

entia rationis sunt $\overline{\text{a Deo}}$, quia $\overline{\text{sunt}}$ verbum mentale
complexum vel incomplexum.

$\overline{\text{Sed}}$ dicis, quod ens rationis distinguitur contra ens
reale, ergo $\overline{\text{non}}$ idem. Respondeo primo $\overline{\text{per}}$ Commentatorem vi⁰ *Metaphysicae* in fine,* quod Philosophus
loquitur de entibus, quae sunt complexa, quae distinguuntur contra entia quae sunt per se sub praedicamentis et quae distinguuntur contra incomplexa, et hoc
sufficit Philosopho. Et postea incomplexum dividit in
decem praedicamenta. Aliter potest dici, quod ista est
divisio vocis in sua significata, non per opposita. Et
non est inconveniens $\overline{\text{ibi}}$, quod membra coincidant. Sic
enim i⁰ *Priorum* † dividit contingens in communi in
contingens ad utrumlibet, necessarium et possibile, et
tamen tam contingens ad utrumlibet quam necessarium
est possibile. Sic in proposito.

Ad tertium dico, quod non sunt talia esse obiectiva
quae nec sunt nec possunt esse entia realia ; nec est
unus alius parvus mundus $\overline{\text{esse}}$ obiectivorum. Sed illud,
quod nulla res est, omnino nihil est, sicut dicit Augustinus i⁰ *De doctrina Christiana*.‡

Si dicis, secundum Augustinum *De Trinitate* § possum
fingere talem hominem qualem vidi : $\overline{\text{dico}}$, quod illa
fictio est intellectio, quae est communis omnibus hominibus, et si nihil in re sibi correspondeat, $\overline{\text{est}}$ mendosa
intellectio.

Similiter ad illud de peccatis potest dici, quod omnis
res quae est peccatum, est a Deo, tamen Deus non
peccat, quia non tenetur ad oppositum, cum nullius
debitor sit.

Ad quartum dico, quod privationes, quae sunt in-

---

* Averroes *In VI Metaph.* comm. viii (ed. Venice 1551, f. 75)
† (25ᵃ, 37 sqq.)   ‡ cap. ii. ii (Migne *PL*, TOM. XXXIV, col. 20)
§ VIII, iv. vii (Migne *PL*, TOM. XLII, col. 951)

God, since they are mental words, either non-complex or complex.

You object, however, that logical being (*ens rationis*) is contrasted with real being (*ens reale*), hence they are not the same. I answer first with the Commentator on the sixth book of the *Metaphysics, ad fin.* : 'The Philosopher speaks of beings which are propositions. They are contrasted with beings which of themselves fall under the categories ; and also with non-complex terms. Later the Philosopher divides non-complex terms into the ten categories'. We could answer in another way by saying that this is the division of a name in relation to the things it signifies, and not by opposites. And there is nothing improper in the fact that here subdivisions coincide. For in like manner the Philosopher, in the first book of the *Prior Analytics*, divides 'contingent' in general into 'contingent as regards being and non-being', 'necessary' and 'possible'. Nevertheless what is contingent as regards being and non-being is possible and what is necessary is possible also. Now it is the same in our case.

To the third I reply that there are no such thought-objects (*esse objectiva*) ; they neither are nor can be real beings. Nor is there another little world made up of thought-objects. But whatever is not a thing is absolutely nothing, as St Augustine says in the first book of his *De doctrina Christiana*.

If you object that according to St Augustine in the *De Trinitate* I can mentally picture such a man as I have seen, I reply : Such a mental picturing is an act of thinking which refers to all men ; and if nothing in reality corresponds to it, it is a faulty act of thinking.

In a similar manner, the objection concerning sins can be answered. Everything that is a sin is from God. But God does not sin, since He is not obliged to do the opposite of that which is a sin, because He is debtor to no one.

To the fourth I reply : privations, being intelligible,

telligibiles vere sunt aliquid, quia vel sunt conceptus
mentis vel voces vel res extra animam, quia videtur,
quod caecus et caecitas significant omnino idem et pro
eodem possunt supponere. Et ideo sicut conceditur,
quod caecus est res extra animam, ita et caecitas ut
supponit personaliter, non autem ut supponit simpliciter.

Ad aliud de veritate dico, quod veritas illius propositionis : Deus nihil causat, potest causari a Deo, quia
veritas istius propositionis non est nisi ista propositio,
quae potest causari a Deo.

Si dicis, ponatur in esse : dico, quod non potest poni
in esse, quia positio eius in esse includit contradictionem,
scilicet quod 'Deus nihil causat', et : 'Deus aliquid
causat' ; quia si ponatur in esse, tunc haec est vera :
'Deus causat hanc veritatem : "Deus nihil causat",' et
per consequens, Deus aliquid causat ; et si causat hanc
veritatem : 'Deus nihil causat', haec est vera : 'Deus
nihil causat'. Exemplum, haec est vera : 'Album potest
esse nigrum', et tamen non potest poni in esse, quia tunc
haec esset vera : 'Album est nigrum'. Aliter potest dici,
quod si ponatur in esse, non debet sic poni in esse :
'Deus causat hanc veritatem', sed sic : 'Deus causat
hanc propositionem (pro qua supponit "veritas"): "Deus
nihil causat".' Sed tunc non erit veritas sed falsitas ;
sicut haec propositio : 'Album potest esse nigrum', debet
sic poni in esse : 'Haec est possibilis : "Sortes (pro quo
supponit 'album') est niger".'

Ad argumentum principale patet ex dictis.

are something, because they are either concepts of the
mind or words or things outside the mind ; for it seems
that 'blind' and 'blindness' signify absolutely the same
and can stand for the same.   Therefore, just as we
concede that a blind man is something outside the soul,
so also is blindness, provided it has personal *suppositio* ;
not, however, if it has simple *suppositio*.

To the other part of this objection, that concerning
truth, I reply : the truth of the proposition 'God causes
nothing' can be caused by God, since the truth of this
proposition is only the proposition itself, and that can
be caused by God.

If you reply, 'Let us assume that this possibility is a
fact', I answer, it is not possible to do so, since assuming
it as a fact involves a contradiction, viz. that God causes
nothing, and that God causes something.   For if it is
assumed as a fact, then this proposition is true, 'God
causes the truth "God causes nothing" ;' consequently,
God causes something.   But if God causes the truth
'God causes nothing', then the proposition 'God causes
nothing' is true.   An example may explain this.   The
proposition 'Something white can be black' is true ;
nevertheless, the possibility cannot be assumed as a fact,
since then the proposition 'Something white is black'
would be true.   Another answer would be the following :
If our proposition is assumed as a fact, it must not be
done like this, 'God causes this truth', but like this,
'God causes this proposition (for which the term "truth"
stands): "God causes nothing".'   But in that case the
proposition will not be truth but falsity ; just as the
proposition, 'Something white can be black', has to be
assumed to be a fact thus, 'This proposition is possible :
"Socrates (for whom 'white' stands in fact) is black".'

The answer to the main argument is clear from the
aforesaid.

Utrum Deus habeat scientiam determinatam et necessariam
omnium futurorum contingentium?

2. Ideo dico ad quaestionem, quod indubitanter est tenendum, quod Deus certitudinaliter et evidenter scit omnia
futura contingentia. Sed hoc evidenter declarare et
modum quo scit omnia futura contingentia exprimere
est impossibile omni intellectui pro statu isto.

Et dico, quod Philosophus diceret,* quod Deus non
scit evidenter et certitudinaliter aliqua futura contingentia ; et hoc propter istam rationem : Quia illud
quod non est in se verum, non potest sciri pro illo tempore, quo non est in se verum. Sed futurum contingens
dependens simpliciter a potentia libera, non est in se
verum, quia non potest secundum eum assignari ratio,
quare plus est una pars vera quam alia, et ita vel utraque
pars est vera vel neutra ; et non est possibile quod
utraque pars sit vera, igitur neutra est vera ; et per
consequens neutra scitur. Ista ratio non concludit
secundum viam Philosophi nisi de his quae sunt in
potestate voluntatis ; in his autem quae non sunt in
potestate voluntatis, sed dependent simpliciter a causis
naturalibus, non concludit, sicut quod sol orietur, et sic
de aliis. Et hoc quia causa naturalis determinatur ad
unam partem, nec possunt omnes causae naturales
impediri nisi per causam liberam, per quam tamen
possunt impediri respectu unius effectus determinati,
quamvis non respectu cuiuslibet.

Ista tamen ratione non obstante tenendum est, quod
Deus evidenter cognoscit omnia futura contingentia.
Sed modum exprimere nescio. Potest tamen dici, quod
ipse Deus vel divina essentia est una cognitio intuitiva

---

* *Cf. Perihermenias* (19ª, 23-29)

God's foreknowledge of future contingent facts

2. Therefore I reply to the question that it has to be held without any doubt that God knows all future contingent facts evidently and with certainty. But to explain this evidently, and to express the manner in which He knows all future contingent facts, is impossible for any intellect in this life.

And I say that the Philosopher would maintain that God does not know all future contingent facts evidently and with certitude, and he would maintain this for the following reason : That which is not true in itself cannot be known at that time when it is not true. But a future contingent fact simply depends on a free power and hence is not true in itself, because, according to the Philosopher, no reason can be assigned why one side of the contradiction is true rather than the other, and therefore either each part is true, or neither one is true. But it is not possible that each part be true ; therefore neither part is true, consequently neither part is known as true.

This proof is conclusive, according to the way of the Philosopher, only as regards facts which are in the power of the will. As regards those facts which are not in the power of the will but which simply depend on natural causes, as for instance that the sun will rise, and the like, the argument is not conclusive. The reason for this is that a natural cause is determined to one side [of a contradiction], nor can any natural causes be impeded except by a free cause, by which, however, they can be impeded only in regard to one determinate effect, not in regard to every effect.

Notwithstanding this argument, it has to be held that God evidently knows all future contingent facts. The manner in which he knows them, I, however, do not know. Yet it can be said that God Himself or the divine

tam sui ipsius quam omnium aliorum factibilium et
infactibilium tam perfecta et tam clara, quod ipsa etiam
est notitia evidens omnium praeteritorum, futurorum et
praesentium, ita quod sicut ex notitia intuitiva intellectiva
nostra extremorum potest intellectus noster cognoscere evidenter aliquas propositiones contingentes, ita ipsa divina
essentia est quaedam cognitio et notitia, qua non tantum
scitur verum necessarium et contingens de praesenti, sed
etiam scitur, quae pars contradictionis erit vera et quae
erit falsa. Et hoc forte non est propter determinationem
suae voluntatis. Sed etiam posito per impossibile quod,
ipsa divina cognitione existente ita perfecta sicut modo
est, non est causa effectiva nec totalis nec partialis
effectuum contingentium, adhuc esset notitia, qua evidenter sciretur a Deo, quae pars contradictionis erit
falsa et quae erit vera. Et hoc non esset, quia futura
contingentia essent sibi praesentia, nec per ideas tamquam rationes cognoscendi, sed per ipsammet divinam
essentiam vel divinam cognitionem, quae est notitia
qua scitur quid est falsum et quid est verum, quid fuit
falsum et quid fuit verum, quid erit falsum et quid
erit verum.

Ista conclusio, quamvis per rationem naturalem nobis
possibilem et a priori probari non possit, tamen per
auctoritates Bibliae et Sanctorum, quae sunt satis notae,
potest probari. Sed transeo de eis ad praesens.

Verumtamen pro aliquibus artistis est sciendum, quod
quantumcumque Deus sciat de omnibus futuris contingentibus, quae pars erit vera et quae falsa, tamen haec
non est necessaria : 'Deus scit, quod haec pars erit vera',
immo haec est contingens in tantum, quod quantumcumque haec sit vera : 'Deus scit quod haec pars contradictionis erit vera', tamen possibile est, quod haec
numquam fuit vera. Et ita in isto casu potentia est ad

essence is an intuitive cognition both of Himself and
of all things which can or cannot be made, and that this
intuitive cognition is so perfect and so clear that it is
also an evident knowledge of past, future and present
facts. Just as our intellect is able to know contingent
propositions from our intuitive intellectual cognition of
their terms, so the divine essence itself is an intuitive
cognition by which are known not only necessary truth
and contingent truth about a present fact; but also which
side of a contradiction will be true and which will be
false. The reason for this, perhaps, is not determination
by God's will. But even if we made the impossible
assumption that God's will is not the total or partial
effective cause of contingent effects, and nevertheless the
divine cognition remained just as perfect as it is now,
that cognition would still be the means by which God
would evidently know which side of a contradiction was
going to be false and which true. And this is probably
not because the future contingent facts are present to
Him, nor because of ideas that are the means of this
knowledge, but because of the divine essence or the
divine knowledge, which is a cognition by which He
knows what is true and what is false, what was true and
what was false, what will be true and what will be false.

Although this conclusion cannot be proved by any
a priori natural reason possible to us, yet it can be proved
from authentic texts of the Bible and from the saints,
which are well known. But I omit them for the present.

But for certain members of the Faculty of Arts it must
be pointed out that no matter how much God knows
about all future contingent facts, and as to which side
of a contradiction will be true and which false, nevertheless the proposition 'God knows that this side will
be true' is not a necessary but a contingent proposition.
This means that no matter how true the proposition
'God knows that this side of the contradiction will be
true' may be, nevertheless it is possible that this never

oppositum illius sine omni successione, quia possibile
est, quod numquam fuerit.   Sed sic non est de voluntate
creata.   Quia postquam voluntas creata aliquem actum
habuerit, non est possibile, quod postea sit verum dicere,
quod numquam habuit talem actum.

was true. And in this case there is a possibility of the
other side without any succession, because it is possible
this proposition should never have been true. But it
is different as regards a created will. For after a created
will has had an act it is not possible that it should later
on be true to say that it never had this act.

XI
PHYSICS AND ETHICS

Sources :

De quantitate

1. Ideo est alia opinio de quantitate, quae mihi videtur esse de mente Aristotelis, sive sit haeretica sive catholica, quam volo nunc recitare, quamvis nolim eam asserere. Et ideo, quando illam opinionem posui et scripsi super Philosophiam, non scripsi eam tamquam meam sed tamquam Aristotelis, quam exposui ut mihi videbatur. Et eodem modo nunc sine assertione recitabo eam.

Est autem ista opinio, quam etiam multi theologi tenent et tenuerunt, quod scilicet nulla quantitas est realiter distincta a substantia et qualitate, sive tales propositiones : 'Substantia est quantitas', 'Qualitas est quantitas', sint concedendae sive non.

Et de quantitate quidem continua permanente tenetur per istum modum, scilicet, quantitas continua permanens nihil aliud est nisi res una habens partem situaliter distantem a parte, ita quod ista duo 'quantitas continua permanens', et 'res una habens partem distantem a parte', sint aequivalentia in significando in tantum, quod erunt termini convertibiles, nisi aliquis modus syncategorematicus vel aliqua determinatio inclusa aequivalenter in uno impediat convertibilitatem et praedicationem unius de altero. Et ideo cum substantia habeat partem situaliter distantem a parte, et similiter qualitas, aliqua quantitas non erit alia res a substantia, et aliqua quantitas non erit alia res a qualitate. Nec videtur multum consonum theologiae dicere, quod Deus non posset facere istas partes substantiae distare situaliter, nisi rem aliam absolutam coniungat eisdem. Quod si potest facere, vere ista substantia habebit partem distantem a parte sine re absoluta addita eis, et per consequens erit quanta sine alia re absoluta. Et idem

On quantity

1. There is another opinion concerning quantity which, as it seems to me, is in accordance with Aristotle's mind, be it heretical or Catholic. I will explain it, though I do not assert it. Hence, when I assumed this opinion while writing on the philosophy of Aristotle, I did not write it as my own opinion, but as Aristotle's, which I have explained as seemed right to me. In the same manner I shall now explain it without asserting it.

This is also the opinion which many philosophers held and still hold, namely that no quantity is really distinct from substance and quality, regardless of whether such propositions as 'Substance is quantity', 'Quality is quantity', are to be admitted or not.

According to this opinion continuous quantity is to be explained as follows : Continuous permanent quantity is nothing but a thing with one part locally distant from another part. Therefore the two expressions 'permanent quantity' and 'a thing having part distant from part' are so much equivalent in signification that the terms are convertible, unless there is some syncategorematic mode or some determination equivalently included in one of such expressions which prevents their convertibility and prevents one from being predicated of the other. For this reason, when a substance (and, likewise, when a quantity) has part locally distant from part, then some quantity is nothing other than a substance, and some quantity is nothing other than a quality. Nor does it seem to be much in harmony with theology to state that God cannot make these parts of a substance to be locally distant unless He joins some other non-relative reality (*rem absolutam*) to them. If He can do this, then this substance has truly part distant from part without a non-relative reality being added to it, and consequently

argumentum potest fieri de qualitate. Et ideo cum
substantia potest esse quanta sine quantitate quae sit
alia res, et similiter qualitas, quantitas talis media inter
substantiam et qualitatem videtur omnino superfluere.

Propter quod dicunt, quod nulla est quantitas alia
a substantia et qualitate, sicut nulla res est habens
partem situaliter distantem a parte nisi substantia et
qualitas. Unde et de Sacramento Altaris dicunt, quod
post consecrationem corporis Christi una quantitas, quae
praecessit, erat eadem realiter cum substantia panis, et
illa non manet ; sed praeter illam manet una quantitas,
quae est eadem cum qualitate, in qua tamen quantitate
non est aliqua qualitas subiective. Sed omnia accidentia
remanentia post consecrationem remanent simul cum
corpore Christi sine omni subiecto quia per se substantia.
Sic igitur dicunt de quantitate continua.

De quantitate autem discreta dicunt, quod numerus
nihil est aliud quam ipsae res numeratae. Unde dicunt,
quod sicut unitas rei non est aliquod accidens additum
illi rei, quae est una, ita numerus non est aliquod accidens
illis rebus quae sunt numeratae. Quod autem unitas
non sit aliquod accidens additum rei, quae est una,
potest ostendi. Quia si sit accidens, secundum omnes
oportet quod sit relativum vel absolutum. Non relativum,
quia nullum terminum realem habere potest. Unde ad
hoc, quod aliquid sit unum, non oportet quod sit alicuius
unum, nec quod sit alicui unum, et sic de aliis casibus,
sub quibus aliquid dicitur ad aliud. Nec est accidens
absolutum, quia tunc vel esset qualitas, quod evidenter
patet esse falsum, vel est quantitas, et tunc continua vel
discreta, quorum utrumque patet esse falsum. Relin-

it will be quantitative without there being another non-relative reality. The same argument can be made in regard to quality. Since, therefore, a substance can be quantitative apart from any quantity which is a different thing from it, and the same is true of quality, a quantity which is midway between substance and quality seems to be entirely superfluous.

For this reason they say that there is no quantity different from substance or quality, just as there is no thing with part locally distant from part except a substance or quality. Hence concerning the Sacrament of the Altar they maintain that after the consecration of the body of Christ a quantity which was really the substance of the bread was there before, but does not remain ; besides this, however, there remains a quantity which is identical with a quality ; but there is no quality that has this quantity as a subject of inherence. Rather, all the accidents remaining after the consecration remain along with the body of Christ without any subject, since they subsist by themselves. This is their opinion concerning continuous quantity.

Concerning discrete quantity they maintain that number is nothing but the actual numbered things themselves. Hence they say that just as unity is not an accident added to the thing which is one, so number is not an accident of the things which are numbered. We can show that unity is not an accident added to the thing which is one. For if it is an accident, then according to all it must be either a relative or a non-relative accident. It is not a relative one, since it cannot have any real term of relation ; for in order that something should be one it need not be one *of* something, nor one *for* something, and similarly for the other cases used in predicating a relation. Nor is it a non-relative accident, for then it would be either a quality, which is certainly false, or it would be a quantity, and then either a continuous or discrete quantity, both of which are manifestly

quitur igitur, quod unitas non est aliquod accidens
realiter distinctum ab illo, quod est unum et additum
sibi in re extra. Et eadem ratione nec numerus est
accidens additum rebus numeratis.

De loco etiam et tempore dicunt, quod non sunt res
aliae. Sed de hoc in libro Physicae perscrutatum est.
De oratione autem dicunt, quod non est nisi ipsae voces
prolatae.

His visis consequenter habent positores praedictae
opinionis ponere, quod punctus, linea et superficies et
corpus et numerus non sunt res totaliter distinctae et
realiter, nec inter se nec a substantia et qualitate.
Verumtamen secundum eos, non obstante identitate
eorum, quae importantur per omnia ista, tamen istas
praedicabilia sunt distincta et sunt distinctae species
quantitatis. Aliquando enim praedicabilia habent
eadem significata, et tamen in tantum distinguuntur,
quod praedicatio unius de altero est impossibilis. Isti
enim termini 'homo' et 'homines' idem significant, et
tamen haec est impossibilis : 'Homo est homines'. Ita
est in proposito, quod omnia ista easdem res significant
et tamen sunt distinctae species et distincta praedicabilia.

2. Item notandum, quod in motu proiectionis est magna
difficultas de principio motivo et effectivo illius motus :
Quia non potest esse proiiciens, quia potest corrumpi
existente motu ; nec aer, quia potest moveri motu con-
trario, sicut si sagitta obviaret lapidi. Nec virtus in
lapide, quia quaero : A quo causatur illa virtus ? Non
a proiiciente, quia agens naturale aequaliter approximatum passo aequaliter semper causat effectum ; sed

false. It remains, therefore, that unity is not an accident really distinct from that which is one, and added to it in reality outside the mind. For the same reason, number is not an accident added to the numbered things.

Concerning place and time they maintain likewise that they are not distinct things. But about that we inquired in the book of *Physics*. Concerning speech they assert that it is nothing but the words uttered.

In consequence, those who hold the aforesaid opinion have to maintain that point, line and surface, and body, and number are not things wholly and really distinct, neither amongst themselves, nor from substance and quality. Nevertheless, according to them, in spite of the identity of the things signified by all such terms these predicates are distinct, and are distinct species of quantity. For sometimes predicates signify the same objects and nevertheless are distinct to such an extent that it is impossible to predicate one of the other. The terms 'man' and 'men' signify the same, nevertheless the proposition 'A man is men' is impossible. It is the same in our case. All of these terms signify the same things and nevertheless they are different species and different predicates.

[On projectile motion]

2. One other point has to be noted. There is a great difficulty concerning the moving and efficient principle in projectile motion. It cannot be the projecting body, since this body can be destroyed while the motion is still going on. Nor can it be the air, since the air may be being moved in the opposite direction, as when an arrow meets a stone [moving in the opposite direction] ; nor can it be some power in the [projected] stone. For, I ask, by what is this power caused ? Not by the projecting body, because a natural agent which is brought equally near to its object always causes an effect in the

proiiciens quantum ad omne absolutum et respectivum
in eo potest aequaliter approximari lapidi et non movere,
sicut quando movet ; potest enim manus mea tarde
moveri et approximari alicui corpori, et tunc non movet
ipsum localiter, et potest velociter et cum impetu moveri,
et tunc approximari eidem sicut prius, et tunc causabit
motum, et prius non ; ergo ista virtus quam tu ponis,
non potest causari ab aliquo absoluto vel respectivo in
proiiciente. Nec a motu locali ipsius proiicientis, quia
motus localis nihil facit ad effectum nisi approximat
activa passivis, sicut saepe prius dictum est, sed omne
positivum in proiiciente aequaliter approximatur pro-
iecto per motum tardum sicut per motum velocem.

Ideo dico, quod ipsum movens in tali motu per
separationem mobilis a primo proiiciente est ipsum
motum secundum se et non per aliquam virtutem
absolutam in eo vel respectivam, ita quod hoc movens
et motum est penitus indistinctum.

Si dicit, quod effectus novus habet aliquam causam,
sed motus localis est effectus novus : dico quod motus
localis non est effectus novus absolutus nec respectivus,
et hoc negando *ubi*, quia non est aliud nisi quod mobile
coexistit diversis partibus spatii, ita quod cum nulla una
coexistat, dum contraria verificantur. Unde licet quaelibet pars spatii, quam transit mobile, sit nova respectu
mobilis transeuntis, quatenus mobile nunc transit per
illas partes, et prius non, tamen nulla pars est nova

same manner. Now the projecting body, in regard to every absolute or relative feature of it, can be brought near to a stone in the same manner as when it moves the stone, and nevertheless not move the stone. For my hand can be moved slowly and brought near to a body, but it does not move it from its place. My hand can also be moved swiftly and with an impetus, and be brought near to the same body as before. But now it causes a motion, whereas in the former case it did not. Therefore that power which you assume cannot be caused by something absolute or relative in the projecting body. Nor can it be caused by the local motion of the projecting body, since local motion has only the effect of bringing the agents near to the objects they act upon, as we have said many times before. But every positive feature of the projecting body is equally brought near the projected body in slow motion and in fast motion.

For that reason I maintain, that in such motion as occurs through the separation of a movable object from its first projecting body, the moving agent is the very thing that is moved and not some power in it, whether absolute or relative, so that this mover and the thing it moves are absolutely indistinguishable.

If the opponent says that the new effect has some cause ; but local motion is a new effect, etc., I answer : A local motion is not a new effect, neither an absolute nor a relative one. I maintain this because I deny that position (*ubi*) is something. For motion is nothing more than this ; the movable body coexists with different parts of space, so that it does not coexist with any single one while contrary statements are made true. Therefore, though every part of the space which the movable body traverses is new in regard to the moving body—in so far as the moving body is now traversing these parts and previously it was not—nevertheless no part is new without qualification. About this we have spoken else-

simpliciter. De hoc dictum est alias. Mirabile enim
esset, si manus mea causaret aliquam virtutem in lapide
per hoc quod motu locali tangit lapidem.

3. *Utrum possit demonstrari quod anima intellectiva sit forma
corporis?*

Quod sic : Quia experimur, quod intellectio est in
nobis, et intellectio est operatio hominis, ergo est efficiens
et subiectum recipiens ; sed hoc in nobis non potest esse
intelligentia separata, quia operationem talis substantiae
non possumus experiri ; nec esset talis operatio alicuius
compositi ; ergo receptivum illius operationis est aliquid
hominis : non materia, ergo forma.

Contra : Anima intellectiva est forma incorruptibilis ;
ergo non est forma corporis corruptibilis.

In ista quaestione sunt duae difficultates. Una, utrum
possemus intelligere per animam intellectivam, quamvis
non esset forma corporis. Alia, an posset evidenter sciri
per rationem vel per experientiam, quod intelligamus,
accipiendo intelligere pro aliquo actu proprio substantiae
immateriali, cuiusmodi ponitur anima intellectiva, quae
est ingenerabilis et incorruptibilis, quae est tota in toto
et tota in qualibet parte.

Quantum ad primam difficultatem videtur, quod sic :
Quia multa attribuuntur uni rei per aliam per communi-
cationem idiomatum, quae nec est materia nec forma

where. For it would be astonishing if my hand caused a power in a stone through coming into contact with the stone by local motion.

[*The existence of an intellective soul*]

3. *Whether it can be demonstrated that the intellective soul is a form of the body?*

It can : For we experience that an act of intellect occurs in us ; and the act of intellect is a human activity and therefore it has an efficient cause and a subject of inherence ; now, in our case this cannot be a separate intelligence, since we cannot experience within ourselves the activity of such a substance ; nor could such an activity belong to a composite substance ; hence the subject of inherence of this activity is something that belongs to man [as a part] : now this is not matter, therefore it must be a form.

On the contrary : The intellective soul is an incorruptible form ; hence it is not a form of a corruptible body.

Concerning this question there are two problems. One, whether we could perform an act of intellect by the intellective soul, even if it were not a form of the body. The other, whether it could be evidently known either by reason or experience, that we do perform an act of the intellect, if we understand by an act of the intellect an act proper to an immaterial substance such as we assume the intellective soul to be, namely, a substance which is incapable of being generated or corrupted, and which exists entire in the entire body and entire in each part.

As regards the first problem, it seems that we can have an act of intellect by the intellective soul, even if it were not the form of the body. For by communication of attributes many properties are attributed to one thing

nec pars eius, sicut dicimus, aliquid attribuitur alteri
propter instrumentum vel propter vestimentum et
similia ; quemadmodum dicimus istum hominem esse
remigatorem a remo, vel fossorem, et illum dicimus
vestitum et calciatum et armatum. Et dicimus, quod
ille homo tetigit alium, quia panni sui tetigerunt vel
arma sua. Talis est communicatio inter Filium Dei et
naturam assumptam, ubi neutrum est forma. Ergo
eodem modo potest aliquid attribui corpori moto propter
motorem absque hoc quod iste motor sit forma eius.
Exemplum patet de angelo Tobiae, propter quem
tamquam propter motorem dicebatur constitutum ex
corpore assumpto et angelo comedere et bibere et
ambulare, intelligere et iudicare ; ergo non obstante,
quod anima solum sit motor corporis et nullo modo
forma, possumus dici intelligere per animam intellectivam.

Quantum ad secundam difficultatem dico, quod
intelligendo per animam intellectivam formam im-
materialem et incorruptibilem, quae tota est in toto
corpore et tota in qualibet parte, non potest evidenter
sciri per rationem vel per experientiam, quod talis forma
sit in nobis, nec quod intelligere talis substantiae proprium sit in nobis, nec quod talis anima sit forma
corporis. Quidquid de hoc senserit Philosophus, non
curo ad praesens, quia ubique dubitative loqui videtur.
Sed ista tria solum credimus.

Quod autem non possit demonstrari patet, quia omnis
ratio probans ista accipit dubia homini sequenti rationem
naturalem, nec per experientiam probantur, quia solum
experimur intellectionem et volitionem et consimilia. Sed
omnia ista diceret sequens rationem cum experientia esse
operationes et passiones causatas et receptas in forma illa,

through another which is neither its matter nor its form nor a part of it, as we say that something is ascribed to somebody else in respect of his instrument or his clothes or the like. For instance, we call this man an oarsman (from his oar), or a digger, and another is said to be clothed or to be shod or to be armed. And we say that this man touched another because his linen or his weapons touched him. Such is the communication between the Son of God and the assumed nature, where neither is a form. Hence, in the same manner, something can be attributed to a body that is moved in respect of what moves it, without this mover being its form. An instance of this is manifest in the angel of Tobias. Because this angel was a kind of mover, the composite of the angel and an assumed body was said to eat, to drink, to walk, to think and to judge. Hence even if the soul were only the mover of the body and by no means its form, it could still be said of us that we understand by the intellective soul.

Concerning the second problem, I maintain that if we understand by 'intellective soul' an immaterial and incorruptible form which exists entire in the entire body and entire in each part, it cannot be evidently known by reason or experience that such a form exists in us, nor that the understanding proper to such a substance exists in us, nor that such a soul is a form of the body. Whatever the Philosopher thought of this does not now concern me, because it seems that he remains doubtful about it wherever he speaks of it. These three things are only matters of belief.

It is clear that these things cannot be demonstrated ; for every reason by which we try to prove them assumes something that is doubtful for a man who follows only his natural reason. Neither can they be proved by experience ; for we experience only acts of intellect and the will and the like. But a man following reason and experience would say that all these are operations and

per quam poneret hominem distingui a brutis. Et licet
secundum fidem ista sit anima intellectiva, quae est
forma incorruptibilis, tamen talis diceret, quod esset
forma extensa et corruptibilis et generabilis. Nec
videtur, quod experientia aliam formam concludat.

Et si quaeras, utrum possit evidenter probari, quod
ista, quam sequens rationem concludit per experientiam,
sit forma corporis, respondeo quod sic per tale medium
forte : Omne compositum differens specie ab alio
composito vel differt se toto vel per partem ; sed homo
differt specie ab asino, et non se toto, quia habent
materiam eiusdem rationis ; ergo per partem ; non
per materiam, ergo per formam. Et forte in ista ratione
accipiuntur aliqua dubia. Si autem ponatur, sicut
ponimus secundum veritatem, quod anima intellectiva,
quae est forma immaterialis et incorruptibilis, sit in
nobis, et quod per eam intelligamus, tunc rationabilius
est ponere ipsam esse formam corporis quam quod sit
solus motor : quia si esset motor, aut moveret corpus
motu locali aut alterationis. Non primo modo, quia
tunc aequaliter moveret corpus pueri et adulti. Similiter
ad movendum corpus motu locali sufficit anima quae
est forma corporis ; ergo superfluum est ponere alium
motorem. Nec secundo modo, quia ad omnem altera-
tionem corporalem sufficiunt alia agentia corporalia ;
ergo talis motor superfluit. . . .

Ad principale concederet sequens rationem naturalem,
quod experimur intellectionem in nobis, quae est actus

impressions caused and received in that form by which, according to him, man is distinct from brute animals. Though this form, according to faith, is the intellective soul, which is an incorruptible form, nevertheless such a man would maintain that it is an extended and corruptible and generable form. Nor does it appear that experience argues another form.

If you ask whether it can be evidently proved that this form, which a man following reason establishes from experience, is the form of the body, I answer that it can be done, perhaps by this means : Every compound different in species from another compound differs from it either totally or in part. But man differs in species from a donkey, although not totally, since they have matter of the same kind. Therefore they differ only in part. But a man and a donkey do not differ in matter, therefore they differ by their form. But perhaps some doubtful points are assumed in this proof.

If, however, it is assumed (as we assume according to the truth) that the intellective soul, which is an immaterial and incorruptible form, exists in us and that we understand by means of it, then it is more reasonable to maintain that it is the form of the body and not only its mover. For if it were only its mover, then it would move the body either by local motion or by motion of alteration. Not in the first manner, for then it would move equally the body of a boy and that of a grown man ; likewise, in order to move the body by local motion, a soul which is form of the body is sufficient ; hence it is superfluous to assume another mover. Nor does it move the body in the second manner [by alteration], since the other agents which are corporeal are sufficient for every such alteration. Hence such a mover is superfluous. . . .

In regard to the main argument, one who followed natural reason would concede that we experience an act of understanding in us, but would maintain that it is

formae corporeae et corruptibilis. Et diceret consequenter, quod talis forma reciperetur in materia extensa.
Non autem experimur illam intellectionem quae est
operatio propria substantiae immaterialis ; et ideo per
intellectionem non concludimus illam substantiam incorruptibilem esse in nobis tamquam formam. Et forte,
si experiremur illam intellectionem esse in nobis, non
possemus plus concludere, nisi quod eius subiectum est
in nobis sicut motor, non autem sicut forma.

4. *Utrum solus actus voluntatis sit necessario virtuosus vel vitiosus?*

Quod non : Quia omnis actus voluntatis potest elici
intentione mala ; ergo omnis actus voluntatis potest
esse malus.

Contra : Diligere Deum est actus solus virtuosus et
non est alius quam virtuosus ; ergo ille actus est solus
virtuosus.

Ad istam quaestionem dico, quod ista propositio exclusiva
posita in quaestione habet duas exponentes. Unam
negativam, quae est, quod nullus actus alius ab actu
voluntatis est necessario virtuosus ; et aliam affirmativam, scilicet quod aliquis actus voluntatis est necessario
virtuosus.

Quantum ad negativam exponentem dico, quod est
simpliciter vera, quia omnis actus alius ab actu voluntatis, qui est in potestate voluntatis, sic est bonus, quod
potest esse malus, quia potest fieri cum malo fine et
mala intentione. Similiter omnis alius actus potest elici
naturaliter et non libere, et nullus talis est necessario
virtuosus.

Praeterea : Omnis actus alius a voluntate potest fieri

an act of a corporeal and corruptible <u>form</u>. Consequently he would say that such a form would inhere
in extended matter. However, we do not experience in
ourselves that act of understanding which is the activity
proper to an immaterial substance. Hence from an act
of understanding we do not conclude that such an
incorruptible substance exists in us as a form. Or
perhaps if we did experience that such an act of understanding existed in us, we could not conclude any more
than that its subject exists in us as a mover ; not, however, as a form.

[The basis of morality]

4. *Whether only an act of will is necessarily virtuous or vicious ?*

No : For every act of will can be elicited with a bad
intention ; hence every act of will can be bad.

On the contrary : To love God is an act that is only
virtuous and nothing but virtuous ; hence this act is
only virtuous.

I reply to this question : The exclusive proposition found
in the formulation of this question is exponible as a pair
of propositions. One is negative, viz. 'No act different
from the act of will is necessarily virtuous'. The other
is affirmative, viz. 'Some act of the will is necessarily
virtuous'.

Concerning the negative part of the explanation, I
maintain that this proposition is simply true. For every
act other than an act of will which is in the power of the
will is good only in such a manner that it can be bad
because it can be performed for a bad end and with a
bad intention. Furthermore, any other act can be performed naturally and not freely ; and no such act is
necessarily good. Again, every act other than an act
of will can be brought about by God's sole action ;

a solo Deo, et per consequens non est necessario virtuosus creaturae rationali.

Praeterea : Quilibet alius actus ide mmanens potest indifferenter esse laudabilis et vituperabilis, et primo laudabilis et postea vituperabilis, secundum quod potest successive conformari voluntati rectae et vitiosae ; patet de ire ad ecclesiam primo bona intentione, postea mala intentione.

Praeterea : Nullus actus est virtuosus nec vitiosus nisi sit voluntarius et in potestate voluntatis, quia peccatum adeo est quia est voluntarium ; sed actus alius potest primo esse in potestate voluntatis et postea non, puta quando aliquis voluntarie demittit se in praecipitium, et postea poenitet, et habet actum nolendi illum descensum meritorie propter Deum ; sed in descendendo non est in potestate voluntatis ; ergo iste descensus non est necessario vitiosus.

Circa affirmativam exponentem dico primo, quod de virtute sermonis nullus actus est necessario virtuosus. Hoc probatur : Tum quia nullus actus necessario est, et per consequens non est necessario virtuosus. Tum quia quilibet actus potest fieri a solo Deo, et per consequens non est necessario virtuosus, quia talis actus non est in potestate voluntatis.

Tamen aliter potest intelligi actum esse virtuosum, ita quod non posset esse vitiosus stante divino praecepto. Similiter, non potest causari a voluntate creata nisi sit virtuosus. Et sic intelligendo 'actum virtuosum' dico secundo, quod sic potest aliquis actus esse virtuosus necessario.

Quod probo : Quia impossibile est, quod aliquis actus contingenter virtuosus, ita quod indifferenter potest dici virtuosus vel vitiosus, fiat determinate virtuosus nisi propter alium actum necessario virtuosum. Hoc

consequently it is not necessarily virtuous for a rational creature.

Furthermore, every act, remaining identically the same, can be indifferently laudable or blameworthy ; and it can be first laudable and afterwards blameworthy inasmuch as it can be successively in accordance with a righteous and with a vicious will. This becomes clear if we consider the act of going to church, first with a good intention, and then with a bad intention.

Furthermore, no act is virtuous or vicious unless it is voluntary and in the power of the will, because a sin is a sin only because it is voluntary ; but another act can be in the power of the will at first and then afterwards beyond the power of the will. For instance, in the case where someone voluntarily jumps off a precipice, and then repents and has an act of not willing his fall, and that meritoriously for God's sake ; but the fall itself is not any more in the power of the will ; hence this fall is not necessarily vicious.

Concerning the affirmative part of the explanation I maintain : First, literally speaking, no act is necessarily virtuous. Proof : No act exists necessarily ; and consequently, no act is necessarily virtuous. Again, every act can be performed by God's sole action ; consequently it is not necessarily virtuous, since such an act [caused by God] is not in the power of the will.

However, another meaning can be attached to saying that an act is virtuous, viz. that it cannot be vicious while God's commandment stands ; or, again, that such an act cannot be caused by a created will without being virtuous. If we understand 'virtuous act' in this sense, then I maintain that an act may be necessarily virtuous. Proof : It is impossible that any contingently virtuous act, that is an act which can be called indifferently virtuous or vicious, can be determined to be a virtuous act, except by reason of another necessarily virtuous act. This is

probatur : Quia actus contingenter virtuosus, puta actus
·ambulandi, fit determinate virtuosus per conformitatem
ad alium actum. Quaero de isto secundo actu : aut
est necessario virtuosus modo praedicto, et habetur propositum, quod est aliquis actus in homine necessario
virtuosus, aut est contingenter virtuosus, et tunc iste fit
virtuosus determinate per conformitatem ad alium actum
virtuosum. Et de illo quaerendum est sicut prius. Et
erit processus in infinitum, vel stabitur ad aliquem actum
necessario virtuosum.

Tertio dico, quod iste actus necessario virtuosus modo
praedicto est actus voluntatis, quia actus quo diligitur
Deus super omnia propter se est huiusmodi ; nam iste
actus sic est virtuosus, quod non potest esse vitiosus, nec
potest iste actus causari a voluntate creata, nisi sit
virtuosus : Tum quia quilibet pro loco et tempore
obligatur ad diligendum Deum super omnia, et per
consequens, iste actus non potest esse vitiosus ; tum quia
iste actus est primus omnium actuum bonorum.

Praeterea, solus actus voluntatis est intrinsece laudabilis vel vituperabilis.

Praeterea, secundum Sanctos nullus actus est laudabilis
vel vituperabilis nisi propter intentionem bonam vel
malam ; intentio autem est actus voluntatis ; ergo etc.

Praeterea, secundum Anselmum * sola voluntas puni-
tur, quia sola voluntas peccat, ergo etc.

Si dicatur, quod Deus potest praecipere, quod pro
aliquo tempore non diligatur ipse, quia potest praecipere,
quod intellectus sit intentus circa studium et voluntas
similiter, ut nihil possit illo tempore de Deo cogitare :
tunc volo, quod voluntas tunc eliciat actum diligendi

* *De conceptu virginali et de originali peccato*, cap. iv (Migne *PL*,
TOM. CLVIII, col. 438; *Opera omnia*, ed. Schmitt, VOL. II, p. 415,
17 sqq.)

proved as follows : A contingently virtuous act, let us say an act of walking, is determined to be a virtuous act by its conformity with another act. About this second act I ask : Is it necessarily virtuous in the sense explained ?—and then we have our intended thesis—or is it contingently virtuous and determined to be a virtuous act by some other virtuous act ? About this third act we have to ask as before. Thus, either we go on *ad infinitum*, or we stop at some necessarily virtuous act.

Thirdly I maintain that a necessarily virtuous act, in the sense explained above, is an act of will, since the act by which God is loved above all and for His own sake is such an act. For this act is virtuous in such a way that it cannot be vicious, nor can this act be caused by a created will without being virtuous. First, because everyone is bound (according to time and place) to love God above all, and consequently this act cannot be vicious ; secondly, because this act is the first of all good acts. Furthermore, only an act of will is essentially laudable or blameworthy. Again, accòrding to the saints, every act is laudable or blameworthy only because of its good or bad intention ; but an intention is an act of the will ; therefore, etc. Again, according to St Anselm, only the will is punished, because only the will sins ; therefore, etc.

The objection may be made : God can command that He be not loved for a certain time, because He can command that the intellect be occupied with study and the will likewise, so that at this time it cannot think anything about God. I now assume that the will then performs an act of loving God ; then this act is either

Deum, et tunc aut ille actus est virtuosus—et hoc non
potest dici, quia elicitur contra praeceptum divinum—
aut non est virtuosus, et habetur propositum, quod actus
diligendi Deum super omnia non sit virtuosus.

Respondeo : Si Deus posset hoc praecipere, sicut
videtur quod potest sine contradictione, dico tunc, quod
voluntas non potest pro tunc talem actum elicere, quia
ex hoc ipso, quod talem actum eliceret, Deum diligeret
super omnia ; et per consequens impleret praeceptum
divinum : quia hoc est diligere Deum super omnia,
diligere quidquid Deus vult diligi. Et ex hoc ipso quod
sic diligeret, non faceret praeceptum divinum per casum,
et per consequens sic diligendo Deum diligeret et non
diligeret, faceret praeceptum Dei et non faceret. Posset
tamen diligere simplici amore et naturali, qui non est
dilectio Dei super omnia, sicut ponendo quod aliquis
non credat Deum esse, non potest eum diligere, quia
nihil potest diligi nisi quod est vel potest esse.

Quarto dico, quod solus habitus voluntatis est intrinsece et necessario virtuosus, quia quilibet alius habitus
inclinat indifferenter ad actus laudabiles et vituperabiles.

Ad *argumentum principale* nego assumptum, quia aliquis
actus voluntatis nullo modo cum intentione mala potest
elici, sicut patet ex dictis.

virtuous—but that cannot be said, since it is performed against the divine command—or it is not virtuous, and then we have our intended thesis that an act of loving God above all is not virtuous.

I answer : If God could command this—and it seems that He can do it without contradiction—then I maintain that the will in this situation cannot perform such an act, because merely by performing such an act the will would love God above all and consequently would fulfil the divine precept. For to love God above all means to love whatever God wills to be loved. But by the mere fact of loving God in this way one would not (according to our assumption) fulfil the divine command. Consequently by loving God in this manner one would love God and not love God ; one would fulfil the precept of God and not fulfil it. However, one could have an act of a simple and natural love, which is not the same as the love of God above all ; just as, if someone did not believe in God, he could not love Him, since nothing can be loved unless it exists or can exist.

Fourthly I maintain that only a habit of the will is essentially and necessarily virtuous, since every other habit indifferently inclines to laudable and blameworthy acts.

In regard to the main argument I deny the premise, for there is an act of the will which, as it is clear from the aforesaid, cannot be performed with a bad intention.

APPENDIX
OCKHAM: *PHILOSOPHICAL WRITINGS*
TEXT CORRECTIONS
BY STEPHEN F. BROWN

1. Prologue to the *Expositio in libros Physicorum Aristot.* (OP IV, 4–14)   2
2. L: *for* super . . . Physicorum *read* in libros Physicorum Aristot.
   for sum etiam *read* sum
   for reprehendi *read* resilire
   E: *for* super . . . Physicorum *read* in libros Physicorum Aristot.
   for to . . . corrected *read* to withdraw my opinion
3. L: *for* alicuius *read* autem eius
   for videtur *read* videtur satis
   E: *for* author *read* author like Aristotle
   for clear *read* clear enough
4. L: *for* quae nihil *read* quae
   for non est *read* est
   for si *read* etsi
   E: *for* only . . . ready *read* something that it did not have before is more ready
5. L: *for* Philosophus *read* Philosophus in
   for includentem *read* includente
8. L: *for* color *read* calor
   for habet *read* habet tantum
   E: *for* the colour *read* heat
9. L: *for* accidens *read* accidens ipsius
   for Philosophus *read* Philosophus 'subiectum'
   E: *for* intellect *read* intellect itself
10. L: *for* aliud *read* aliud est primum
    for tale *read* aliud
11. L: *for* secundario *read* et secundario
12. L: *for* multae *read* multae res
    for ideo *read* et ideo

148

for notitia *read* notitia et scientia
for quod *read* dico quod

E: *for* real knowledge *read* real knowledge or real science

13. L: *for* communi *read* communi supponente
for generabilibus *read* generabilibus et corruptibilibus

E: *for* For . . . impossibilities *read* For this term 'impossible' is a term common to all impossibilities, and something may rightly be said of such a common term that stands for all impossible things
for generable *read* generable and corruptible

14. L: *for* termini *read* termini 'res mutabilis'

15. L: *for* quod *read* quod ista

17. 1   Prologue to the *Scriptum in I Sent.*, q. 1 (OT I, 15–33)   18
    2   *Quodlibet VI*, q. 6 (OT IX, 604–607)   25
    3   *Quodlibet I*, q. 13 (OT IX, 72–78)   27
    4   *Summa logicae*, I, 14 (OP I, 47–49)   32
    5   *Summa logicae*, I, 15 (OP I, 50–54)   35
    6   *Summa logicae*, I, 16 (OP I, 54–57)   37
    7   *Scriptum in I Sent.*, d. 2, q. 8 (OT II, 271–276)   41
    8   *Expositio in librum Perihermenias Aristot.* (OP II, 351–355)   43

19. L: *The sentence* et . . . etc. *is found only in the second redaction*
for scientiam *read* et scientiam
for et proxima *read* proxima

E: *The sentences* On the . . . distinct *are found only in the second redaction*

20. L: *for* est *read* sit

21. L: *for* rerum importatarum, vel *read* rerum vel *and realize that this phrase is found only in the second redaction*
for rerum, vel *read* rerum importatarum vel *and realize that this whole phrase is found only in the second redaction*
The clause et per . . . diligit *is found only in the second redaction*

E: *The clause* or . . . stand *is found only in the second redaction*
The phrase or things *is found only in the second redaction*
The clause and . . . loves *is found only in the second redaction*

22. L: *The phrase* etiam . . . sensibilium *is found only in the second redaction*

The sentence Utrum . . . distinctam *is added in the second redaction*

for abstractiva *read* abstracti a

The sentence Et si . . . opposito *is added in the second redaction*

E: *The phrase* and has . . . facts *is added in the second redaction*

The words But . . . thing *are found only in the second redaction*

The statements If such . . . contrasted *are found only in the second redaction.*

23. L: *The clause* nisi . . . impedimentum *is found only in the second redaction*

The words seu . . . rerum *are only found in the second redaction*

E: *The clause* unless . . . impediments *is only found in the second redaction*

The phrase or things *is only found in the second redaction*

24. L: *The phrase* terminorum . . . significatarum *is added in the second redaction*

The phrase vel res *is added in the second redaction*

The phrase vel re *is added in the second redaction*

E: *The phrase* of terms . . . by terms *is added in the second redaction*

The phrase or things *is added in the second redaction*

The phrase or thing *is added in the second redaction*

25. L: *for* quidlibet *read* quodlibet

26. L: *for* visionem *read* visionem sui

for non *read* nec

for in *read* ad

27. L: *for* videat *read* videt

for et *read* et tamen

28. L: *for* qualibet *read* quacumque

for sic est *read* est

for singularis *read* singulari

for probatur sic *read* probatur

29. L: *for* Secundum *read* Secundum assumptum

for respectu sibi simillimi *read* sibi simillimae

for demonstratur *read* detur

for si cognitio *read* si

30. L: *for* Quartum dubium *read* Quartum
    for causatur *read* causetur
    for potest *the editor suggests* potest <ab altero>
  E: *for* it can . . . other *read* it is caused by one object and not by another, and it is not even possible that it be caused by another.
31. L: *for* aliquod *read* aliquid compositum
    for Respondeo . . . si *read* Responsio: dico quod causae, quandocumque auctae et intensae
    for longitudinis et talis *read* longitudinis
    for illud *read* istum conceptum
    for Sed *read* Sed si
    for alio *read* aliquo
  E: *for* I answer . . . otherwise not *read* Response: I say that whenever causes are increased and intensified and cannot cause an effect that is specifically the same, then they are specifically different; otherwise they are not.
    for by . . . together *read* it is by means of this composite concept that
32. L: *for* est *read* esset
33. L: *for* plures *read* plures res
34. L: *for* dicitur autem *read* et dicitur etiam
  E: *for* on the . . . called *read* and it is also called
35. L: *for* quod *read* quare
    for res *read* substantia
    for aut . . . detur *read* aut est plures res aut una et non plures. Si secundum detur, sequitur quod est singularis; si primum detur
  E: *for* everything *read* a substance
    for Is this . . . second *read* 'Is this many things, or is it one thing and not many?' If the second alternative is granted, then it follows that it is singular; if the first
36. L: *for* sed . . . individui *read* si aliquod individuum
    for sequitur *read* sequeretur
    for manent *read* manerent
    for sequitur *read* sequeretur
    for realiter . . . damnato *read* et in damnato est damnata
  E: *for* but . . . pre-exist *read* if any individual were to pre-exist

for do *read* would
for follows *read* would follow
for really . . . damned *read* and in one of the damned would be damned, since it is damned in Judas

38. L: *for* natura *read* natura non
for sequitur *read* sequeretur
for et *read* et natura

39. L: *for* propositum *read* intentum

39–40. L: *for* minuente *read* diminuente

40. L: *for* Philosopho *read* philosophis
for aliquod *read* aliquid

E: *for* Philosopher *read* philosophers

41. L: *after* Et dico *the second redaction adds* probabiliter
for dico *read* hoc
for proportionaliter *read* proportionabiliter

E: *after* I maintain *the second redaction adds* with probability
for What . . . this *read* It has this type of existence in the following way:

42. L: *for* ostendam *the second redactions reads* igitur faciam aliqua argumenta ad probandum
for et *read* et ens

E: *for* I shall . . . show *the second redaction reads* Therefore, first I will present some arguments to prove

43. L: *The phrase* non . . . obiective in anima *is added only in the second redaction*
for possunt *read* poterunt
The word dico *is replaced in the second redaction by the words* diceret ista opinio
The words Dico ergo *are replaced in the second redaction by the words* Posset igitur dici
for animae esse *read* esse

E: *The phrase* and they . . . mind *is added only in the second redaction*
The words I maintain *are replaced in the second redaction by* this opinion could maintain
The words I . . . therefore *are replaced in the second redaction*

by It could therefore be said

44. L: *for* quae *read* et
   for intelligitur per eam *read* ea intelligitur
   for Et ita *read* Ita
   for per quam *read* qua
   for voces supponunt pro rebus *read* voces

45. L: *for* cum non appeteretur *read* tamen non appetitur
   for alia, oportet *read* alia. Oportet
   for discerni *read* distingui
   for ad alia *read* alia
   E: *for* was *read* is

46. 1 *Summa logicae*, I, c. 1 (OP I, 7–9) 47
   2 *Summa logicae*, I, c. 2 (OP I, 9–10) 49
   3 *Summa logicae*, I, c. 4 (OP I, 15–16) 51
   4 *Summa logicae*, I, c. 10 (OP I, 35–38) 52
   5 *Summa logicae*, I, c. 11 (OP I, 38–41) 56
   6 *Summa logicae*, I, c. 13 (OP I, 44–47) 59

47. L: *for* vel *read* et
   for distinctiones *read* divisiones
   for Boethium *read* Boethium in
   for scriptae *read* descriptae

48. L: *for* voces *read* voces semper
   for aliquod *read* aliquid
   E: *for* are *read* are always

49. L: *for* primam *read* primam cognitionem
   for vel *read* vel etiam

50. L: *for* praecise *read* terminus praecise et magis stricte
   for sumeretur *read* sumatur
   for et *read* et etiam
   for Homo *read* Omnis homo
   E: *for* precise *read* precise and more strict
   for A *read* Every

51. L: *for* aliquid *read* aliquis

52. L: *for* aliquid *read* aliud
   for dicendum est *read* est
   for importent *read* important

for idem *read* illud

53. L: *for* aliam *read* aliquam
   for absolutum *read* absolutum saltem
   for in . . . oratione *read* alterius orationis
   for de multis *read* de

54. L: *for* unum terminum *read* unum
   for quod *read* quod illud idem quod
   for quaeratur *read* quaeras
   for dictum *read* dictu
   for humanus *read* humanum
   for habet *read* debet

   E: *for* it . . . asked *read* you ask

55. L: *for* 'connotativum' *read* 'nomen connotativum'
   for 'relativum' *read* 'nomen relativum'

   E: *for* name 'connotative' *read* noun 'connotative name'
   for name 'relative' *read* noun 'relative name'

56. L: *for* sequuntur *read* consequuntur
   for et proprie. Large *read* et

   E: *for* senses . . . strict *read* senses.

57. L: *for* animae *read* animae vel praecise intentiones animae

57-58. E: *for* mental concepts *read* mental concepts or only concepts of the mind

58. L: *for* 'album' *read* 'album', 'ens'
   for sed tam *read* tam
   for 'aliquid', 'unum' *read* 'aliquid'

   E: *for* 'white' *read* 'white', 'being'
   for 'one' and *read* and

60. L: *for* 'homo' . . . primo *read* Primo enim
   for postea *read* postea autem

63. 1 *Summa logicae*, I, c. 63 (OP I, 193–195)   64
    2 *Summa logicae*, I, c. 64 (OP I, 195–197)   65
    3 *Summa logicae*, I, c. 65 (OP I, 197–199)   68
    4 *Summa logicae*, 1, c. 70 (OP I, 209–212)   70

64. L: *for* stricte 'suppositio' *read* stricte
   for supponunt *read* supponit
   for si *read* si terminus

for terminus *read* terminus supponens

65. L: *for* autem *read* igitur
    for Filius Dei *read* ille

66. L: *for* quodcumque *read* quodcumque aliud
    for aliquod *read* aliquid
    for tantum *read* tamen
    for pro dictionibus *read* pro
    for Suppositio *read* quod suppositio

    E: *after* signs; *the Latin demands that you add* because, however, it is
    meant to signify these vocal signs

67. L: *for* quo *read* hoc
    for hic *read* li
    for dissyllaba etc. *read* dissyllaba
    for et *read* et pro
    for vel *read* et

68. L: *for* et *read* et pro

69. L: *for* est *read* est propositio
    for Patris *read* Patris, quia hoc nomen 'Paternitas' significat
    proprietatem Patris
    for supponeret *read* supponat

    E: *for* Father *read* Father, because this noun 'Paternity' signifies a
    property of the Father

70. L: *for* aliis talibus *read* talibus
    for materialem *read* materialem vel personalem
    for et *read* vel
    for sic est *read* est
    for Suppositio autem *read* Suppositio
    for dicatur *read* dicatur quod

    E: *for* material *read* material or personal

71. L: *for* istam *read* eam
    for determinata *read* certa

72. L: *for* homo . . . illud *read* illud
    for Et ideo *read* Ideo
    for tantum *read* tantum et
    for Suppositio *read* Suppositio personalis
    for quacumque *read* quocumque

   for illud *read* illud vel illud

  E: *for* confused *read* confused personal

72–73. L: *for* sub animali *read* animalis

  73. L: *for* convenit *read* contingit

    for nulla *read* nullo uno

    for ille *read* ille homo est animal

    for et *read* et Cicero currit, et

    after aliis *the editor judges it is necessary to add another* <aliis>

   E: *for* it is . . . descent *read* a logical descent takes place

    for running *read* running and Cicero is running

  74. L: *for* confusa *read* confusa et

  75. *Summa logicae*, II, c. 2 (OP I, 249–251)   76

  76. L: *for* Primo dicendum est *read* Primo

    for Unde *read* Circa quod

    for ipsi subiecto *read* subiecto

    for aliquod *read* aliquid

  77. L: *for* falsum *read* falsa

    for et per consequens *read* et

   E: *for* and consequently *read* and

  78. L: *for* est pars *read* pars

  79. 1 *Summa logicae*, II, c. 32 (OP I, 347–349) 80

    2 *Summa logicae*, II, c. 33 (OP I, 349–350) 81

    3 *Summa logicae*, III–1, c. 1 (OP I, 359–360) 83

    4 *Summa logicae*, III–3, c. 38 (OP I, 727–731) 84

  80. L: *for* veritatem *read* veritatem autem

    for Similiter *read* Et similiter

    for quaelibet *read* utraque

    for est *read* sit

  81. L: *for* vel tu es *read* vel

    for altera *read* aliqua

  82. L: *after* requiritur *the editor suggests the addition of* <vel>

    for illius *read* ipsius

    for sit *read* sit aliquando

    for impediens *read* impediens fallaciam consequentis

   E: *for* is *read* is at times

84. L: *for* quando *read* quandocumque
      for consequens *read* conclusionem
   E: *for* consequent *read* conclusion
85. L: *for* totius antecedentis *read* antecedentis
      for Notandum est *read* Notandum
      for sequitur *read* sequatur
      for propositione *read* propositionum
      for sic *read* nam bene sequitur
86. L: *for* Et ex *read* Ex
      for asinus *read* homo
      for homo *read* asinus
      for ista *read* isto
      for ista antecedente *read* ista
   E: *for* donkey *read* man
      for man *read* donkey
87. L: *for* repugnat *read* repugnat etiam
      for istae *read* ista
      for istae *read* ista
      for quia ut nunc *read* quamvis
      for Alia *read* Alia regula est quod
      for Nam *read* quia
      for Sicut *read* Sicut bene
   E: *for* is *read* is also
      for because . . . time *read* even though
88. L: *for* Sed *read* et
      for Notandum *read* Et notandum
      for positum possibile *read* positionem possibilis
      after obligationis *it is necessary to add* . . .
      for nec *read* et ideo istae regulae non
   E: *for* they *read* therefore these rules
89. 1   *Summa logicae*, I, c. 38 (OP I, 106–108)   90
     2   *Summa logicae*, III–2, c. 27 (OP I, 553–555)   92
90. L: *for* puta *read* puta de
91. L: *for* aliquid *read* aliquod
      for IV *read* V

for quasi *read* quod
for clarum est *read* claret
for Musicus *read* Musicum
for alia *read* aliqua
E: *for* at least one *read* some

92. L: *for* distinguitur *read* dividitur
for divisibile *read* dicibile
for Utrum *read* Utrum scilicet
E: *for* divisible . . . actual *read* predicable by potency and by act

93. L: *for* sit *read* est
for absoluta *read* abstracta
for sequitur *read* sequeretur
for est *read* esset

94. L: *for* igitur *read* ideo
for esse *read* esse et non creaturam
E: *for* existence *read* existence, and that creatures are not their very existence

96. 1   *Quodlibet V*, q. 1 (OT IX, 475–480)   97
    2   *Scriptum in I Sent.*, d. 2, q. 9 (OT II, 312–317)   102
    3   *In III Sent.*, q. 5 (OT VI, 335–345)   106

97. L: *for* conclusiones *read* conclusiones scitae
for 'scientia' *read* scientia naturali et theologia
for dico *read* dicam
for habitu . . . theologico *read* habitu
for distinctae *read* dictae
for Ideo *read* Et ideo
E: *for* the . . . meaning *read* known conclusions must necessarily belong to different realms
for distinguish . . . 'knowledge' *read* make a distinction in regard to natural knowledge and theology
for conclusion . . . *habitus read* conclusion
for distinct cognitions *read* natural knowledges, taken in the first sense of the term,

98. L: *for* Hoc *read* Et hoc
for aliquod *read* aliquod ens
for Deus *read* Dei
for Deo *read* eo

for solum probatur *read* sed talis modus probandi solum probat

E: *for* but . . . proved *read* but this way of proving only establishes

98–99 E: *for* conclusion . . . precisely *read* premises, the conclusion and the terms would have

99. L: *for* praecise *read* praemissae et

for tunc *read* cum

for ibi in *read* in

for aliter theologus *read* theologus

E: *for* alternative, *read* alternative, since

for it?' Such *read* it?', such

100. L: *for* alia *read* aliqua

for conceptu *read* conceptu Dei

for est *read* est quaedam

for quaedam . . . subiecti *read* descriptio

partes *is found in the new edition*

E: *for* another *read* any

for concept *read* concept of God

for a . . . subject *read* a certain definition or description

101. L: *for* erit *read* est

for intuitiva *read* intuitiva subiecti

for possit *read* potest

for dicitur *read* oportet

E: *for* cognition *read* cognition of the subject

for subject it is said that *read* subject

102. L: *for* sequitur *read* sequetur

E: *for* follows *read* will follow

103. L: *The words* modo exposito *are found only in the second redaction*

for alterius rei *read* rei

E: *The words* in . . . explained *are found only in the second redaction*

105. L: *The paragraph* Ista . . . praedicabitur *is added in the second redaction*

E: *The paragraph* This proof . . . predicated *is added in the second redaction*

106. L: *for* univocum *read* univocum quibuscumque. Dico tamen quod nihil est univocum

for reperire *read* reperiri aliquid

for sunt *read* sint
for reperire *read* reperiri
for solus *read* solius
for reperire *read* reperiri
for vel ad *read* vel
for et *read* quia

E: *for* univocal *read* univocal to every being whatsoever.
Nevertheless, I say that nothing is univocal
for only . . . species *read* the concept of the lowest species alone

108. L: *for* Accipiendo *read* Similiter accipiendo
for univocus *read* univocus. Non pure aequivocus
for nec *read* nec etiam
for esse *read* esse medius
for hic *read* huius
for perfecta univocatio *read* perfectissima univocatio. . . .

E: *for* For it *read* Not purely univocal, for it
for perfect . . . obtains *read* the most perfect univocation obtains. . . .

109. L: *for* forte *read* forte dicitur

110. L: *for* accidens *read* accidens, nec e converso
for complexa *read* incomplexa
for illa *read* illa cognitio
for alio *read* aliquo

E: *for* accident *read* accident nor the opposite
for understanding . . . (*complexum*) *read* by non-complex knowledge

111. L: *for* alicuius creaturae *read* unius rei
for alterius *read* alterius rei
for quamvis *read* qua
for Sortes *read* forte

E: *for* creature *read* thing
for another *read* another thing
for though *read* by which
for Socrates . . . reality *read* perhaps in reality he

112. L: *for* creaturae *read* creata
for quae *read* qui
for creaturae *read* creata

for dicitur *read* dicitur esse
for talis *read* talis conceptus
for creatura, modo *read* creatura modo,
for communis *read* communis et
for Isto *read* Quia isto
for quod *read* quando
for sed *read* sed etiam

113. L: for et in *read* in
for nec *read* vel

115. L: for particulares *read* partiales
after et *the new edition adds* <quantum ad conservari, in accidentaliter ordinatis secunda tantum dependet a prima quantum ad primum esse et>

E: *after* existence *the new edition adds* and for its conservation; in accidentally ordered causes the second cause only depends on the first for its first existence

117. L: for alia *read* aliqua
for verme *read* verme igitur etc
after aliquando *the new edition adds* <ita>
after simul *the new edition adds* <cum causa particulari>
after perfectior *the new edition adds* <si causetur>
after quam *the new edtion adds* <si causetur>

118. L: after effectus *the new edition adds* <unus>
after ab . . . modo *the new edition adds* <quia omnes causae essentialiter ordinatae simul>

E: for numerically . . . effect *read* an effect that is numerically one

for alone. . . . .they *read* alone, because all essentially ordered causes at the same time

119. L: *for* quod . . . primum *the new edition reads* <in infinitum; igitur etc.>

after probatur *the new edition adds* primo sic: universitas <causatorum>

for causa *read* causata

for igitur *read* igitur ab

for Universitas *the new edition reads* <Tota> universitas

after est *the new edition adds* <quod est>

E: *for ad* . . . first *read* in an infinite regress etc.

for Essentially *read* The universe of essentially

for have a cause *read* is caused

120. L: *for* quodlibet *read* quidlibet

for dependet . . . ordine) *read* dependet

for quam *read* quasi

for aliquid *the new edition has* <nihil>

for conservatione specialiter *read* conservatione

for innitens . . . naturali *the new edition reads* <innitens rationi naturali>; *the manuscripts write* innuens rationem naturalem

for causare cum *read* causari ab

for secundum *read* secundam

for dependeat *read* dependet

E: *for* and . . . succession *read* as it were from a proximate cause which is not part of this succession

for be . . . with *read* be caused by

121. L: *for* sed . . . dependet *the new edition reads* <quod aliter idem dependeret>; *the manuscripts write* sed . . . dependet

for tertium *read* tertiam

for est *read* sit

for sunt . . . finitate *read* sine infinitate

for quartum *read* quartam *and the same holds for all numbers until* septimum *for which you should read* septimam

E: *for* but . . . sense that *the new edition would have us read* namely, that otherwise it would depend on itself, because

for finite *read* not infinite

122. L: *for* potest *read* possit
     for octavum *read* octavam
     after totam *the new edition adds* <successionem>
     for dependet *read* dependeat
     for dictis *read* praedictis
     for actu *read* in actu
   E: *for* total production *read* a total succession

123. L: *for* aliquo *read* alio
     for aliquo *read* alio; *and then the new edition adds* <igitur conservatur ab alio, et>
     for est *read* erit
     after ista *the new edition adds* <ita>
     for Arguitur *read* Arguatur
     for quo *read* suo
     for nec *read* non
   E: *for* something *read* another
     after else *the new edition adds* then it is conserved by something else and
     for From . . . cause *read* About its productive cause

124. L: *for* seipsum *read* seipsam
     for quod non *read* quin

125. L: *for* est *read* esse
     for Sic *read* Et sic
     for Aristotelem *read* Philosophum
     for In read Ad
     for accipiendo Deum *read* accipiendo
     after Deus *the new edition adds* sic accipiendo Deum
     for etiam *read* est
     for [ut] manifestum *read* manifestum
     after est *the new edition adds* igitur etc.
   E: *after* God *the new edition adds* understanding 'God' according to the first description

126. L: *for* Deum esse *read* Deum
     for descriptionem *read* descriptionem, tunc
     for B read B esset
     for Etiam *read* Similiter

        for imperfectior *read* imperfectior quam
        for tamen *read* tamen haec
        for Dei *read* Dei sic accepti
        for potest *read* possit
        for tenemus *read* tenetur
    E: *for* God *read* God, understood in this second sense,
        for we hold *read* may be held

127. 1   *Quodlibet III*, q. 4 (OT IX, 214–220)   128
     2   *Scriptum in I Sent.*, d. 38, q. unica (OT IV, 583–586)   133

128. L: *for* intelligitur *read* intelligit
        for Symbolo *read* Symbolo dicitur
        for in *read* in unum
        for omnipotentem', et sequitur *read* omnipotentem
        for creatorem *read* factorem
    E: *after* Creed *add the words* it is said
        for in *read* in one
        for and then . . . creator *read* maker

129. L: *for* , etc. Item *read* . Item
        for Extra *read* Extravagantes,
        for catholica *read* catholica, c.
        for si *read* si non
        for increatum *read* incausatum
        for Si . . . infinitum *read* Si primo modo, igitur causatur ab ali-
        quo; et de illo quaero, et erit processus in infinitum
        for propositum *read* propositum, quia tale est Deus
        for una *read* aliqua
        for etc. *read* et Deus
        for esset verum *read* esset
        for alia *read* causa
        for sed *read* et
        for voluntate *read* voluntate creata
        for Contra tamen hoc *read* Sed contra ista
        for Primum *read* Primo
    E: *after catholica the new edition adds* in the chapter that begins with
        the word
        for uncreated *read* uncaused

for If the . . . *infinitum the new edition has the reading* If it is caused, then it is caused by something. I then ask about this cause, and there will be an infinite regress

after thesis *the new edition adds* that such a being is God

for therefore, etc. *the new edition has* so then is God its immediate cause

for will *read* created will

130. L: *for* nec *read* nec sunt

for Respondeo *read* Respondeo quod

for potest . . . possibilis *read* est possibilis

for modo *read* modo 'possibile'

for accipitur . . . dicitur *read* dicitur

for de *read* de aliquo

for omnes *read* omnes tales

for talium *read* figmenta

E: *for* can . . . possible *read* is possible

for both these *read* all such

for some of them *read* such imaginary beings

130–131 E: *for* from God *read* real beings

131. L: *for* a Deo *read* realia

for sunt *read* ens rationis est

for Sed *read* Si

for non *read* non sunt

for per *read* secundum

for ibi *read* illi

for esse *read* entium

for dico *read* respondeo

for est *read* est mendacium et

E: *for* since . . . words *read* since a being of reason is a mental word

for You *read* If you

for faulty . . . thinking *read* lie and a deceptive act of thinking

132. L: *for* ita et *read* ita

for dico *read* dico primo

for haec *read* ista

E: *for* answer *read* answer first that

133. L: *for* concludit *read* convenit

134. **L:** *for* Et ita *read* Et
136. 1 *Summa logicae,* I, c. 44 (OP I, 136–139)   137
      2 *Quaestiones in librum tertium Sent,* q. 4 (OT IV 142–144)   139
      3 *Quodlibet I,* q. 10 (OT IX, 62–65)   141
      4 *Quòdlibet III,* q. 14 (OT IX, 253–257)   144
137. **L:** *for* scilicet *read* scilicet quod
       for altero *read* alio
138. **L:** *for* potest *read* possit
       for substantia *read* subsistentia
       for accidens *read* additum
       for relativum *read* respectivum
       for relativum *read* respectivum
     E: *for* of *read* added to
139. **L:** *for* est *read* erit
       for aliae *read* aliae distinctae
       for Physicae *read* Physicorum
       for eorum *read* illorum
       for istas *read* ista
       for altero *read* alio
141. **L:** *for* est *read* eius causa
       for recipiens *read* recipiens est in nobis
       for sed . . . nobis *read* Hoc
       for posset *read* possit
       for per *read* propter
     E: *for* it has . . . case *read* its cause and subject of inherence is in us, and
       for could *read* can
142 **L:** *for* attribuitur *read* attribui
       for vel propter *read* propter
       for Talis *read* Talis etiam
       for et bibere et ambulare, intelligere et *read* bibere, ambulare, intelligere
       for immaterialem et *read* immaterialem
       for non *read* nec
       for talis *read* tali
     E: *for* through *read* because of
       for Such *read* Such also

143 L: *for* fidem *read* fidem et veritatem
     for ista *read* illa forma
  E: *for* faith *read* faith and truth
144. L: *for* reciperetur *read* recipitur
     for materia *read* forma
     for virtuosus vel vitiosus read virtuosus
  E: *for* would inhere . . . matter *read* inheres in an extended form
     for virtuous or vicious read virtuous
145. L: *for* ide mmanens *read* idem manens
     for postea *read* et postea
     for voluntarium *read* voluntarium etc.
     for alius *read* alius ab actu voluntatis
     for quilibet *read* omnis
     for esse *read* esse necessario
     for ita *read* ita scilicet
     for posset *read* possit
  E: *for* act *read* act besides the act of the will
     for is *read* is necessarily
146. L: *for* dicatur *read* dicis
     for sit *read* sit sic
     for possit *read* possit pro
  E: *for* The . . . made *read* If you object that
147. L: *for* tamen *read* tamen Deum
     for ponendo *read* posito
     for dictis *read* praedictis
  E: *for* love *read* love for God

PHILOTHEUS BOEHNER, O.F.M., was born in Lichtenau, Germany, in 1901. Although seriously ill with tuberculosis, he was ordained a priest of the Franciscan order of Saxony in 1920. Subsequently he did graduate studies in philosophy and earned a doctorate in botany. During his long recovery from tuberculosis, Boehner translated into German Etienne Gilson's works on St. Bonaventure (1929), St. Augustine (1930), and St. Bernard (1936) and with Gilson produced in 1937 *Die Geschichte der Christlichen Philosophie*. In 1937 Boehner accepted an invitation from Gilson to lecture at the Pontifical Institute of Mediaeval Studies at Toronto. Before classes began in September, he visited St. Bonaventure College in Olean, New York—on the eve of World War II. After England declared war on Germany, Boehner was not permitted to reenter Canada. Fortunately, he was able to continue his work at St. Bonaventure College, where he edited the first two parts of Ockham's *Summa logicae* and Walter Burley's *De puritate artis logicae Tractatus longior*, wrote *Medieval Logic, An Outline of Its Development from 1250 to c. 1499* (1952), translated and commented on St. Bonaventure's *Itinerarium Mentis in Deum*, and prepared Ockham's *Philosophical Writings*. Before his death in 1955, he established the Franciscan Institute, reorganized *Franciscan Studies*, and founded *Cord* magazine, a journal of Franciscan spirituality.

STEPHEN F. BROWN is chair, Department of Theology, Boston College, where he has taught since 1979. He earned the B.A. degree at St. Bonaventure University (1955), the M.A. at the Franciscan Institute (1959), and the Ph.D. degree at the University of Louvain (1964). He has taught philosophy and chaired the department at St. Bonaventure University and at the University of South, and from 1962 to 1971 he edited *Franciscan Studies*. Author of many articles on medieval philosophy and theology, Stephen Brown has edited several of the volumes that form the modern critical edition of William of Ockham.